PROFESSIONAL LEARN
FOR DIVERSITY, EQUI
DEMOCRACY

This edited volume examines research and practical examples of professional learning approaches for school leaders and teachers in the areas of diversity, equity and democracy – 'big issues' that represent some of the most urgent challenges facing our societies and schools today.

Educators from Ireland, Poland, Spain, Norway and Chile provide unique insights into professional learning programmes that were intentionally and collaboratively designed and put into action *with* and *for* school leaders, teachers and teacher educators. A key principle promoted throughout this book is the commitment to placing individuals, communities and context at the centre. All programmes emphasise the creation of new spaces, where lived experiences, evolving ideas and theoretical frameworks can be explored with honesty, critical depth and moral purpose. They prioritise transformative practice and outcomes through learning together, rather than through mere implementation or replication of programmes or policies.

In offering summaries and critical discussions of key theoretical perspectives, learning materials and thinking points, and ultimately a shared sense of solidarity in the ongoing work of shaping transformative educational change, this book will be useful for school leaders, teachers, teacher educators, teacher professional development providers and policymakers working in the areas of diversity, equity and democracy.

Manuela Heinz is Associate Professor at the University of Galway, Ireland, and Editor of the *European Journal of Teacher Education*.

María Jesús Rodríguez-Entrena is Associate Professor in the Department of Didactics and School Organization, University of Murcia, Spain.

Gerry Mac Ruairc is Emeritus Professor of Education and former Head of the School of Education at the University of Galway, Ireland.

PROFESSIONAL LEARNING FOR DIVERSITY, EQUITY AND DEMOCRACY

Big Ideas for Better Schools

Edited by Manuela Heinz, María Jesús Rodríguez-Entrena, and Gerry Mac Ruairc

Routledge
Taylor & Francis Group
LONDON AND NEW YORK

Designed Cover Image: ©Getty Images

First published 2026
by Routledge
4 Park Square, Milton Park, Abingdon, Oxon OX14 4RN

and by Routledge
605 Third Avenue, New York, NY 10158

Routledge is an imprint of the Taylor & Francis Group, an informa business

British Library Cataloguing-in-Publication Data
A catalogue record for this book is available from the British Library

ISBN: 978-1-032-62926-1 (hbk)
ISBN: 978-1-032-60134-2 (pbk)
ISBN: 978-1-032-62929-2 (ebk)

DOI: 10.4324/9781032629292

Typeset in Sabon
by Apex CoVantage, LLC

CONTENTS

About the editors *viii*
Contributors *ix*
Foreword *xiii*
José Weinstein
Acknowledgements *xvii*

PART ONE
Professional learning for diversity, equity and democracy in schools – context, concepts and rationale **1**

1 School leadership for better futures: Collaborative professional learning *about* and *for* diversity, equity and democracy 3
Manuela Heinz, María Jesús Rodríguez-Entrena, and Gerry Mac Ruairc

2 Big ideas for better schools: A transnational professional learning project 17
Manuela Heinz, Gerry Mac Ruairc, and María Jesús Rodríguez-Entrena

3 Diversity, equity and democracy in school leadership: Troublesome concepts in troubled times 24
Gerry Mac Ruairc, Sara Gartland, Manuela Heinz, and María Jesús Rodríguez-Entrena

4 A model to enable professional learning for transformative school leadership 47
Mary Nihill and Gerry Mac Ruairc

PART TWO
Making it happen – learning from case studies **63**

5 Professional learning with school leaders on diversity, equity and inclusion in Ireland: Deepening understanding and commitment through safe and honest 'big issue' conversations 65
Manuela Heinz, Cáitlin Graham, Art O Neachtain, Gerry Mac Ruairc, Sara Gartland, and Claire Whyte

6 Diversity, equity and democracy: Developing an understanding of complex social phenomena with teachers and students in Poland 87
Jakub Kołodziejczyk, Joanna Kotlarz, Grzegorz Mazurkiewicz, and Joanna Trzópek-Paszkiewicz

7 What is democracy? Recognising diverse perspectives and building shared understandings with school leaders in Spain through a professional learning experience 103
María Jesús Rodríguez-Entrena, Antonio Portela Pruaño, María del Carmen Maldonado López, Francisco Alfonso Hernández López, and Abraham Bernárdez-Gómez

8 Democracy as a central value in a national curriculum: Working with school leaders and teachers to connect values with practice in Norway 128
Eli Ottesen, Ruth Jensen, Bård Halvorsen and Pia Merethe Vinje

9 Education for citizenship under democratic strain: Professional learning for school leaders and teachers in Chile 146
Camila Jara Ibarra, Macarena Sánchez Bachmann, and Javiera Peña Fredes

PART THREE
Review of learning and charting pathways for the future **165**

10 Transformative professional learning in action: Embracing complexity and critical co-inquiry for diversity, equity and democracy 167
Gerry Mac Ruairc, María Jesús Rodríguez-Entrena, and Manuela Heinz

Index *180*

ABOUT THE EDITORS

Manuela Heinz is an associate professor at the University of Galway, Ireland, and a former head of discipline of education. She currently serves as editor of the *European Journal of Teacher Education*. Her research centres on teacher education and school leadership, with an emphasis on diversity, equity, inclusion and school–university partnerships.

María Jesús Rodríguez-Entrena is an associate professor in the Department of Didactics and School Organization at the Faculty of Education, University of Murcia, Spain. She currently serves as the director of the Center for Training and Professional Development at the University of Murcia. Her research interests include at-risk students, teacher education and educational leadership.

Gerry Mac Ruairc is an emeritus professor of education at the University of Galway, Ireland. Previously, Gerry was a primary teacher and a school inspector. He has published widely in the areas of leadership for inclusive schooling, language and social class, and leadership and school improvement for equity and social justice.

CONTRIBUTORS

Macarena Sánchez Bachmann is an associate researcher at the Faculty of Education, Universidad Diego Portales, Chile. She holds an MSc in inequalities and social science from the London School of Economics. She has participated in research projects on political socialisation and citizenship education at the school level and also in teacher professional development initiatives.

Abraham Bernárdez-Gómez holds a PhD in education from the University of Murcia, Spain. His research focuses on socio-educational exclusion, school dropout, educational trajectories and teacher development. He was a postdoctoral 'Margarita Salas' fellow (2022). Since 2023, he has been an assistant professor at the University of Vigo, specialising in didactics and research methods.

Javiera Peña Fredes is an associate researcher at the Faculty of Education, Universidad Diego Portales, Chile. She holds a master's degree in peace and conflict studies from Philipps-Universität Marburg, Germany. She has been a researcher and a co-ordinator in various projects related to educational leadership, school trust and teacher culture.

Sara Gartland holds a PhD from the University of Delaware. She is a secondary mathematics teacher, a mathematics teacher educator and an educational researcher based in the United States. Her research focuses on equity and student voice in mathematics. She contributed to this project while serving as a postdoctoral researcher at the University of Galway.

Cáitlin Graham is a passionate secondary school teacher in the west of Ireland, whose subjects include history; civic, social and political education; and social, personal and health education. Cáitlin is a graduate of a first-class honours BA from Queen's University Belfast and a first-class honours MA in education from the University of Galway, Ireland.

Bård Halvorsen teaches history, religious studies, mathematics and physical education and is an advisor for the student council in a lower secondary school in Norway. Halvorsen's professional interests include the fostering of inclusive classroom environments, teacher–student relationships and creating a school culture where all students feel seen, heard and valued.

Camila Jara Ibarra is an assistant professor at the Faculty of Education, Universidad Diego Portales, Chile. She holds an MSc in statistics and quantitative analysis for the social sciences from KU Leuven and a PhD from Leiden University. Her research focuses on school leadership, citizenship education, teacher education and gender.

Ruth Jensen is a professor of educational leadership at the University of Oslo, Norway, and previously a teacher and leader at the municipal level. She has led and collaborated in projects on educational leadership and workplace learning with specific attention to the use of pedagogical tools, governance, learning and change in institutions. She has written and co-authored many books.

Jakub Kołodziejczyk is an associate professor at the Jagiellonian University, Poland. His research explores educational leadership, focusing on how school management influences student development and well-being. He currently studies the relationship between principals' leadership styles and student safety, including issues of aggression and bullying.

Joanna Kotlarz is a teacher, researcher and project manager at the Institute of Culture of Jagiellonian University in Kraków, Poland. She has authored scientific publications on education and diversity in management. She has research and teaching experience specialising in project management, research methods, educational leadership and management theories, and social diversity research.

Francisco Alfonso Hernández López is a graduate in mathematics and a holder of a diploma in management informatics. A mathematics teacher since 2001, he has worked at the Hellín Teacher and Resource Center (CPR) and as an IT coordinator at IES Valle de Leiva, Spain. He has served as head of studies at IES Valle de Leiva for 12 years, excelling in educational management and innovation.

María del Carmen Maldonado López is a graduate in English philology from the University of Granada, Spain. She worked as head of studies in IES La Contraviesa de Albuñol (Granada) (2007–2010) and in IES Valle de Leiva in Alhama de Murcia (Murcia) (2016–2024). She was also the quality manager (2012–2024), achieving the CAF+500 Education Certification in 2021.

Grzegorz Mazurkiewicz is an associate professor at the Jagiellonian University in Kraków, Poland. He is a researcher, a teacher and a sociologist interested in the theory and practice of educational leadership, educational policy, quality of education, social justice, intercultural education and learning within the frame of expeditionary learning. He has managed projects in the public and non-governmental sectors.

Art O Neachtain, a former primary school teacher, now lectures in the School of Education at the University of Galway, Ireland. He teaches across undergraduate and postgraduate teacher education programmes, with research and teaching interests in literacy, teacher education and school leadership.

Mary Nihill is a second-level school principal in Ireland and currently on secondment to Oide – a support service for teachers and school leaders – as director of leadership. Her PhD research focused on professional learning for school leadership, and she has contributed articles on professional learning for leadership in a number of publications.

Eli Ottesen is a professor emerita in educational sciences at the University of Oslo, Norway. Her professional interests are educational administration and leadership, school development, workplace learning in schools and supervision. She has participated in research projects and published extensively about school administration and leadership, governance and curriculum development.

Antonio Portela Pruaño, PhD, is an associate professor and head of the Department of Didactics and School Organization at the University of Murcia's Faculty of Education, Spain. His research interests are in the areas of teacher development, educational administration and leadership. He is a former secondary school teacher and a department head.

Joanna Trzópek-Paszkiewicz holds a PhD in management and quality sciences and is a research associate in the Department of Leadership and Management in Education at Jagiellonian University, Poland. She has been the co-founder and an active member of a non-governmental educational organisation since 2009. Her research focuses on educational leadership, education management, civil society and democratic values.

Pia Merethe Vinje is an experienced educator with 25 years of service in the Norwegian school system. She has worked in schools in different parts of the country. Vinje holds a master's degree in religion, philosophies of life and ethics.

Claire Whyte is a second-level French and Spanish teacher and a middle leader based in the west of Ireland. She holds a BA (Ed) in languages and a Master of Education in School Leadership from the University of Limerick.

FOREWORD

José Weinstein

I think the expression 'being in the right place at the right time' – people in flesh and blood being present where they are most needed – applies perfectly to this book. We live in times in which the values of diversity, equity and democracy are under threat in many of our societies, and in which citizens' rights, which until recently seemed natural to us, are being questioned and run a serious risk of being relativised and restricted, if not outright violated. In the face of this, education, and in particular, educators who embody these ideas in their daily practice, cannot stand by with folded arms and remain silent.

In these pressing circumstances, this book addresses important educational concerns: How can the major issues of our time, such as diversity, equity and democracy, referred to in this collection as 'big issues', be brought into the classroom? How can teachers, often overwhelmed by the daily grind of teaching and consumed by an encyclopaedic curriculum or by the demand that their students perform on high-stakes tests, make these deeper conversations with their students happen? To construct pedagogical answers, the authors do not start deductively from a theory of *how* 'big issues' *should* be taught. Instead, they seek answers to these questions in direct experiences in schools, where, together with teachers and students, they try to find out how these concepts are understood by the different actors and how discussions can be mobilised and supported in order to make better sense of them. The detailed descriptions of innovative pedagogical approaches and processes, together with supporting resources for professional learning, are highly original and a strong contribution of this book.

The participatory methodologies developed throughout the professional learning projects do not imply that the authors do not have a conceptual framework for understanding the 'big issues' under discussion. On the contrary, they have agreed on definitions that allow them to position themselves in relation to the three concepts individually, as well as making the connections between them visible. If in the school world, from the Salamanca Statement (1994) onwards, diversity has been understood primarily in terms of seeking how not to discriminate against students with special educational needs (SEN), in this book, the definition is extended to include all groups impacted by discrimination. The authors also engage an intersectional view of diversity, highlighting how different characteristics and group belongings form complex and multilayered identities in which the multiplication of advantage or disadvantage often results in having more or less educational opportunities (as it might happen, for example, to a female, poor, lesbian and indigenous student). What is required by way of response to the complexity of diversity as it manifests in schools is an education that seeks to develop the full potential of people regardless of their identities and distinctive characteristics, within the context of a democratic coexistence that allows different groups and individuals to fully exercise their rights, and to resolve their differences peacefully and through dialogue. From the point of view of the proposed educational discussion process, the three concepts are articulated from the starting point of inequalities, since, as the editors write, 'diversity precludes the existence of inequity and consequently necessitates the discussion of equity and democratic processes'.

Although the different experiences of professional learning programmes compiled in this edited collection do not use identical methodologies, the process of discussing 'big issues' in schools sheds light on common (and novel!) aspects of teachers' professional development. For example, the value of *entry points* to these vast topics is explicated – *hooks* that need to motivate the teachers and leaders involved – which vary according to the schools and contexts. The authors also emphasise the importance of systematising and always keeping in mind the intellectual journey that is developed by the participants in the collective discussions on, and engagement with, the 'big issues'. Central to the professional learning approaches are critical enquiry, reflection and ethical responsibility. Throughout the book, the authors develop a forward-looking pedagogical vision in which threshold concepts play an important role and in which discomfort is embraced and troublesome knowledge is interrogated collectively. To effectively practise these critical and non-traditional professional learning methodologies, commitment and decisive action are needed to flatten pre-established hierarchies in schools and between practitioners and academics so that meaningful dialogue can happen in spaces of authentic mutual respect. To create these spaces of collaboration and equality, the authors emphasise the importance of being open and of actively seeking to confront and enrich theoretical perspectives with knowledge from practical experience.

The practical examples described in this book also show that there are certain organisational conditions within the structure and culture of schools, which are decisive for the success of professional learning on 'big issues', for example, the existence of trust between the various school actors. This allows all involved to engage in innovative processes in which risks are taken and dynamic, open-ended initiatives, that are not always guaranteed to succeed, are promoted. Meaningful professional collaboration also plays a significant role, since it allows reflection on complex issues, such as democracy or diversity, to be based on collective professional capacities linked with organisational routines that are already in place.

The role of school leaders is highlighted as essential, since their way of leading and managing the school opens (or closes) opportunities for teachers' professional learning. Thus, it is undeniable that certain specific ways of leading, such as those that promote social justice or cultural responsiveness, enable 'big issues' to be part of not only professional learning processes but also the daily life of schools. Particularly interesting is the description of the transformational professional learning model developed in Ireland, which has, among its pillars, a transformative approach to school leadership. It is framed within a relationship of mutual interdependence between school leaders and teachers, highlighting that 'an absence of professional learning leaves leadership vulnerable to poor models of practice and untimely burnout'.

What is highly original in the collection is the application of a shared thematic focus and shared professional learning principles across five different national contexts. These contexts not only have different school realities but are also experiencing different societal challenges related to diversity, equity and democracy. The comparative approach offered in this book allows the editors to explore similarities and differences in their reflection on the importance of context and on ways in which the promotion of these values within the schools is often influenced by the particular orientation of governments and societies at a specific time. The situations in Ireland, Poland, Spain, Norway and Chile are not the same. In some contexts, efforts to strengthen teacher education align with government guidelines and are even driven by curricular reforms. In others, however, such initiatives have been developed despite limited governmental support – or even in direct contradiction to, or resistance against, official messages. Incidentally, this *coherence*, or lack of coherence, within educational policies has consequences for the possibility that professional learning experiences, such as those proposed here on 'Big Ideas for Better Schools' (BIBS), will prosper, scale up and be sustained over time.

These are extraordinarily challenging times for diversity, equity and democracy across the globe. The education of children and young people is deeply entangled in this struggle. It is, in fact, where the future of society is being shaped. Educators must hold on to a lucid optimism that, without turning a blind eye to the risks and threats that lie ahead, affirms their vital role and empowers them to cultivate democratic values and competencies among the new generations. But, for this enterprise to be successful, the voice of the children and young people themselves must be heard; it must be given a strong role in their educational experience. It is time for real innovation, for new approaches to education to build better schools, and time to ask what 'good schools' (should) really look and feel like. This book offers a powerful vision for, and excellent examples of, educational initiatives that can bring about real change through collaborative professional learning approaches that embrace co-creation. As the poet Antonio Machado masterfully wrote decades ago, 'Caminante no hay camino, se hace camino al andar . . . Traveler, there is no path. The path is made by walking'.

ACKNOWLEDGEMENTS

This edited collection grew out of the 'Big Ideas for Better Schools' (BIBS) project, funded by Léargas (2019-1-IE01-KA201-051528). We are deeply grateful to Léargas for their generous support and would like to extend a special thank you to Weronika Gasior, whose guidance and encouragement were invaluable throughout the project.

The project brought together academic institutions and school partners from Ireland, Norway, Poland and Spain, and we were delighted to extend our collaboration and the reach of this collection to include our wonderful colleagues from Chile. Our shared aim was to deepen educators' conversations, understanding and agency around diversity, equity and democracy through collaborative professional learning. Along the way, we built strong professional relationships, learned with and from one another, navigated challenges together and strengthened our collective commitment to democratic, collaborative school–university partnerships. A heartfelt thank you goes to all our academic and school partners, to the school leaders who supported and participated in the various projects and especially to the teachers and students in the various partner schools – your engagement was the heart of this work, and it continues to inspire us.

We extend our sincere thanks to the colleagues who generously served as peer reviewers for chapters in this collection. Their careful, constructive feedback helped strengthen the work presented here. We especially wish to acknowledge Nataliia Avsheniuk (National Academy of Educational Sciences of Ukraine), Audrey Bryan (Dublin City University), Daniela Frison (University of Florence), Fiona King (Dublin City University), Rory Mc Daid (Marino Institute of Education) and Anja Swennen (Vrije University of Amsterdam). These outstanding scholars have made important contributions to teacher education and to teaching and learning in schools, and we are honoured by their support and collegiality. We are also grateful to the many colleagues in our respective universities who contributed to this project as critical friends and collaborators, offering thoughtful insights and participating in various aspects of the work.

Our sincere thanks also go to AnnaMary Goodall, Kanishka Jangir, Pakhi Pande and the wider team at Routledge for their professionalism, encouragement and ongoing support throughout the preparation and production of this volume.

We are especially grateful to Professor José Weinstein, Director of the School Leadership Program at Diego Portales University, for contributing such a thoughtful Foreword to this collection. His commitment to school leadership, relational trust and supporting vulnerable schools resonates strongly with the themes of this book. We appreciate him finding time in his demanding schedule to share his insights.

And finally, a huge thanks to our families and friends. Their patience, support and understanding, especially when work spilt into weekends and holidays, meant more than we can say. We finish this phase of the work knowing that learning continues – about ourselves, each other and the world we hope to help shape.

PART ONE

Professional learning for diversity, equity and democracy in schools – context, concepts and rationale

1

SCHOOL LEADERSHIP FOR BETTER FUTURES

Collaborative professional learning *about* and *for* diversity, equity and democracy

Manuela Heinz, María Jesús Rodríguez-Entrena, and Gerry Mac Ruairc

Rationale, focus and purpose: *Why this book now?*

This book is about educators' collaborative professional learning *about* and *for* diversity, equity and democracy – 'big issues' that represent some of the most urgent challenges facing our societies and schools today. A persistent problem lies in how these ideals and values are often treated in policy, curriculum frameworks and schools – acknowledged and promoted at the surface level, without the deep engagement and 'thick understanding' that their complexity and difficulty demand (Apple, 2018; Mac Ruairc et al., 2026). Responding to this challenge, the book explores how professional learning programmes can be intentionally and collaboratively designed and implemented *with* and *for* teachers, school leaders, teacher educators and researchers to foster deeper understanding of the theoretical and practical dimensions and of the complex interactions among diversity, equity and democracy. We hope that such a deeper understanding can contribute to strengthening the capacity of educators and schools to engage with these values in more meaningful, context-sensitive and proactive ways.

We are living in deeply unsettling times. Democracies across the globe are under increasing strain, facing mounting political polarisation, the rapid spread of misinformation and disinformation, eroding public trust in governments and a resurgence of populist movements. More and more citizens are disengaging from democratic institutions. Hard-won recognitions and commitments related to equity, diversity and inclusion, as well as emancipatory scholarship and policies, are being positioned as divisive. The Trump administration is actively dismantling numerous justice- and diversity-oriented initiatives, including international aid programmes designed to promote these

DOI: 10.4324/9781032629292-2

values. These political shifts are unfolding alongside intensifying global crises, including the climate emergency, rising economic inequality, outbreak and escalation of wars, forced displacement and global health threats, along with the rapid advancement of, and concerns about the impact of, artificial intelligence. We are facing challenges of historic scale and urgency.

In the midst of all this, it can be hard to believe that the world can become a better place for everyone. Yet, as educators, we need to hold on to hope, and that hope must fuel determined action for change (Fielding, 2012; Riley, 2022). This book grew out of our shared commitment to make a meaningful difference, an ambition to help shape and lead transformative change. Like many others around the globe – educators, activists, young people, grassroots movements, non-governmental organisations and scholars – we believe that genuine, lasting change is still possible if we collectively challenge exclusion, inequality, injustice and the relentless exploitation of our planet for profit. Education can make a difference because it is shaped not only by context and politics but also by the courage, care and persistence of those who work on the ground to make schools better places where all children can learn and grow to become responsible global citizens.

Long-term commitments to social justice, peace and sustainability – in international policy frameworks such as the 2030 Agenda for Sustainable Development – offer fuel for hope, and no small measure of relief, in our troubled times. While these frameworks are far from perfect and have rightly been criticised (Elfert & Morris, 2022), we believe that they need to be recognised as vital foundations for collective action (Heinz & Swennen, 2025). The Sustainable Development Goals (SDGs) affirm inclusive and equitable quality education (SDG 4) not only as a fundamental human right but also as a crucial pathway for achieving broader goals like advancing gender equality (SDG 5), reducing inequalities (SDG 10) and fostering peace, justice and strong institutions (SDG 16). UNESCO's (2021) report, 'Reimagining Our Futures Together', positions education as a deeply transformative force – one that 'is key to creating just, inclusive and sustainable futures' as it can help us reimagine how we 'relate to each other, to the planet, and to the technologies shaping our lives'. At the heart of that vision are teachers, described as 'key figures on whom possibilities for transformation rest' (p. 80). We fully agree: Teachers are key influencers in schools. While real and lasting societal change also depends very significantly on wider political commitment and decisive action to address broader societal barriers such as poverty, housing, health and discrimination, schools are critical sites for transformation. This is because young people's relationships, values and behaviours are deeply shaped within school environments, making education a powerful force for nurturing inclusive, equitable and democratic societies.

As we have already stated in the opening of this chapter, this book is about educators' collaborative professional learning *about* and *for* diversity, equity and democracy. It offers a collection of chapters co-written by teachers, school leaders, teacher educators and other academics, who came together to inquire into, and deepen, their understanding of these 'big issues' and to share and in/transform their professional practice. Working across schools and universities, teachers, school leaders and teacher educators stand at the intersections of values and realities, hope and hardship, theory and practice, and policy and implementation. While teacher educators often receive less attention in international transformation agendas, this book highlights the important role they can play when working in partnership with teachers and school leaders – supporting one another, inquiring together into theory and practice and working collectively towards the aim of creating more inclusive, democratic and socially just educational environments. The programmes and experiences shared in this collection place collaboration and co-learning at the heart of professional learning. They reflect a 'holistic approach' that values the real-life experiences of teachers and teacher educators and that creates space for shared reflection and sense-making, 'deepening learning about themselves, each other, and the changing world around them – both now and in the future' (Heinz, 2024).

It takes courage, clarity, deep moral purpose and emotional resilience to uphold values under pressure, and even more to bring them to life in schools and classrooms. That is why professional collaboration, support and learning matter, especially now and especially the kind that goes beyond technical proficiency to nurture educators as thoughtful, ethical and future-oriented leaders – leaders who can hold space for complexity, act with care and inspire others in times of uncertainty. We wrote this book out of a shared desire and commitment to defend, strengthen and enact visions of dignity, equity, inclusion and care for the future. We know that change does not happen overnight, nor through a single project, and we are aware that education itself has often played a role in (re)producing social inequalities. But, through our work with young people in schools across varied contexts, we are reminded again and again of the possibilities education offers, even in increasingly challenging times, when teachers are empowered to imagine – and enact – more inclusive, equitable and democratic futures.

This collection has particular implications for school leadership, understood in its broadest sense, because engaging with the concepts of diversity, equity and democracy is a shared responsibility that involves the entire school community. At the same time, there are specific imperatives that demand the visible and sustained commitment of 'formal' school leaders, particularly the principal and senior leadership team, whose willingness to lead by example and to model and champion inclusive, socially just and emancipatory practices deeply shapes school cultures and priorities (Neves et al., 2023; Lee, 2019). We emphasise the applied intellectual journey of leaders, in the Gramscian sense as 'organic intellectuals' whose task is not only to understand but also to transform (Gramsci, 2011). The core focus of this work for leaders, and the conceptual foundation of this collection, is therefore *transformative leadership* – for inclusion, for social justice and for emancipatory outcomes (as developed by Shields & Hesbol, 2020; Theoharis, 2024; Mac Ruairc et al., 2013).

Key concepts: *How do we conceptualise diversity, equity and democracy?*

Before we go any further, it is important to clarify our understandings and approaches to exploring the three 'big issues' – diversity, equity and democracy. We were/are acutely aware that focusing on three individually complex – and deeply interrelated – concepts sets an ambitious and demanding agenda for our work, too ambitious and too demanding in many ways. We grapple(d) with the tensions and challenges that emerged from this wide scope, and we fully acknowledge the limitations it entails. Each of our central themes – diversity, equity and democracy – has a rich body of scholarship, research traditions and philosophical foundations, as do the domains of professional learning and school leadership. We do not claim to address these bodies of work in comprehensive depth, neither within the professional learning programmes we designed nor in the pages of this book.

Nonetheless, in practice, education – leading schools and teaching and learning – is constantly challenging us to pursue, balance and make sense of complex and intertwined values, ideas and concepts. There is nothing new there, except for the question of how understanding can be deepened and practice transformed and/or enriched in the midst of such complexity. As all the chapters throughout this book demonstrate, theory matters in professional learning and, therefore, one challenge for us lies in selecting the right amount and the right kind(s) of theory/theories. We had enough experience to recognise the importance of making theory accessible within the restricted time available for professional learning in schools. We also understood the need to present theoretical ideas in ways that respected the expertise of the experienced educators involved – without coming across as lecturing or, worse, patronising. We will delve deeper into the interpersonal dynamics of practitioner–academic interactions in a 'third space' (Heinz & Fleming, 2019; Zeichner, 2010) later, especially in Chapter 5 (Heinz et al., 2026a). Coming back to the challenge of conceptualising our key concepts, in this book, we will only briefly look at them in relation to broader society, mainly to set the context for the various case study chapters. Our core focus will be on how the concepts of diversity, equity and democracy are relevant for, manifest in and can be influenced (in a transformative way) in/by schools. In Chapter 3, we offer a concise overview of the theoretical frameworks and debates that have informed our thinking (Mac Ruairc et al., 2026).

Our aim is not to provide an exhaustive review but rather to highlight perspectives we have found particularly useful in practice, both for ourselves and for those involved in professional learning. For readers seeking to explore these concepts in greater scholarly depth, we recommend further engagement with the relevant literature.

So here then is a very brief overview (refer to Chapter 3 for more detail) of our conceptualisation of the three key concepts. Overall, we see 'diversity' as a social reality precluding the existence or lack of equity and, consequently, necessitating discussions and action towards equity and democratic processes. Diversity is an increasingly relevant and important construct to unpack (Cerna et al., 2021). For our work with schools and teachers, we felt that an expansive definition of diversity was needed, even if that complicated matters. Our conceptualisation encapsulated diversity as multidimensional and inextricably linked with identity. Both concepts are intersectional, constructed of multiple, overlapping dimensions or layers of individual or group membership, based on a variety of socio-economic, cultural, geopolitical, educational and personal factors. In our collaborative explorations, we considered diversities in schools at the intersection of students' and teachers' gender, age, socio-economic status, sexual orientation, disability/ability, race/ethnicity, religious affiliation/worldview, language, geographical location, migration status, family background and family/social situation. Key in exploring diversity critically is the recognition that many identities are marginalised, stigmatised and essentialised and that advantages or disadvantages are accrued to different identities. In our work, we hoped to engage educators in discussions that problematise practices and approaches that ignore and/or perpetuate patterns of marginalisation, exclusion and disadvantage.

Like diversity, 'equity' is intersectional (Crenshaw, 1989). Through our work, we realised that to problematise equity, *in*equity needs to preclude any discussions of equity because *in*equity is the current state across the globe (Cerna et al., 2021; Heinz et al., 2025; OECD, 2025). Given that educators are, in most contexts, members of majority groups (Keane et al., 2023) and less often from significantly marginalised and/or disadvantaged backgrounds, such discussions will always create discomfort or even resistance. However, laying bare how current and historic policies and practices across societies and schools have created, recreated and sustained inequities is crucial if we want to move beyond rhetoric and towards meaningful change in understandings, attitudes and action. From there, professional learning and education work can focus on equity as a process of fairness, which is not the same as 'sameness' (Gutiérrez, 2011), in educational and related economic outcomes for all, irrespective of personal and social circumstances. In agreement with Cerna et al. (2021), we see equity as encompassing the provision of 'support for all students to achieve their full educational potential, including in relation to developing a sense of belonging, wellbeing and self-worth, irrespective of their personal and social circumstances'. In terms of working towards more equitable practices in education, we also draw on four key themes: (1) Equity can be enhanced through collaborative development of equity literacy in schools (Ainscow, 2020; Gorski & Swalwell, 2015), (2) sustained equity success requires both individual and systems level action, (3) authentic incorporation of student voice promotes equity in a variety of educational spaces (Patterson, 2019), and (4) a critical socio-political perspective fosters meaningful and responsive change (Gutiérrez, 2011).

Finally, 'democracy', like equity, can be conceptualised as a process. In education, it is often framed as a nuanced process of co-construction that supports decision-making, typically highlighting relational aspects and balancing the needs of individuals with the needs of groups. In its broadest sense, democracy is about relating to and living with others and about co-constructing social norms and realities informed by individuals' and groups' values (Alongi et al., 2016; Ben-Porath, 2012; Biesta, 2019). It is also a form of government. Definitions about and conceptualisations of democracy abound in the academic literature, highlighting processes, intended outcomes and the importance of education for democracy. In our conceptualisation of, and when discussing, democracy alongside diversity and equity, we paid particular attention to the ways in which diversity influences relational interactions and the ways in which such interactions, in turn, influence (in)equity. We also explored how democratic processes can be leveraged to promote equity and social justice (Alongi et al., 2016; de Groot, 2017), with particular attention to the need for pedagogical approaches that actively amplify student voice (Bessant et al., 2016; Fielding, 2012; Scotton, 2020). Traditional teacher-centred pedagogical approaches, which continue to dominate across many education systems, stand in stark contrast to the collaborative and deliberative ethos of democracy. This tension was already recognised by Dewey (1903, p. 197), who posed the critical question of 'how we can justify our belief in democratic principles and then go entirely against it when we come to education?' In our work, we deliberately foregrounded the inherently political nature of teaching while also acknowledging the real pressures and risks teachers face – particularly in the current climate of intensified political push-back – when engaging in this work. This tension was central to our thinking, shaping our conviction that, to fulfil the vital role of reaffirming the democratic purpose of education, teachers need a 'thick understanding' of diversity, equity and democracy as interconnected principles, alongside sustained, practical support and authentic empowerment.

Contexts: *Where did the work take place?*

What makes this volume especially rich and interesting is the wide range of national contexts we bring together: In Ireland, a complex postcolonial history, significant emigration and rapid recent demographic change have shaped current educational structures and debates. The dominance of faith-based schools and a largely homogeneous teaching profession present challenges for inclusion, despite legislative and policy efforts. Core values such as respect, equality, and justice are now firmly embedded in education policies and curriculum frameworks, yet teachers struggle and the realities of practice often lag behind policy intentions. In Spain, democratic citizenship is increasingly visible in education policy, with the recent introduction of a subject focused on civic and ethical values. While this reflects a clear effort to promote active citizenship, implementation varies across the country's autonomous regions. Spain, like many other systems, is grappling with how to move from policy statements to sustained, system-wide engagement with democratic and inclusive education. In Norway, democracy and inclusion are embedded within the structure of the national curriculum, which was revised in 2020. One of its core principles is the integration of democratic values across all subjects, aiming to make these themes a living part of everyday teaching and learning. Norway's approach illustrates how values-based education can be systematically supported through curriculum design and teacher development. In Poland, the legacy of a socialist past and a relatively recent democratic transition continue to shape civic culture. Civic participation is often framed in terms of political change, and surveys suggest a growing resistance to diversity, particularly among young people. Although anti-discrimination principles are included in legal frameworks, equality-focused education policy remains underdeveloped. Poland's extensive response to the war in Ukraine is an example of a significant recent societal challenge related to diversity, equity and democracy. In Chile, citizenship education has become a national priority amid ongoing social and political transformation. Following the end of a military dictatorship in 1990, the country has faced declining voter turnout, public disillusionment and large-scale protests in 2019 that led to a constitutional reform process. These developments have brought renewed attention to the role of schools in fostering democratic engagement. A new national plan for citizenship education reflects a strategic effort to strengthen democratic culture in response to growing populism, authoritarian rhetoric and social division.

Each country involved in this project brings its own unique history, culture and set of challenges related to diversity, equity and democracy, both within education systems and in broader society. While many issues are shared – such as demographic change, rising polarisation or persistent gaps between policy and practice – there are also significant differences in political systems and educational policy landscapes. These variations reveal how efforts to promote diversity, equity and democracy are always deeply contextual, shaped by national histories, cultural norms and institutional structures. The diversity of histories, experiences and perspectives not only broadened the reach and value of this collection but also profoundly enriched our collaborative learning journey. The opportunity to learn about one another's contexts and lived realities brought a critical, reflective dimension to our transnational work, which deepened both our professional relationships and our collective understanding of the complex, context-bound nature of educational work (Heinz et al., 2026b).

The audience – *who is this book for, and how can it be used?*

This book is written for educators and policymakers who believe in education's transformative power to advance justice, inclusion and democracy – even in the most challenging times. We hope that it will speak to those seeking practical tools as well as theoretical ideas, collaborative strategies and a shared sense of solidarity in the ongoing work of educational change. It is for those who dare to imagine schools as spaces where knowledge and ideas are shared openly and discussed with honesty and critical depth, and where everyone has the right to learn, change and shape the future with compassion, courage and care. We wrote this book with teachers, school leaders, teacher educators, academics and policymakers in the broad field of education in mind, and we think that it will also be of interest to academics in sociology, philosophy, psychology, leadership, management and other related fields.

The practical case study chapters in Part Two offer ideas, conceptual models and resources for teacher educators, school leaders and professional development bodies to design context-sensitive professional learning programmes that enhance educators' understanding, agency and skills related to diversity, equity and democracy in schools. These chapters include sample activities, discussion points and reflections from both programme facilitators and participants. Educators can dip in and out, adapt a full professional learning programme or create their own by mixing ideas from the different initiatives described here. They can also draw on Chapters 3 and 4 to deepen their understanding of key concepts and select suitable professional learning approaches. Particularly useful are the conceptual tools explained throughout the programmes, as well as the recommendations for developing positive collaborative learning cultures.

Overview of content: *What is in this book?*

Part One – Professional learning for diversity, equity and democracy in schools – context, concepts and rationale – consists of four introductory, context and theory-/rationale-based chapters. Following this introductory chapter, where we, the editors of this collection, outline the rationale, focus, background and content of the book, the second chapter, 'Big Ideas for Better

Schools': A transnational professional learning project', provides a brief overview of the Erasmus-funded transnational BIBS project, which supported the collaborative work we share in this book, especially with regard to its background, objectives and approach.

In Chapter 3, 'Diversity, equity and democracy in school leadership: Exploring troublesome concepts in troubled times', Gerry Mac Ruairc, Sara Gartland, Manuela Heinz and María Jesús Rodríguez-Entrena explore the rationale for professional learning programmes in the areas of diversity, equity and democracy for school leaders and teachers drawing on, and synthesising, key research and policy from relevant fields. Positioned in the context of the current anti-diversity, equity and inclusion (DEI) wave of discourse, this chapter provides an overview of conceptualisations of diversity, equity and democracy, specifically addressing how these concepts intersect in symbiotic ways at both theoretical and practical levels. Recent research, policy and legislation related to these three 'big issues' will be examined to explicate current perspectives and practice. The chapter thus serves as a helpful foundation and conceptual guide for researchers and practitioners exploring the three themes.

Chapter 4, written by Mary Nihill and Gerry Mac Ruairc and titled 'A model to enable professional learning for transformative school leadership', examines teacher professional learning research, theories and policies. The authors argue for an approach to professional learning that encourages engagement with the specifics of school contexts as a core feature in the design and implementation. Central to the model is an emphasis on the leader as a professional as well as a person. This dual focus is essential, since many of the policies related to diversity and equity draw on the hearts, minds and souls of leaders and teachers. The proposed professional learning model explicitly encourages participants to engage in a process of sense-making of new developments so that the understanding of the 'why' in its broadest and most empowering sense is at the core of the 'how' of the on-the-ground implementation of developments and innovation.

Part Two – Making it happen – learning from case studies – showcases five professional learning programmes for teachers and school leaders implemented in Ireland, Poland, Spain, Norway and Chile. These case studies provide accounts of how the various professional learning programmes were designed and implemented and what we learned – both individually and collectively – throughout the process. They are written with educators, school leaders and professional development providers in mind, offering conceptual tools, practical ideas, materials and inspiration for those working to advance equity and democratic practice in schools.

The chapter from Ireland, 'Professional learning with school leaders on diversity, equity and inclusion in Ireland: Deepening understanding and commitment through safe and honest 'big issue' conversations', is written by

Manuela Heinz, Cáitlin Graham, Art O Neachtain, Gerry Mac Ruairc, Sara Gartland and Claire Whyte. This chapter presents a professional learning programme designed for school leaders and teachers in Ireland, focused on exploring DEI in education as interlinked theoretical and practical concepts. The authors describe and discuss the collaborative design process, identifying key considerations that informed the development of guiding principles for collaborative professional learning. The chapter highlights the importance of creating safe spaces and fostering a shared understanding of learners' rights to express and refine evolving ideas throughout a collective learning journey.

In Chapter 6, 'Diversity, democracy and equity: Developing an understanding of complex social phenomena with teachers and students in Poland', Jakub Kołodziejczyk, Joanna Kotlarz, Grzegorz Mazurkiewicz and Joanna Trzópek-Paszkiewicz explore a collaborative professional learning initiative aimed at deepening school leaders' and teachers' understanding of the complex societal constructs of diversity, equity and democracy. The initiative involved academics, teachers and high school students in Poland. Following the collection of data from students to capture their understandings and perspectives towards the 'big issues' of diversity, equity and democracy, students, with the support of teachers, used semantic analysis of concepts to collaboratively create definitions based on their own responses to three surveys. The discussions among students unfolding during this process of analysis and the resulting definitions (semantic fields) provided teachers with new and deep insight into their students' understanding of the concepts and served as a foundation for designing future activities and lessons.

In Chapter 7, titled 'What is democracy? Recognising diverse perspectives and building shared understandings with school leaders in Spain through a professional learning experience', written by María Jesús Rodríguez-Entrena, Antonio Portela Pruaño, María del Carmen Maldonado López, Francisco Alfonso Hernández López and Abraham Bernárdez-Gómez, a change-oriented professional learning model was implemented to create spaces for debate, reflection and joint teacher learning. The authors provide insights into the professional learning activities used and the outcomes of these, detailing lessons they learnt from the critical analysis of training materials, field notes and pre- and post-programme surveys conducted with participants. In the conclusion, they identify both barriers and opportunities that schools face in offering students educational experiences that cultivate the competencies required for active participation in democratic societies and communities. The chapter emphasises the importance of developing communities of practice where collaborative learning is fostered in schools. Additionally, it highlights the significant benefits of partnerships between universities and schools and of leveraging real-world experience to enhance educational outcomes.

Chapter 8, 'Democracy as a central value in a national curriculum: Working with school leaders and teachers to connect values with practice in Norway', by Eli Ottesen, Ruth Jensen, Bård Halvorsen and Pia Merethe Vinje, provides insights into a professional learning initiative for democracy education implemented in Norway. The 2020 curriculum renewal for primary and secondary schools in Norway aims to more closely align educational content with the country's central values, placing particular emphasis on democracy as a central educational value. This chapter draws on a professional learning programme implemented in a rural school in Norway to explore some of the persistent challenges in realising education *about*, *through* and *for* democracy in practice – highlighting the gap between curricular intent and implementation. Grounded in analyses of the workshop materials and data collected through teacher interviews and pupil surveys, the authors identify and discuss the role of conceptual models as tools for collective discourses and in-service professional learning, the need for time and leadership, and the importance of dealing with past experiences, ongoing actions and hopes and concerns about the future.

In Chapter 9, 'Education for citizenship under democratic strain: Professional learning for school leaders and teachers in Chile', Camila Jara Ibarra, Macarena Sánchez Bachmann and Javiera Peña Fredes present professional development tools designed for school leaders and teachers in Chile to support the planning and delivery of civic and citizenship education. In a context marked by growing public distrust in representative democracy and the rise of disruptive forms of political participation, citizenship education has gained increasing prominence in Chile's educational and policy agenda. The professional development activities were guided by the 3Cs framework – culture, curriculum and community – as well as by two key dimensions of citizenship education – the civil and the civic dimensions. Participants found the programme effective, especially for its practical tools, which can support school-based planning. They also underscored the importance of leadership involvement and the benefits of discussing strategies for addressing controversial topics in the classroom.

Part Three – Review of learning and charting pathways for the future – brings the threads of the book together. It synthesises key insights that emerged across the chapters and offers reflections on what effective professional learning in these areas can look like. In 'Transformative professional learning in action: Embracing complexity and critical co-inquiry for diversity, equity and democracy', Gerry Mac Ruairc, María Jesús Rodríguez-Entrena and Manuela Heinz synthesise learning from the previous chapters in order to make recommendations for future research, policy and practice. The authors pay particular attention to the importance of 'calling out' complexities, of explicitly addressing difficulties and discomfort with terminologies and of positioning practice and theory as closely interconnected. They also reflect on approaches that contributors used to 'dig deeper' into the 'big issues' – especially ways in which they connected real experiences and contextual data with relevant 'threshold concepts'. Finally, they emphasise the importance of, and share key principles for, the development of equal and mutually respectful school–university partnerships. This final chapter can inform the ongoing development of theories and practical approaches to school leaders' professional learning. It offers a succinct summary of challenges as well as promoters to professional learning and envisions a teaching and school leadership force that is more engaged in, informed about and ready to respond to issues related to increasingly diversified student populations as well as the pressing need for greater equity and social justice in more authentic democratic societies.

Acknowledgement of funding

Erasmus+ project, funded by Léargas (Ireland) 2019-1-IE01-KA201-051528

References

Ainscow, M. (2020). Promoting inclusion and equity in education: Lessons from international experiences. *Nordic Journal of Studies in Educational Policy*, *6*(1), 7–16.

Alongi, M. D., Heddy, B. C., & Sinatra, G. M. (2016). Real-world engagement with controversial issues in history and social studies: Teaching for transformative experiences and conceptual change. *Journal of Social Science Education*, *15*(2), 26–41.

Apple, M. W. (2018). The struggle for democracy in education. In M. W. Apple, L. Armando, S. Liu, A. Meshulam, & E. Schirmer (Eds.), *The struggle for democracy in education* (pp. 1–19). Routledge.

Ben-Porath, S. (2012). Citizenship as shared fate: Education for membership in a diverse democracy. *Educational Theory*, *62*(4), 381–395. https://doi.org/10.1111/j.1741-5446.2012.00452.x

Bessant, J., Farthing, R., & Watts, R. (2016). Co-designing a civics curriculum: Young people, democratic deficit and political renewal in the EU. *Journal of Curriculum Studies*, *48*(2), 271–289. https://doi.org/10.1080/00220272.2015.1018329

Biesta, G. (2019). What kind of society does the school need? Redefining the democratic work of education in impatient times. *Studies in Philosophy and Education*, *38*(6), 657–668. https://doi.org/10.1007/s11217-019-09675-y

Cerna, L., Mezzanotte, C., Rutigliano, A., Brusino, O., Santiago, P., Borgonovi, F., & Guthrie, C. (2021). Promoting inclusive education for diverse societies: A conceptual framework. *OECD Education Working Papers, No. 260*. OECD Publishing. https://doi.org/10.1787/94ab68c6-en

Crenshaw, K. (1989). Demarginalising the intersection of race and sex: A Black feminist critique of antidiscrimination doctrine, feminist theory and antiracist politics. *University of Chicago Legal Forum*, *1*(8). http://chicagounbound.uchicago.edu/uclf/vol1989/iss1/8

de Groot, I. (2017). Mock elections in civic education: A space for critical democratic citizenship development. *Journal of Social Science Education*, *16*(3), 83–95.

Dewey, J. (1903). Democracy in education. *The Elementary School Teacher*, *4*(4), 193–204.

Elfert, M., & Morris, P. (2022). The long shadow between the vision and the reality: A review of the UNESCO report reimagining our futures together. *Quaderni di Pedagogia della Scuola*, *1*(2), 37–44.

Fielding, M. (2012). Más allá de la voz del alumnado: patrones de colaboración y las exigencias de la democracia profunda. *Revista de Educación*, *359*, 45–65.
Gorski, P. C., & Swalwell, K. (2015). Equity literacy for all. *Educational Leadership*, *72*(6), 34–40.
Gramsci, A. (2011). *Prison notebooks* (Vols. 1–3). Columbia University Press.
Gutiérrez, R. (2011). Context matters: How should we conceptualize equity in mathematics education? In B. Herver-Eisenmann, J. Choppin, D. Wagner, & D. Pinn (Eds.), *Equity in discourse for mathematics education: Theories, practices, and policies* (pp. 17–33). Springer.
Heinz, M. (2024). Holistic teacher education: Emphasising relationships, pedagogies and environments. *European Journal of Teacher Education*, *47*(3), 409–414. https://doi.org/10.1080/02619768.2024.2366580
Heinz, M., & Fleming, M. (2019). Leading change in teacher education: Balancing on the wobbly bridge of school-university partnership. *European Journal of Educational Research*, *8*(4), 1295–1306.
Heinz, M., Graham, C., O Neachtain, A., Mac Ruairc, G., Gartland, S., & Whyte, C. (2026). Professional learning with school leaders on diversity, equity and inclusion in Ireland: Deepening understanding and commitment through safe and honest 'big issue' conversations. In M. Heinz, M. J. Rodríguez-Entrena, & G. Mac Ruairc (Eds.), *Professional learning for diversity, equity and democracy: Big ideas for better schools* (pp. 65–86). London: Routledge.
Heinz, M., Mac Ruairc, G., & Rodríguez-Entrena, M. J. (2026). Big ideas for better schools: A transnational professional learning project. In M. Heinz, M. J. Rodríguez-Entrena, & G. Mac Ruairc (Eds.), *Professional learning for diversity, equity and democracy: Big ideas for better schools* (pp. 17–23). London: Routledge.
Heinz, M., Mc Daid, R., & Keane, E. (2025). The essential role of teacher diversity in creating equitable and inclusive learning environments: An interdisciplinary conceptual framework. *Learning Environments Research*, 1–21.
Heinz, M., & Swennen, A. (2025). Teacher education research must shape and drive transformative change towards more sustainable, socially just and inclusive futures. *European Journal of Teacher Education*, 1–9.
Keane, E., Heinz, M., & Mc Daid, R. (2023). Diversifying the teaching profession: Representation matters. In E. Keane, M. Heinz, & R. Mc Daid (Eds.), *Diversifying the teaching profession: Dimensions, dilemmas and directions for the future* (pp. 3–21). Routledge.
Lee, C. (2019). Courageous leaders: Promoting and supporting diversity in school leadership development. *Management in Education*, *34*(1), 5–15. https://doi.org/10.1177/0892020619878828
Mac Ruairc, G., Gartland, S., Heinz, M., & Rodríguez-Entrena, M. J. (2026). Diversity, equity and democracy in school leadership: Troublesome concepts in troubled times. In M. Heinz, M. J. Rodríguez-Entrena, & G. Mac Ruairc (Eds.), *Professional learning for diversity, equity and democracy: Big ideas for better schools* (pp. 24–46). London: Routledge.
Mac Ruairc, G., Ottesen, E., & Precey, R. (Eds.). (2013). *Leadership for inclusive education: Values, vision and voices* (Vol. 18). Springer Science & Business Media.
Neves, C., Almeida, A. P., & Ferreira, M. (2023). Headteachers and inclusion: Setting the tone for an inclusive school. *Education Sciences*, *13*(2), 129. https://doi.org/10.3390/educsci13020129
OECD. (2025). Reducing inequalities by investing in early childhood education and care. *Starting strong*. Paris: OECD Publishing. https://doi.org/10.1787/b78f8b25-en
Patterson, A. D. (2019). Equity in groupwork: The social process of creating justice in a science classroom. *Cultural Studies of Science Education*, *14*(2), 361–381.

Riley, K. (2022). *Compassionate leadership for school belonging*. UCL Press.
Scotton, P. (2020). Knowing, understanding, living, dissenting and countering: The educational moment in the enhancement of democratic citizenship. *Studies in Philosophy and Education*, *39*(1), 71–844.
Shields, C. M., & Hesbol, K. A. (2020). Transformative leadership approaches to inclusion, equity, and social justice. *Journal of School Leadership*, *30*(1), 3–22.
Theoharis, G. (2024). *The school leaders our children deserve: Seven keys to equity, social justice, and school reform*. Teachers College Press.
UNESCO. (2021). *Reimagining our futures together: A new social contract for education*. Paris: United Nations Educational, Scientific and Cultural Organization.
Zeichner, K. (2010). Rethinking the connections between campus courses and field experiences in college-and university-based teacher education. *Journal of Teacher Education*, *61*(1–2), 89–99.

2

BIG IDEAS FOR BETTER SCHOOLS

A transnational professional learning project

Manuela Heinz, Gerry Mac Ruairc, and María Jesús Rodríguez-Entrena

Introduction – background and key objectives of the 'Big Ideas for Better Schools' project

The idea for this book originated and took shape while we worked on the Erasmus+-funded project 'Big Ideas for Better Schools: Professional Learning for Diversity, Equity and Democracy'. The project was funded by Léargas (Ireland, 2019-1-IE01-KA201-051528) and started in 2019. As we are still working on the themes and objectives related to the project, it is hard to say that it is complete. However, the funded period came to an end in 2023. The project brought together academic institutions and school partners from Ireland, Norway, Poland and Spain. Our goal was to deepen educators' conversations about, understanding of, and agency in diversity, equity and democracy through collaborative professional learning. Along the way, we formed strong professional relationships, learned from one another, struggled through challenging times and deepened our understanding and commitment to democratic collaborative school–university partnership work. The outputs we developed together – country portfolios, professional learning programmes and cross-curricular toolkits – served as both scaffolds and springboards for rich conversations and meaningful change in schools.

In 2018, we wrote in our funding application:

> There has been a worrying rise in anti-diversity discourse and policy over the past decade in the US and in EU countries and beyond. These recent developments have compounded many other well-established forms of inequity. The outcome of this has been the increasing popularity of the political right, especially that of the extreme right. The increasingly

DOI: 10.4324/9781032629292-3

> unchecked 'escalator' approach whereby extreme, often unchecked, views can lead to either support for terrorism or direct negative action against specific individuals or groups has resulted in many forms of victimisation and marginalisation.
>
> Overcoming negative beliefs about others is not just a matter of legislation but of developing perspectives and attitudes that promote a sense of 'shared humanity'. This requires a focus at the most basic level on what we have in common rather than what divides. This is of particular relevance to how schools respond to diversity, and to how children and young people experience, and are shaped by, these responses and actions in school. As children grow, their views develop and become more established. Once discriminatory attitudes become embedded, they are hard to shake or change. Increasing tolerance and reducing discrimination requires deliberative and specific action on the part of education. Schools are often ill-equipped to engage with the critical ideas and conversations needed to prepare young people for, and enable them to contribute to, a society more firmly based on diversity, equity and democracy. In many cases, there is a lack of deep knowledge and understanding among teachers and school leaders regarding these concepts, coupled with limited opportunities to engage in meaningful professional learning to enhance their awareness and expertise. Additionally, schools often provide little, if any, space for robust, in-depth deliberation on broader societal issues and transformative ideas.

When this project took off in 2019, we could not have foreseen the scale of global and regional events that would unfold over its lifetime – events that would not only shape but also, in many ways, intensify the urgency of our project's focus. The COVID-19 pandemic, the political shifts across Europe (particularly in Poland and Hungary), Brexit, the growing global Black Lives Matter movement, the refugee crisis triggered by the war in Ukraine, especially affecting our colleagues in Poland, violent conflict in Israel, the re-election of Trump and the increasingly weakening position and influence of international institutions – all of these developments challenged the very values at the heart of this project. Each of our three core concepts – diversity, equity and democracy – has been, and is, increasingly tested and contested since we started our work on this project, sharpening their relevance and the urgency of addressing them.

As our collaboration unfolded, we felt compelled to share what we were learning. Writing this book together became a natural extension of our work. It is our way of capturing not only the insights and innovations that emerged from the project but also the spirit of collaboration and mutual learning that defined it. At the heart of the volume are three deeply connected themes – diversity, equity and democracy – around which our professional dialogue consistently revolved.

The core objectives of the project were to:

- support and encourage, and provide space for, the engagement of school leaders and teachers with each of the three topics – diversity, equity and democracy – in order to enhance and deepen their professional knowledge and understanding,
- encourage school leaders and teachers in project schools to develop critical perspectives, ask questions, be innovative and creative and contribute to school improvement by exploring and addressing school-identified issues related to diversity, equity and democracy,
- provide opportunities for sustained transnational exchange and collaboration to expand and deepen thinking and understanding about and for diversity, equity and democracy,
- ensure that the outcomes of the project are translated into more democratic forms of engagement among leaders, teachers and students, approaches that are better aligned with the kinds of needs many students have in making sense of their complex social worlds,
- support schools in making more explicit efforts to include the complexity of children's and young people's social realities in their education, and
- identify ways to enhance student engagement so that all students are included as meaningful participants in their education.

From the outset, our aim was to bring deeper conversations about these 'big issues' into schools through professional conversations. A core focus of the 'Big Ideas for Better Schools' project was the development of professional learning programmes to support teachers and leaders to engage with these themes in ways that were theoretically informed, critically reflective and practice-oriented. A central ambition of the project was to shift the focus from the portrayal and announcement of these values as aspirational statements – commonly found in school ethos or policy documents – to the realm of real, critical and sustained dialogue. We began with the understanding that issues of diversity, equity and democracy extend well beyond the scope of policy. While we acknowledge the significance of national policies and global frameworks – particularly in a time when these values face increasing political push-back – we contend that a genuine commitment to promoting them demands much more than compliance or surface-level engagement. It requires deep, critical understanding that goes far beyond 'common sense', general kindness or the assertion that one is merely 'following the required policy documents' (Edling & Mooney Simmie, 2020).

We were very aware that in the busy, often reactive, life of schools, such themes are frequently acknowledged but rarely interrogated in depth. In addition, majority-oriented normative school cultures are often taken for granted and largely invisible to homogeneous teaching bodies that are predominantly drawn from majority group backgrounds (Heinz et al., 2023). By deliberately scaffolding discussion and reflection in professional learning spaces through to classroom practice, the project aimed to create new opportunities to revisit, rethink and action these ideas in more grounded and practical ways. Ultimately, we hoped that these discussions would bring the values to life – begin to shape school life in its broadest sense – everyday interactions, relationships and judgements about priorities and educational practices that shape school communities. Drawing on Dewey's (1916) conception of democracy as a lived experience and building on the distinction between thin and thick (or strong) democracy (Apple, 2018; Barber, 1984), as well as notions of strong equity (Cochran-Smith & Stringer Keefe, 2022), the project aimed to cultivate thick*er* (or strong*er*) understandings of these values – not as abstract ideals or words on ethos statements but as critically examined principles deeply woven into the everyday fabric of school life.

Project philosophy and approach

We always felt that the project needed to target the minds and hearts of the participants. We knew we had ambitious expectations for transformative outcomes, but we were not naive enough to think that designing and implementing a professional learning programme focused on diversity and equity, for example, was going to change the world. We had hoped, however, that it might begin to change the questions asked, the assumptions that gave rise to these questions and the directions in which teachers and school leaders were looking as well as the ambitions they set for themselves, their students and schools. A comprehensive review of contemporary literature related to the three themes formed a key part of this work and laid the foundation for the development of the professional learning programmes. The concepts of diversity, equity and democracy were understood as deeply interconnected and further linked to a wider set of key ideas – including culture, power, identity, justice, inclusion and intersectionality (see Mac Ruairc et al., 2026) – which collectively shaped the design and focus of the programmes.

Overall, the project involved and reached 22 teachers/school leaders and 150 students in Ireland, 12 teachers/school leaders and 200 students in Spain, 15 teachers/school leaders and 200 students in Norway and ten teachers/school leaders and 100 students in Poland. Working alongside teachers and leaders in a genuinely collaborative process allowed us to shape and refine project materials in ways that remained responsive to the realities of school life while also supporting professional engagement with diversity, equity and democracy in tangible, thought-provoking ways. From the outset, academics, teachers and school leaders collaborated in the design, development, implementation and ongoing evaluation of the project. All university partners brought long-standing national relationships with schools to the project, which proved particularly valuable when COVID-19 disrupted activity just six months into the timeline.

The main methodology used in this project was based on the co-construction and piloting of materials and resources for use in 1) professional learning programmes for staff and 2) cross-curricular lessons or learning units for students focused on three core concepts – diversity, equity and democracy. At the core of this work, and the starting point, was the development of more nuanced and aware conversations in schools on topics related to the three key themes – diversity, equity and democracy. From an academic point of view, the university partners were very aware of the contested nature of the themes and the fact that they are widely viewed as difficult and challenging ideas to incorporate into professional discussions and teaching and learning content and pedagogy. Our intention was to work together to break down any barriers, either real or imagined, between the knowledge that exists in research and scholarship, and the pedagogy and practice in schools.

In working towards our aims, we began not with abstract theories but with the realities of the schools and – importantly – the voices of the students and teachers themselves. We wanted to ground the project in the realities of each participating school and national context. Each country team gathered data through surveys with students and teachers, designed to explore their current understandings, lived experiences, questions and aspirations in relation to the core themes of diversity, equity and democracy. These findings were compiled and analysed within country-specific portfolio reports, which also outlined the relevant policy, legal and curricular contexts, and were shared across the partnership during our international meetings. Together, these portfolios offered a vivid, real-time picture of how these complex and often contested themes were being lived out in very different school settings. What stood out most strongly was the impact of student voices on teachers and school leaders. Many were surprised not only by the depth and clarity of the views expressed by some students but also by the thought-provoking questions that were raised. In more than one case, teachers commented that they felt some students were ahead of them – more articulate, more reflective and more willing to engage with uncertainty and complexity. This was a humbling and energising moment. It helped shift the focus of our work – not just towards 'teaching' these concepts but towards creating spaces where meaning could be co-constructed.

The value of transnational collaboration

While the chapters in this book will provide detailed descriptions of how we conceptualised and grappled with the three complex concepts, as well as how we designed and implemented professional learning programmes across various national contexts, we want to highlight the immense value of international exchange and collaboration here. Central to the success of this project was the funding that enabled teachers, school leaders and teacher educators to come together for international meetings and workshops and, crucially, provided the time, space and substitution support needed for teachers to participate fully. Throughout the project, participants consistently emphasised the importance of learning from diverse situations and approaches across countries, identifying shared challenges and collaboratively developing solutions. Many described these experiences as 'insightful', 'inspirational' and 'deeply meaningful', recognising 'reciprocal learning' and 'changed perspectives' in programme evaluations. These transnational exchanges encouraged participants to question existing practices, affirm best practices, open up dialogue, reflect critically and foster both personal and professional growth. Ultimately, this international collaboration was a key motivator for all involved, creating rich opportunities for discussion and thoughtful feedback on the professional learning programmes we developed and implemented within our different national contexts.

As one teacher reflected in the final project evaluation, the greatest gratification came from seeing students actively engage in the project and witnessing the positive impact it had on them. 'We cannot forget', they reminded us, 'that we are working in the formation and education of the future generations of our society'. Throughout the project, there was a genuine sense of shared purpose – pursuing high ideals while remaining deeply aware that we were navigating fragile and complex terrain.

We all believe that this work has uncovered something vital. In many ways, we have just opened Pandora's box, beginning a challenging but necessary journey into these critical topics with leaders, teachers, students and, crucially, as a central focus for the future, communities. There is still much work to be done.

Acknowledgement of funding

Erasmus+ project, funded by Léargas (Ireland) 2019-1-IE01-KA201-051528

References

Apple, M. W. (2018). The struggle for democracy in education. In *The struggle for democracy in education* (pp. 1–19). Routledge.

Barber, B. R. (1984). *Strong democracy: Participatory politics for a new age*. University of California Press.

Cochran-Smith, M., & Stringer Keefe, E. (2022). Strong equity: Repositioning teacher education for social change. *Teachers College Record*, *124*(3), 9–41.

Dewey, J. (1916). *Democracy and education*. New York: Macmillan.

Edling, S., & Simmie, G. M. (2020). *Democracy and teacher education: Dilemmas, challenges and possibilities*. Routledge.

Heinz, M., Keane, E., & Mc Daid, R. (2023). Charting pathways toward a more diverse, equitable and inclusive teaching profession. In E. Keane, M. Heinz, & R. Mc Daid (Eds.), *Diversifying the teaching profession: Dimensions, dilemmas and directions for the future* (pp. 226–240). Routledge.

Mac Ruairc, G., Gartland, S., Heinz, M., & Rodríguez-Entrena, M. J. (2026). Diversity, equity and democracy in school leadership: Troublesome concepts in troubled times. In M. Heinz, M. J. Rodríguez-Entrena, & G. Mac Ruairc (Eds.), *Professional learning for diversity, equity and democracy: Big ideas for better schools* (pp. 24–46). London: Routledge.

3

DIVERSITY, EQUITY AND DEMOCRACY IN SCHOOL LEADERSHIP

Troublesome concepts in troubled times

Gerry Mac Ruairc, Sara Gartland, Manuela Heinz, and María Jesús Rodríguez-Entrena

Introduction

And then there was . . .

When we started to work on this collection, we were in a very different world in terms of the discourses framing diversity, equity and democracy. When we set out on this journey in 2019, there were many danger signs on the horizon. Questions were being asked in relation to the legitimacy of many previously hard-won recognitions and positions relating to equality and equity, particularly as they referred to diversity. What was unimaginable at that time, but has since become clearly identifiable, is the extent and speed of the rebuttal to this well-established, dominant worldview:

> Whereas the fascist authoritarian extreme right was a marginal political phenomenon in many democratic countries 30 years ago, it has in a relatively short period of time become a strong, and emboldened segment of the mainstream right with ideas and viewpoints once considered deviant and morally repugnant today confidently asserted as the new common sense and increasingly shaping public policy.
>
> *(Cammaerts, 2022, p. 2)*

Negative connotations and accusations of being 'woke' have increasingly become part of the articulation of the backlash against so many concepts that have informed education policy for decades. Before we look at the anti-woke perspective, it is worth focusing on what is now defined as 'woke', so we can have a shared understanding of what is being rejected by current challenges. Woke is intrinsically tied to Black consciousness and anti-racist struggles. Now that it has become weaponised by the far right, it has been decoupled

DOI: 10.4324/9781032629292-4

from its initial meaning in the struggle for civil rights (Cammaerts, 2022) into an insult used against anyone engaged in the struggle against fascism, racism and other forms of injustices and discrimination. In current discourse and across the full suite of social media, those who became demonised as 'woke' are advocates:

> promoting social justice and human rights, embracing social and sexual pluralism thus opposing homophobia, racism, sexism, and more recently transphobia . . . being woke entails a commitment to fairness, dignity and respect in the way that people are governed and treated so that women and minorities are not governed or treated as second-class citizens because they do not conform to the patriarchal, heteronormative, white definitions of normality.
>
> *(Dorey, 2024, p. 94)*

For those of us who have argued for years for a more inclusive democratic education system that seeks to minimise the impact of marginalisation of all kinds on the life-chances of children and young people, it is hard to imagine an education system that would aspire to anything other than a very overt and solid alignment with the intention and direction of these perspectives. This book is premised on this worldview and its incumbent ambition for all education systems. It is difficult, therefore, to imagine, let alone respond to, a view where practices condemning discrimination and contesting hate speech are silenced by a deliberate denouement of their marginalised realities accompanied by a mis-characterisation of this marginalisation (Gupton & O Sullivan, 2024). These emancipatory perspectives are increasingly framed as an intolerant ideological stance, part of political correctness gone mad and part of an aberrant, crazy, elitist and irrational mob, out of touch with common sense (Cammaerts, 2022). They are often positioned by this new order as divisive perspectives and labelled as divisive concepts in policy documents (White House, 2020 cited in Schoorman, 2024). Voicing racist, sexist or LGBTQ-phobic views has now re-emerged as a legitimate opinion and as worthy of consideration and recognition as any other view. Those who oppose these views are positioned as part of the 'cancel culture' movement, attempting to silence opposing voices to what is considered leftist ideology. These perspectives are gaining momentum with anti-woke academic rhetoric emerging as intellectual scaffolding for ideological and political efforts that undermine the hard-earned legal and organisational advances in the area of DEI made over the last several decades (Ajnesh & Śliwa, 2024). Most recently, in the Trump 2.0 era, these perspectives have become more and more legitimatised and fuelled by the deliberate shutting down of diversity-based programmes led by US federal policy. These trends are coupled with, and to varying degrees enabled by, an 'undermining of democracy by curriculum' in schools in some states in the United States (Schoorman, 2024; Roberts et al., 2025). These practices have also extended beyond the United States – into US companies located worldwide and also emerging in the United Kingdom (see Dorey, 2024, for a good overview of UK developments) and European Union (EU) (see Wunsch & Chiru, 2024· on democratic backsliding in the EU and Gergorićk et al., 2025, for trends related to gender and anti-feminism in particular). This is very regrettable considering that, traditionally, both the United Kingdom and the EU were very strong advocates and allies of more liberal, inclusive societies. Increasingly, this anti-DEI turn is accompanied by a surveillance regime (Willard, 2024) that serves to create a culture of epistemic, symbolic, material and physical violence that the current types of surveillance perpetuate (Willard, 2024, 68). In more and more states in the United States, what is taught to, and read by, students is increasingly subject to 1) censorship particularly as it relates to race, gender and sexuality and 2) surveillance by parents, other teachers and sometimes students themselves, all of whom are encouraged to report those teachers deemed to be teaching inappropriate content (Bylica et al., 2024). Essentially, we are now in a Gramscian war of position (Gramsci) – a 'metapolitics' that is shaping a very oppositional culture war (Cammaerts, 2022), a form of ideological warfare (Asen, 2024) aimed at changing hearts and minds for the long term.

All of these factors create a context for schools and school leaders that makes diversity work more problematic. In Ireland, there is some evidence of far-right ideology having an impact on educational institutions. Some individual institutions and academics have been targeted by far-right conservative groups. Colleagues at the University of Galway were subjected to significant abuse on social media following the publication of a paper detailing the lack of diversity in the teacher profession and among teacher education students in Ireland. More recently, a phrase that JD Vance used at a national event 'The professors are the enemy' (invoking Richard Nixon) was spray-painted at the main entrance to the St. Pat's Campus, Dublin City University, in August 2024. While there is no overt sign that this type of influence is currently impacting how education is conceptualised at the policy level, this does not mean that the ground has not shifted from a place where there was a much stronger and more secure sense that the prevailing shared view of the world was one where diversity was recognised and affirmed, and to varying degrees in schools, equity and democracy were foundational principles of how the system responded to this diversity. Even under these more favourable conditions, many policies and practices in the domain of diversity lacked efficacy. They were, at least broadly, aligned with the commitment to more inclusion in our schools. Now that it is possible to legitimately challenge this trajectory of policy and practice, school leaders stand in a less secure position and will need to be more prepared to take on challenges to school policies that prioritise diversity actions.

Notwithstanding this, years of thinking, research and scholarship on DEI have left a strong legacy of discourse that cannot be simply erased by the current trends. In formulating a response to current challenges, it will be necessary to draw on this body of scholarship to frame responses while remaining committed to delivering on the promise of more inclusive and empowering schools and classrooms. While anti-woke may well be the current 'new kid in town' (Dorey, 2024) in political circles and, to different extents, beyond, it is our view that it has no place in the pedagogical world. It is inconceivable to imagine a school system that would overtly turn the clock back on years of progress towards more equitable outcomes for education. Education remains one of the great equalisers; while it has struggled to alter persistent patterns of successes and failures for different social groups over time, it has at least tried to move things on (Labaree, 2012). The remainder of this chapter will explore recent scholarship in relation to the concept of trilogy explored in this book. This is not to negate years of scholarship that provided the bedrock for these more recent scholars but rather to highlight the amount of work in these areas that has been and continues to be undertaken all over the globe.

The United Nations 2030 Agenda for Sustainable Development (2015) and related SDGs (2022) position education as both a right and a tool to unlock individual life-chances. Building on the United Nations Convention on the Rights of the Child (UNCRC), which states that all children have the right to education (2010), SDG 4 calls for member nations to 'ensure inclusive and equitable quality education and promote lifelong learning opportunities for all' (2022). This firmly positions not only education but also inclusive, equitable and quality education as a right. Other SDGs – such as SDGs 5 (Gender Equality), 10 (Reduced Inequalities) and 16 (Peace, Justice and Strong Institutions) – position education as a tool to be used in achieving these goals. This broad policy framework provides imperatives to the different nation-states that have signed up to these goals to ensure that their education systems perform in ways that achieve these outcomes. It will not be easy to walk away from these commitments, particularly as even with current efforts, education, to date, has largely reproduced many of the social harms, injustices and inequities that lead to, or exacerbate, poverty and other social issues (Bourdieu, 2018; Cerna et al., 2021). The persistent nature of these outcomes has been rehearsed in scholarship and practice nationally and internationally for decades. More recently, intensive and active patterns of globalisation and migration have led to rapidly increasing levels of diversity in countries around the world (Ainscow, 2020; Cerna et al., 2022). This evolving and emerging context for education systems is mediated differently by different countries; however, one key driver of any system focused on creating a more socially transformative education system is the need to ensure access to inclusive, equitable and quality education that helps to sustain justice in other areas, and by consequence, it is essential that key educators are informed by perspectives that explore the complexity of diversity and equity in education while seeking to recognise the authentic democratic processes typically associated with the type of transformative educational practices that support diversity and equitable outcomes (Biesta, 2019). The importance of intentional and responsive teacher and leadership professional learning on these types of topics emerges from scholarship as linked to positive outcomes (Abawi et al., 2018; Bjørnsrud & Nilsen, 2019; López-Azuaga & Suárez Riveiro, 2020; McGillicuddy & Machowska-Kosciak, 2021; Meléndez-Luces & Couto-Cantero, 2021; Raphael & Allard, 2013; Shevlin et al., 2013; Tuters, 2015). There was a clear focus in this body of scholarship on consistent and critical teacher reflection, on developing understandings and exploring experiences of diversity with respect to classroom context(s), both individually and in community with others, identifying a need to foster the development and refinement of culturally responsive pedagogy (Bartz & Bartz, 2018; Bjørnsrud & Nilsen, 2019; Hajisoteriou & Angelides, 2017; Raphael & Allard, 2013; Tuters, 2015; Gay, 2023; Ladson-Billings, 1995; Ladson-Billings & Tate, 1995).

Exploring how to design and implement ways of enriching thinking and enhancing insight on diversity, equity and democracy was the main impetus for this collection. The experience of working in teacher education among participants in this study provided a clear insight into the challenges of asking practitioners to engage deeply with these complex and challenging topics in a professional learning context (see Heinz et al., 2026a for teacher educators' considerations and Bryan, 2016 for good examples of how teacher education students react to the exploration of race in a university seminar). Each of these can be considered threshold concepts (Meyer & Land, 2005), and difficult knowledge (Bryan, 2016) (see Nihill & Mac Ruairc, 2026 for more details on these). Threshold concepts are transformative, in that grasping a threshold concept involves a conceptual shift (changing what you know) as well as an ontological shift (changing your sense of being). In a professional learning context, this pedagogy of discomfort (Boler, 1999 in Bryan, 2016) needs to acknowledge and respond to the disruptive emotional impact of this type of professional learning among participants. The 'learning outcomes' of working with these threshold concepts can often be irreversible, in that once a threshold concept is understood, the learner is unlikely to forget it (this does not exclude subsequent modification or rejection of the concept for a more refined or rival understanding). Threshold concepts are integrative insofar as they expose the hidden interrelatedness of the phenomenon. They are conceptually bound, in that 'any conceptual space will have terminal frontiers, bordering with thresholds into new conceptual areas' (Meyer & Land, 2005, p. 6). And finally, in the context of this and other chapters in the collection, threshold concepts usually involve 'troublesome knowledge'. Troublesome knowledge is 'that which appears counter-intuitive, alien (emanating from another culture or discourse), or seemingly incoherent' (Meyer & Land, 2005, p. 7).

Sharpening the sword

As part of the development of materials for the professional learning programmes, the university team in Ireland conducted a systematic review of the literature on each of the topics. A key feature of the review focused on the interrelatedness of the three constructs. The overall outcome of this work led to the view that diversity precludes the existence of inequity and, consequently, necessitates the discussion of equity and democratic processes. Additionally, diversity, equity and democracy inherently involve an acknowledgement of other constructs such as culture, power, identity, justice, intersectionality, inclusion and justice. The complexity and interrelatedness of the three constructs became clearer as our review of scholarship progressed; however, at the same time, the approach to how to present the topic to educators became less challenging. Because of the close interconnectedness of the ideas and concepts, the entry into exploration and learning could begin at a number of points. Essentially, for the purposes of this professional learning work in schools, and consequently for the purpose of this collection, we considered diversity as foundational insofar as diversity is there – it simply is. Linked to this are considerations of identity and intersectionality. Equity is a principle that should guide how schools and their leaders respond to this reality, and, in this way, education should have a positive impact on life-chances and outcomes. A focus on equity rather than equality facilitates a more nuanced consideration of practice in schools. Democracy and democratic approaches are viewed as the most optimal ways to achieve equity in support of diversity. We hoped that by integrating the three concepts in this way, we could facilitate the development of a more inclusive and holistic learning journey that would resonate better with the individual teacher and leader participants (see also Heinz et al., 2026b). In Figure 3.1, we present a general overview of how we frame each of the concepts individually and how each one contributed to the overall interrelatedness of the three core concepts.

Diversity

We began with diversity because, as noted above, it is a social reality that precludes and/or necessitates discussion of the other two constructs. Diversity is an increasingly relevant and important construct to unpack and clearly define due to the rapid acceleration of globalisation (Cerna et al., 2021). As we progressed, we identified a variety of definitions for diversity presented in

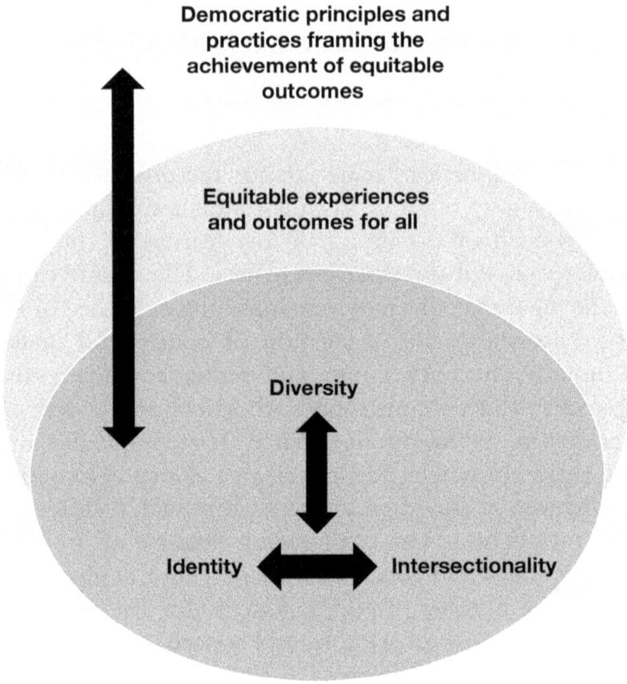

FIGURE 3.1 Diversity, equity and democracy: A conceptual map

the literature while working towards the objective of providing a singular set of descriptors that could aid in the understanding of the constructs of equity and democracy. The literature included presented a diverse range of definitions for diversity. Some characterised diversity as follows:

- cultural difference (Álvarez & Montoto, 2018; Gonzáles-Falcón et al., 2016; Meléndez-Luces & Couto-Cantero, 2021; Moss et al., 2017; Nikolaou et al., 2019; Rodríguez-Izquierdo, 2018; Virta, 2016),
- academic difference (Arvelo-Rosales et al., 2021; Bjørnsrud & Nilsen, 2019; Gilor & Katz, 2021; Raphael & Allard, 2013; Tomlinson, 2015),
- worldview difference (Bartz & Bartz, 2018),
- sexual orientation difference (Kjaran & Lehtonen, 2018) and
- (dis)ability difference (Murray et al., 2020) within a particular population.

These more narrowly defined conceptions of diversity served a particular purpose within the framing of the papers or the studies included in our review. While we appreciated that the experiences along specific dimensions of diversity are necessary and important, such understanding must not lead to a premature focusing on specific dimensions without acknowledging the broader conceptualisation of diversity. Therefore, we came to the view that a more expansive definition of diversity is needed, even if it complicates matters. Diversity is a descriptor that indicates a broad range of differences across a variety of social, economic, cultural, personal, geopolitical and educational factors (Cerna et al., 2021; Adam, 2021; Arvelo-Rosales et al., 2021; Hardy & Woodcock, 2015; Kovač & Vaala, 2021). Diversity is socially constructed, which means it is inextricably linked with conceptions of otherness as defined by the dominant group in a society, organisation or system (OECD, 2023). As Åberg (2020) warns, the term 'diversity', while often treated as 'a fact or an increasing tendency', is also a 'linguistic realisation of certain conceptions of difference' (p. 157) that impact 'those creating and those experiencing diversity' differently, often positioning 'the "diverse" parts of the population at the margins' (p. 169).

Identity

Identity is fundamentally linked to diversity (Back, 2025) in that diversity influences how identities are formed and subsequently recognised in society. Individual and collective identities impact how diverse groups present, interact and coexist, which, in turn, shapes social dynamics and patterns of exclusion and inclusion (Banks, 2024; Kirton & Green, 2021) within education and in society more broadly. Of all of the concepts explored in this book, identity is arguably the one that has created the most controversy. It is interesting that something so fundamental to humanity – 'who we are' has become so highly contested and divisive (Davies et al., 2017). The role schools play in young people's emerging identities is very significant; given how much time children and young people spend 'growing up' in schools, educational settings are an essential part of their identity formation. One of the core missions of most schools is to actively affirm and encourage the development of students' identities and individuality. Recent developments in the sociology of childhood and related fields have clearly identified this growing-up phase as essential in the developing young person. Childhood is not just about becoming something for the future – a preparation for adulthood; it is a discrete time in life where what happens has both contemporaneous and future building dimensions (Uprichard, 2008).

Identities evolve through relational interactions, which, again, position the school at the centre of this process, as so many relational experiences for young people happen in schools (Mullen & Robertson, 2021). These school relationships are different from those formed in family or community settings for many reasons, not least of which is the degree of agency young people have in forming these friendships (Rose et al., 2022; Leszczensky et al., 2022;

Crocetti et al., 2022; Branje, 2022). How children and young people choose to express their identities either aesthetically, linguistically, behaviourally or otherwise has been the source of considerable scholarship and indeed moral panic on the part of some (see Silcox, 2022, for example). Children and young people for many generations have created cultural and subcultural identities, based around a particular set of norms, the purpose of which is to signify a 'presentation of the self or the group' (Goffman, 1963) in a specific identifiable way – punks, mods, goths, etc. The outcome of all this identity work can be far from harmonious with the result that identity can have far-reaching implications for individuals; many identities are marginalised or viewed as undesirable. Different aspects of an identity, particularly the more stigmatised parts (James, 2022), can skew or overly influence how one is perceived by others, leading to processes of essentialisation, which can have very negative connotations (Gross & Protera, 2025; Fuligni, 2007; Goffman, 1963). It is beyond the scope of this chapter to provide a detailed overview of identity. What is intended here is to 1) note its link to diversity, 2) point out how it has become such a fraught space and 3) explore briefly how it manifests in schools.

There are a number of features of current and past models of schooling as they relate to identity that need to be problematised when working with school leaders. In order to build on some recent improvements in terms of inclusion in many systems, schools need to look more critically at identity on a number of fronts: ethnic, gender, disability, sexuality, indigenous culture, etc. (Sadowski, 2021), both in terms of representation in texts and curricula and in terms of how the diversity of the whole school community is included in all aspects of school life (Graham, 2006; Mac Ruairc, 2020a; Sadowski, 2021; Keane et al., 2018). Patterns of exclusion on the basis of a range of presentations of self are embedded in the system and in the rituals, practices and outcomes that frame, to different extents, all our education systems and normative school cultures (Graham, 2019; Heinz et al., 2023; Slee, 2010; Mac Ruairc, 2020a). Often, these ways of working can lead to exclusion and segregation, ultimately protecting an education system that does not sufficiently cater for individual identities (Slee, 2010; Mac Ruairc, 2020b). Examples of marginalising practices include:

- Individualising failure (Good, 2024)
- Deficit thinking (Bertrand & Marsh, 2021)
- Essentialising people – their lives, potential, hopes and possibilities (Eisenberg, 2013)
- Subtractive schooling (Valenzuela, 2005; Golden, 2023)

One of the features of schools that requires much more in-depth scrutiny is the functioning of social norms. In most schools, there can be a preference for a particular way of being – a requirement to present an identity that the school sees as valued (Bourdieu, 2018). This becomes the norm, and schools are good at defining, delimiting and policing the reproduction of this norm. In many contexts, a key task of schooling has focused on normalising difference by stabilising the 'other' in an environment that provides a buffer to enable schools to remain the same. A more critical analysis of what these norms are, where they come from, whose interests they serve and who they marginalise is needed. The imperative for maintaining the centre is derived from this view – that the natural order needs a centre and that it needs a cohesive system. However, the reality is that this cohesive 'centre' has privileged and continues to privilege particular social groups (Graham & Slee, 2008; Mac Ruairc et al., 2013).

Intersectionality

If identity were one-dimensional or made visible on a single-axis framework (Crenshaw, 1991), a lot of the complexity would be removed. This is not the case, however, as identity is never singular (King et al., 2025). While this does not mean that singular manifestations of identity function to essentialise people, the complexity of multiple identity signifiers in each individual remains. Intersectionality, originally developed by Crenshaw (1991), is a conceptual framework that helps conceptualise how different aspects of a person's identity, for example race, gender, sexuality, class and ability/disability (see Figure 3.2), interact and overlap, creating and shaping each individual experience of the world. It provides a way of exploring the multiple and intersecting functions of power and privilege (Shirley & Hargreaves,

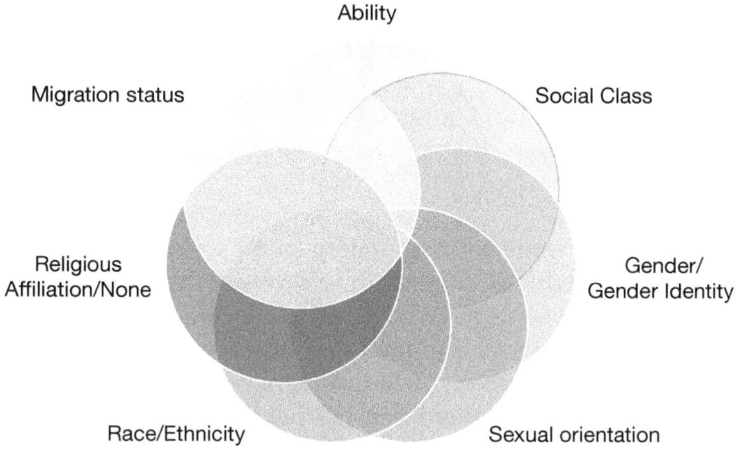

FIGURE 3.2 Intersectionality and intersecting identities

2024; Thomas & Macnab, 2022). It adds depth and nuance to how we understand identity by foregrounding explicitly that no single aspect of who we are exists in isolation. This framework provides a kind of superstructure that facilitates a consideration of multiple components of identities. It is all too frequently underused within education as a conceptual framework for guiding and shaping equitable and democratic responses to diversity. It is, in our view, the most transformative of the threshold concepts that needs to be explored with school leaders, as it holds significant potential to profoundly reshape a lot of what happens in schools and in classrooms. Shirley and Hargreaves (2024, pp. 113–117) have identified three forms of intersectionality that are useful to consider in the context of this collection. These include:

1. Critical intersectionality: This requires us to look at sources of marginalisation and oppression not as isolated issues needing single interventions but as reflections and matrices of domination that implicate us all.
2. Constructive intersectionality: Here, intersectionality is used as a way of ensuring inclusion and of creating a space where the different forms and manifestations of identities are deliberately used as the basis for inclusion. When operating in the domain of constructive intersectionality in a school, a culture prevails where everyone identifies and utilises the multiple and overlapping strengths [and challenges] that each student brings to their learning in the school' (Shirley & Hargreaves, 2024, p. 117).
3. Conflicting intersectionality: This is an important development of how intersectionality and power and privilege function, not in a zero-sum way; people who may be privileged in some respects may also be marginalised in others. Some people come from families or cultures that are both oppressed and oppressors. This dimension of intersectionality creates the greatest challenges for schools and school leaders. It is difficult to hold the positive and negative dimensions of these perspectives side by side. More work is needed here in order to see how the dilemmas created by this dynamic operate in practice – we might then be able to learn how these realities are best addressed in the school context.

Equity

A key issue derived from our exploration of equity in the context of this study revealed that critically attending to diversity at any level – from the teacher to the classroom, to the school and to education as a system – brings *in*equities and *ex*clusions of various types into focus (Cerna et al., 2021; Hippe et al., 2016). Inequity is a consequence of scarcity, a by-product of zero-sum logic and a social condition reproduced through systems such as education (McGhee, 2021). Just as diversity is intersectional, so too is inequity (Crenshaw, 1991). Inequity precludes any discussion of equity because the current state of affairs across the globe is an inequitable one. Equity, the study of equity and conversations about equity are necessary because of the existence of inequity and exclusion. Therefore, we begin with an understanding that inequity must be named, despite any discomfort that might create. Moving forward with that understanding is crucial to this work in schools with educators.

A key aspect of exploring equity in education is a focus on equity as a process of working towards fairness in educational and related economic outcomes with an intentional focus on access and identity. Three perspectives from the literature place explicit focus on defining equity in the context of education and frame and inform our synthesised view of equity as a process. Safir & Dugan (2021) define equity as 'an approach to ensuring equally high outcomes for all by removing the predictability of success or failure that currently correlates with any racial, social, economic, or cultural factor'. Similarly, Cerna et al. (2021) define equitable education systems as those that ensure that 'achievement of educational potential is not the result of personal and social circumstances, including factors such as gender, ethnic origin, Indigenous background, immigrant status, sexual orientation and gender identity, special education needs, and giftedness' (p. 27). Furthermore, Gutiérrez (2012) describes equity as 'fairness not sameness' to distinguish the concept of equity from equality, which is important because providing every student with the same supports, unfortunately, does not ensure equitable outcomes (Heinz et al., 2025). We identified four key themes related to equity that have powerful implications for practice and policy. First, individuals and schools committed to ongoing, and often collaborative, development of equity literacy (Gorski & Swalwell, 2015) more consistently created opportunities for equity within their curricula and learning communities (Ainscow, 2020; Barton et al., 2017; Jurow, 2016; Lambrecht et al., 2020). Second, sustained equity success requires both individual- and systems-level actions. Third, authentic incorporation of student voice promotes equity in a variety of educational spaces (Patterson, 2019). Fourth, a critical socio-political perspective fosters meaningful and responsive changes in instruction (Gutiérrez, 2012; Gorski, 2016; Louie, 2017; Morales-Doyle, 2019; Patterson, 2019) and/or policy (Leonardi & Moses, 2021; Syeed, 2022) with respect to equity.

Democracy

An exploration of democracy concludes our review of the three core themes included in the collection. Positioning democracy at this juncture is deliberate because, in theory, democratic processes are often identified as mechanisms through which equity can be addressed and equity outcomes can be achieved. In practice, however, democratic processes sometimes amplify the social reproduction of inequities in society and in the classroom. Thus, an examination of democracy and democratic practices in education is best situated *after* a critical understanding of diversity and (in)equity has been established.

Like equity, democracy is often conceptualised as a process. However, as Davies (1999) warns: 'democracy and equity, while linked, are not equivalent or synonymous concepts' (p. 130). This is because 'democracy presupposes the existence of three types of rights – political, economic and social: the right to participate in the political process; to enjoy a fair distribution of resources; and to be free from oppression' (p. 129). Equity – or, more specifically, inclusion and/or belonging, access to resources and/or opportunities, and justice – is a process initiated and sustained through democratic mechanisms (Biesta, 2019; Bolin, 2017; de Groot, 2017; Feu et al., 2017; Sant et al., 2021; Scotton, 2020). Some authors explicitly define constructs such as democracy, democratic education or democratic ideals (Biesta, 2019; Bolin, 2017; Feu et al., 2017; Jónsson & Garces Rodriguez, 2021; Scotton, 2020; Warren, 2016; Waterson & Moffa, 2016). Others implicitly characterise democracy through discussions of related concepts such as citizenship education for democracy or mock elections (Alongi et al., 2016; Ben-Porath, 2012; Jeliazkova, 2015; Wahrman & Hartaf, 2021). Democracy within the education domain is often framed as a nuanced process of co-construction that supports decision-making, typically focused on balancing the needs of individuals with the needs of groups (Ben-Porath, 2012; Bessant et al., 2016; de Groot, 2017; Guérin, 2017; Lundahl & Olson, 2013; Mathé, 2020; Payne et al., 2020; Sant et al., 2021; Shultz & Guimaraes-Iosif, 2012). Some characterise democracy in a strictly procedural manner (de Groot & Lo, 2022; Jeliazkova, 2015; Kopińska, 2019; Wahrman & Hartaf, 2021; Waterson & Moffa, 2016). It is important to note that the difference between the co-construction and the procedural definitions is that the former emphasises the relational aspects of the process, while the latter simply lists formal procedures for enacting democracy. Others characterise democracy as a means for managing conflict (Alongi et al., 2016; Parra et al., 2021; Warren, 2016). Such views are related to the co-construction framing in that they acknowledge the relational nature of democratic processes; however, they differ in that they centre conflict and operate from the perspective that a co-constructed solution may not be possible. It is worth noting that many of the characterisations of democracy identified highlight the relational aspects of democracy or of democratic processes. This is important to note, especially when discussing democracy alongside constructs such as diversity and equity. Diversity influences relational interactions (Åberg, 2020; Kovač & Vaala, 2021; Parra et al., 2021; Payne et al., 2020), and the effects of such interactions influence (in)equity (Bolin, 2017; Louie, 2017; Payne et al., 2020). This orientation towards diversity, equity and democracy *together* informs a synthesised view of democracy that can guide both research and practice.

Democracy is a process for relating to and living with others (Ben-Porath, 2012; Biesta, 2019; Bolin, 2017; Guérin, 2017; Jónsson & Garces Rodriguez, 2021; Mathé, 2020; Parra et al., 2021; Payne et al., 2020) that is also a form of government. Democratic processes are mechanisms for co-constructing social norms and realities informed by individuals' and groups' values and identities (Alongi et al., 2016; Ben-Porath, 2012; Biesta, 2019; de Groot, 2017; Parra et al., 2021). Democracy and democratic processes are emotional (Scotton, 2020), deliberative (Guérin, 2017; Shultz & Guimaraes-Iosif, 2012; Waterson & Moffa, 2016), dynamic (Biesta, 2019) and, at times, agonistic (Parra et al., 2021; Sant et al., 2021; Scotton, 2020). Furthermore, democracy and democratic processes can be leveraged to promote equity and social justice (Alongi et al., 2016; de Groot, 2017; Sant et al., 2021) if critical consciousness (Bolin, 2017; Scotton, 2020) is fostered. It is this view of democracy – focusing on the content *and* the process for teaching and learning about democracy – that informed the work we carried out in schools.

A pedagogical approach that models and embeds the skills and dispositions needed to flourish in a democratic society tends to support learning of democratic principles *in addition to* equity literacy and critical awareness of diversity (de Groot, 2017; Gorski, 2016; Mathé, 2020; Payne et al., 2020; Scotton, 2020). For example, Mathé (2020) explains, 'educating for democracy necessarily involves equipping students with knowledge about democratic structures and processes and with the skills and dispositions to engage with them' (p. 70). Additionally, pedagogical approaches that support connections with students' lived experiences, critical reflection on current events and authentic peer-to-peer discourse (that sometimes involves conflict) support learning about democracy *and* participation in democracy in ways that honour diversity and promote equity. One of the key features of pedagogical approaches that focus on more democratic outcomes seeks out and amplifies student voice (Bessant et al., 2016; Guérin, 2017; Lundahl & Olson, 2013; Sant et al., 2021; Scotton, 2020). Pedagogical approaches that centre and amplify student voice and that support learning about democracy *and* participation in democracy in ways that honour diversity and promote equity are essential. However, these approaches are not without risk and significant disagreement and rebuttal. Recent discourses challenging some of the fundamental principles of democracy combined with the current 'anti woke' challenges to decades of discourse and developments with respect to diversity are creating a much more challenging and contested space for work in this domain. Despite the fact that teaching, simply by virtue of deciding what to include in a curriculum, is a political act (Gorski & Swalwell, 2015; Scotton, 2020), teachers often face backlash for being too political when teaching about and for democracy using the types of pedagogical approaches described above. In addition, lest we think that all was well before the woke debate began, for a multitude of reasons, traditional teacher-centred pedagogical approaches persist at all levels of schooling. Such approaches are directly oppositional to the collaborative and deliberative nature of democracy and democratic approaches to teaching (Alongi et al., 2016; Bessant et al., 2016; Mathé & Elstad, 2018). Dewey (1903, p. 197) mused: 'How can we justify our belief in the democratic principle elsewhere, and then go back entirely upon it when we come to education?' The challenge persists, but we must push against it in research and in practice. As Shultz and Guimaraes-Iosif (2012) note, 'schools need to create new sites and scales of struggle that empower students and educators to perform acts of citizenship that transform' (p. 244). A lack of attention to equity literacy and to diversity among school community members – administrators, teachers and students alike – is a barrier to teaching and learning about democracy (Mathé & Elstad, 2018; Scotton, 2020). Therefore, understandings of diversity, equity and democracy are inextricably linked in the context of education.

Critical socio-political orientations

Teaching is a political act regardless of curricular area (Freire, 1970; Gutiérrez, 2012; Hooks, 2014). Politics is a dynamic of power (Kendi, 2019) and a process associated with decision-making and resources. As noted above, the literature tends to characterise diversity, equity and democracy as constructs related to, or involving, power dynamics, decision-making and the allocation of resources. Problematising these concepts within a professional learning context is essential. Leading and teaching that is specifically focused on diversity, equity and democracy is necessarily political, and any attempt to avoid considering it to be political actively prohibits justice (Francis et al., 2017; Freire, 1970; Hooks, 2014; Galloway & Ishimaru, 2015). A critical socio-political orientation towards school leadership and teaching and learning is a lens that foregrounds root causes of social issues, in-depth analyses of power dynamics within systems, questioning of the status quo and scrutinising tradition and hierarchy (Blandy, 1991; Freire, 1970; Hooks, 2014; Ladson-Billings & Tate, 1995) often through processes of collaboration with others (Mathé, 2020; Roegman et al., 2021). This socio-political perspective refers to the context for the analysis, a significant level of questioning and reflection of socially constructed norms, power dynamics, structures and processes (Gutiérrez, 2013; Hooks, 2014; Leonardi & Moses, 2021; Morales-Doyle, 2019; Rodriguez & Morrison, 2019; Szostkowski & Upadhyay, 2019).

A key factor in harnessing the potential for critical interrogation that draws on the socio-political perspective explored above is the connections that prevail among access, identity, power and outcomes. More specifically, access to resources and opportunities, an individual's multiple intersectional identities and power dynamics influence the sort of educational and economic outcomes that are typically the focus of practice, policy and research. Therefore, a focus on the outcomes without an interrogation or acknowledgement of the related issues of access, identity and power within specific contexts is irresponsible and detrimental to justice work (Morales-Doyle, 2019). Implicitly, if not explicitly, literature included in this review focused on access, identity and/or power alongside discussions of the educational and/or economic outcomes typically cited in discussions of diversity, equity and democracy in education.

Concluding comments

As noted in the introduction, education is often positioned as an essential tool for achieving several of the SDGs set out in the United Nations 2030 Agenda. However, it has also been demonstrated that it can be a significant obstacle to achieving these outcomes, always retaining the potential to reproduce social injustice (Bourdieu, 2018; Cerna et al., 2021), always creating winners and losers (Labaree, 2012) and almost always in the same place and among the same groups (Mac Ruairc, 2020a). Disrupting these cycles of reproduction is difficult, not least because they possess a very persistent resistance to change. It is this conundrum that frames the work of this project and the thinking behind this collection. It is vital, therefore, that, at the core of all the work, the push for transformation remains front and centre. In embarking on this 'threshold' work, we recognised that we were taking on a vast territory, and many of the limitations of this broad focus are directly attributable to the scope factor. In many ways, it is too broad, too specific and too close to everyday practice – all at the same time. In choosing to explore three constructs simultaneously, we signalled a commitment to a broad, holistic, complex focus while remaining flexible as to the approach we would use with our partner schools. As it turned out, the 'in school' phase of the work was not as problematic as we had anticipated. In all cases, as you will see in the second section of the book, the focus was narrowed by the schools involved in collaboration with each university team. In all cases, the schools led out on the choice as to where to start. In this way, the breadth and scope, originally viewed as a constraint, in practice provided multiple entry points for participants into the conversations and subsequent seminars. The act of selecting itself became an impetus for participation and provided for the initial explorations and discussions. Because of the interlinked nature of the themes, discussions and conversations invariably drew in all three. Many cognate areas of practice, including discourses of inclusion and exclusion, belonging and marginalisation, also emerged in conversations. The review work we had done, as outlined in this chapter, provided us with a conceptual scaffold that acknowledged the linkages between ideas and concepts while, at the same time, allowing for the focus to be maintained on the main area of exploration for each school. Arguably, all of these concepts are pointing in the same direction; they all require an ontological alignment with complexity and a turn towards troubled and troubling types of knowledge typical of these types of contested threshold concepts. This type of learning for school leaders, teachers and teacher educators is a process, one that is ongoing and will continue to be such. The initial step is probably the most significant; in some ways, that step is often a threshold of its own. It signals a recognition of a gap in knowledge and understanding that acts as an imperative to pursue some additional insights. We were glad to be there on – and share – that learning pathway with these leader educators and look forward to extending this work further into the future.

References

Abawi, L.-A., Bauman-Buffone, C., Pineda-Báez, C., & Carter, S. (2018). The rhetoric and reality of leading the inclusive school: Socio-cultural reflections on lived experiences. *Education Sciences*, *8*(2).

Åberg, I. B. (2020). Diversity is the others: A critical investigation of 'diversity' in two recent education policy documents. *Intercultural Education*, *31*(2), 157–172.

Adam, H. (2021). When authenticity goes missing: How monocultural children's literature is silencing the voices and contributing to invisibility of children from minority backgrounds. *Education Sciences*, *11*(1), 1–18.

Ainscow, M. (2020). Promoting inclusion and equity in education: Lessons from international experiences. *Nordic Journal of Studies in Educational Policy*, *6*(1), 7–16.

Ajnesh, P., & Martyna Śliwa, M. (2024). Critiquing the backlash against wokeness: In defense of DEI scholarship and practice. *Academy of Management Perspectives*, *38*(2), 245–259.

Alongi, M. D., Heddy, B. C., & Sinatra, G. M. (2016). Real-world engagement with controversial issues in history and social studies: Teaching for transformative experiences and conceptual change. *Journal of Social Science Education*, *15*(2), 26–41.

Álvarez, I. M., & Montoto, I. (2018). Teachers' intercultural competence: A requirement or an option in a culturally diverse classroom? *International Journal of Inclusive Education*, *22*(5), 510–526.

Arvelo-Rosales, C. N., De La Rosa, O. M. A., & Guzmán-Rosquete, R. (2021). Initial training of primary school teachers: Development of competencies for inclusion and attention to diversity. *Education Sciences*, *11*(8).

Asen, R. (2024). Anti-woke publics. *Political Communication*, *41*(6), 1029–1034.

Back, M. (2025). Identity, diversity, equity, and inclusion. In C. Fäcke, X. Gao, & P. Garrett-Rucks (Eds.), *The handbook of plurilingual and intercultural language learning*. https://doi.org/10.1002/9781394165957.ch1

Banks, J. A. (2024). Educating citizens in diverse societies. In *Intercultural education* (pp. 17–25). Routledge.

Barton, A. C., Tan, E., & Greenberg, D. (2017). The makerspace movement: Sites of possibilities for equitable opportunities to engage underrepresented youth in STEM. *Teachers College Record*, *119*(6). https://doi.org/10.1177/016146811711900608

Bartz, J., & Bartz, T. (2018). Recognizing and acknowledging worldview diversity in the inclusive classroom. *Education Sciences*, *8*(4). https://doi.org/10.3390/educsci8040196

Ben-Porath, S. (2012). Citizenship as shared fate: Education for membership in a diverse democracy. *Educational Theory*, *62*(4), 381–395. https://doi.org/10.1111/j.1741-5446.2012.00452.x

Bertrand, M., & Marsh, J. (2021). How data-driven reform can drive deficit thinking. *Phi Delta Kappan*, *102*(8), 35–39. https://doi.org/10.1177/00317217211013936 (Original work published 2021).
Bessant, J., Farthing, R., & Watts, R. (2016). Co-designing a civics curriculum: Young people, democratic deficit and political renewal in the EU. *Journal of Curriculum Studies*, *48*(2), 271–289. https://doi.org/10.1080/00220272.2015.1018329
Biesta, G. (2019). What kind of society does the school need? Redefining the democratic work of education in impatient times. *Studies in Philosophy and Education*, *38*(6), 657–668. https://doi.org/10.1007/s11217-019-09675-y
Bjørnsrud, H., & Nilsen, S. (2019). Joint reflection on action – a prerequisite for inclusive education? A qualitative study in one local primary/lower secondary school in Norway. *International Journal of Inclusive Education*, *23*(2), 158–173. https://doi.org/10.1080/13603116.2018.1427153
Blandy, D. (1991). Conceptions of disability: Toward a socio-political orientation to disability for art education. *Studies in Art Education*, *32*(3), 131–144.
Bolin, T. D. (2017). Struggling for democracy: Paulo Freire and transforming society through education. *Policy Futures in Education*, *15*(6), 744–766. https://doi.org/10.1177/1478210317721311
Bourdieu, P. (2018). Cultural reproduction and social reproduction. In *Knowledge, education, and cultural change* (pp. 71–112). Routledge.
Branje, S. (2022). Adolescent identity development in context. *Current Opinion in Psychology*, *45*. https://doi.org/10.1016/j.copsyc.2021.11.006
Bryan, A. (2016). The sociology classroom as a pedagogical site of discomfort: Difficult knowledge and the emotional dynamics of teaching and learning. *Irish Journal of Sociology*, *24*(1), 7–33.
Bylica, K., Hawley, D., & Lewis, S. (2024). 'Walking on eggshells': Music educator perceptions of agency in times of surveillance and divisive concept laws. *Arts Education Policy Review*, 1–10. https://doi.org/10.1080/10632913.2024.2357289
Cammaerts, B. (2022). The abnormalisation of social justice: The 'anti-woke culture war' discourse in the UK. *Discourse & Society*, 1–14. https://doi.org/10.1177/09579265221095407
Cerna, L., et al. (2021). Promoting inclusive education for diverse societies: A conceptual framework. *OECD Education Working Papers, No. 260*. Paris: OECD Publishing. https://doi.org/10.1787/94ab68c6-en
Crenshaw, K. (1991). Mapping the margins: Intersectionality, identity politics, and violence against women of color. *Stanford Law Review*, 1241–1299.
Crocetti, E., Albarello, F., Meeus, W., & Rubini, M. (2022). Identities: A developmental social-psychological perspective. *European Review of Social Psychology*, *34*(1), 161–201.
Davies, A. W. J., Vipond, E., & King, A. (2017). Gender binary washrooms as a means of gender policing in schools: A Canadian perspective. *Gender and Education*, *31*(7), 866–885.
Davies, L. (1999). Comparing definitions of democracy in education. *Compare: A Journal of Comparative and International Education*, *29*(2), 127–140.
de Groot, I. (2017). Mock elections in civic education: A space for critical democratic citizenship development. *Journal of Social Science Education*, *16*(3), 83–95.
de Groot, I., & Lo, J. (2022). Cultivating student participation in the context of mock elections in schools: Practices and constraints in secondary education in the Netherlands. *Journal of Social Science Education*, *21*(1), 33–54.
Dewey, J. (1903). Democracy in education. *The Elementary School Teacher*, *4*(4), 193–204.
Dorey, P. (2024). The conservative right's 'war against woke' in towards a very British version of the 'culture wars'. In A.-P. Bonnet, & R. Kilty (Eds.), *Populism, social fractures and political communication*. Taylor & Francis.

Eisenberg, A. (2013). Identity politics and the risks of essentialism. In *Liberal multiculturalism and the fair terms of integration* (pp. 159–176). London: Palgrave Macmillan UK.
Feu, J., Serra, C., Canimas, J., Làzaro, L., & Simó-Gil, N. (2017). Democracy and education: A theoretical proposal for the analysis of democratic practices in schools. *Studies in Philosophy and Education*, *36*(6), 647–661.
Francis, B., Mills, M., & Lupton, R. (2017). Towards social justice in education: Contradictions and dilemmas. *Journal of Education Policy*, *32*(4), 414–431.
Freire, P. (1970). *Pedagogy of the oppressed*. New York: Continuum.
Fuligni, A. (Ed.). (2007). *Contesting stereotypes and creating identities social categories, social identities, and educational participation*. New York: Russell Sage.
Galloway, M. K., & Ishimaru, A. M. (2015). Radical recentering: Equity in educational leadership standards. *Educational Administration Quarterly*, *51*(3), 372–408.
Gay, G. (2023). *Educating for equity and excellence: Enacting culturally responsive teaching*. Columbia University: Teachers College.
Gergorićk, M., Ghosh, K., & Kuteleva, A. (2025). The rise of anti-gender and anti-feminist discourses in international politics. *POLITIKON: The IAPSS Journal of Political Science*, *59*(1).
Gilor, O., & Katz, M. (2021). From normalisation to inclusion: Effects on pre-service teachers' willingness to teach in inclusive classes. *International Journal of Inclusive Education*, *25*(4), 466–481.
Goffman, E. (1963). *Stigma notes on the management of spoiled identities*. Simon and Schuster.
Golden, N. A. (2023). 'Why should I bother if the school didn't bother with me?': Navigating the effects of subtractive schooling in an alternative learning program. *Journal of Latinos and Education*, *22*(4), 1761–1775.
González-Falcón, I., Coronel, J. M., & Correa, R. I. (2016). School counsellors and cultural diversity management in Spanish secondary schools: The role of relations with other educators and intervention models used in care of immigrant students. *Intercultural Education*, *27*(6), 615–628.
Good, T. L. (2024). Reflecting on decades of teacher expectations and teacher effectiveness research: Considerations for current and future research. *Educational Psychologist*, *59*(2), 111–141.
Gorski, P. C. (2016). Rethinking the role of 'culture' in educational equity: From cultural competence to equity literacy. *Multicultural Perspectives*, *18*(4), 221–226.
Gorski, P. C., & Swalwell, K. (2015). Equity literacy for all. *Educational Leadership*, *72*(6), 34–40.
Graham, L. J. (2006). Caught in the net: A Foucaultian interrogation of the incidental effects of limited notions of inclusion. *International Journal of Inclusive Education*, *10*(1), 3–25.
Graham, L. J. (Ed.). (2019). *Inclusive education for the 21st century: Theory, policy and practice* (1st ed.). Routledge.
Graham, L. J., & Slee, R. (2008). An illusory interiority: Interrogating the discourse/s of inclusion. *Educational Philosophy and Theory*, *40*(2), 277–293.
Gross, B., & Portera, A. (2025). Intersectionality in intercultural education and intercultural educational research. *Intercultural Education*, 1–5.
Guérin, L. (2017). Group problem solving as a different participatory approach to citizenship education. *Journal of Social Science Education*, *16*(2), 7–17.
Gupton, J. T., & O'Sullivan, A. (2024). Critically framing Florida's anti-woke education reform movement. *Journal of Educational Administration and History*, *56*(4), 419–423.

Gutiérrez, R. (2012). Context matters: How should we conceptualize equity in mathematics education? In *Equity in discourse for mathematics education* (pp. 17–33). Dordrecht: Springer.
Gutiérrez, R. (2013). The sociopolitical turn in mathematics education. *Journal for Research in Mathematics Education*, *44*(1), 37–68.
Hajisoteriou, C., & Angelides, P. (2017). Collaborative art-making for reducing marginalisation and promoting intercultural education and inclusion. *International Journal of Inclusive Education*, *21*(4), 361–375.
Hardy, I., & Woodcock, S. (2015). Inclusive education policies: Discourses of difference, diversity and deficit. *International Journal of Inclusive Education*, *19*(2), 141–164.
Heinz, M., Graham, C., O Neachtain, A., Mac Ruairc, G., Gartland, S., & Whyte, C. (2026a). Professional learning with school leaders on diversity, equity and inclusion in Ireland: Deepening understanding and commitment through safe and honest 'big issue' conversations. In M. Heinz, M. J. Rodríguez-Entrena, & G. Mac Ruairc (Eds.), *Professional learning for diversity, equity and democracy: Big ideas for better schools* (pp. 65–86). London: Routledge.
Heinz, M., Graham, L., & Maulana, R. (2025). Towards more equitable and inclusive learning environments: Forging new connections and research directions. *Learning Environments Journal*, 1–21.
Heinz, M., Keane, E., & Mc Daid, R. (2023). Charting pathways toward a more diverse, equitable and inclusive teaching profession. In E. Keane, M. Heinz, & R. Mc Daid (Eds.), *Diversifying the teaching profession: Dimensions, dilemmas and directions for the future* (pp. 226–240). Routledge.
Heinz, M., Mac Ruairc, G., & Rodríguez-Entrena, M. J. (2026b). Big ideas for better schools: A transnational professional learning project. In M. Heinz, M. J. Rodríguez-Entrena, & G. Mac Ruairc (Eds.), *Professional learning for diversity, equity and democracy: Big ideas for better schools* (pp. 17–23). London: Routledge.
Hippe, R., Araújo, L., & da Costa, P. D. (2016). *Equity in education in Europe*. Luxembourg: Publications Office of the European Union.
Hooks, B. (2014). *Teaching to transgress*. Routledge.
James, A. (2022). Talking of children and youth: Language, socialization and culture. In *Youth cultures* (pp. 43–62). Routledge.
Jeliazkova, M. (2015). Social science teachers on citizenship education: A comparative study of two post-communist countries. *Journal of Social Science Education*, *14*(1), 31–46.
Jónsson, Ó. P., & Garces Rodriguez, A. (2021). Educating democracy: Competences for a democratic culture. *Education, Citizenship and Social Justice*, *16*(1), 62–77.
Jurow, A. S. (2016). Kris Gutiérrez: Designing with and for diversity in the learning sciences. *Cultural Studies of Science Education*, *11*(1), 81–88.
Keane, E., Heinz, M., & Eaton, P. (2018). Fit(ness) to teach?: Disability and initial teacher education in the Republic of Ireland. *International Journal of Inclusive Education*, *22*(8), 819–838.
Kendi, I. X. (2019). *How to be an antiracist*. Random House.
King, A. M., Davis, C. J., Darby, C., Proudfoot, D., & Burrow, A. L. (2025). The identity disclosure matrix: A conceptual framework for why and how we share our identities. *Identity*, *25*(2), 227–241.
Kirton, G., & Greene, A.-M. (2021). *The dynamics of managing diversity and inclusion: A critical approach* (5th ed.). Routledge.
Kjaran, J. I., & Lehtonen, J. (2018). Windows of opportunities: Nordic perspectives on sexual diversity in education. *International Journal of Inclusive Education*, *22*(10), 1035–1047.

Kopińska, V. (2019). Country report: Civic and citizenship education in Polish school. *Journal of Social Science Education*, *18*(1), 172–202.

Kovač, V. B., & Vaala, B. L. (2021). Educational inclusion and belonging: A conceptual analysis and implications for practice. *International Journal of Inclusive Education*, *25*(10), 1205–1219.

Labaree, D. F. (2012). *Someone has to fail*. Harvard University Press.

Ladson-Billings, G. (1995). Toward a theory of culturally relevant pedagogy. *American Educational Research Journal*, *32*(3), 465–491.

Ladson-Billings, G., & Tate, W. F. (1995). Toward a critical race theory of education. *Teachers College Record*, *97*(1), 47–68.

Leszczensky, L., Pink, S., Kretschmer, D., & Kalter, F. (2022). Studying youth' group identities, intergroup relations, and friendship networks: The friendship and identity in school data. *European Sociological Review*, *38*(3), 493–506.

López-Azuaga, R., & Suárez Riveiro, J. M. (2020). Perceptions of inclusive education in schools delivering teaching through learning communities and service-learning. *International Journal of Inclusive Education*, *24*(9), 1019–1033.

Louie, N. L. (2017). Supporting teachers' equity-oriented learning and identities: A resource-centered perspective. *Teachers College Record*, *119*(2), 1–42.

Lundahl, L., & Olson, M. (2013). Democracy lessons in market-oriented schools: The case of Swedish upper secondary education. *Education, Citizenship and Social Justice*, *8*(2), 201–213.

Mac Ruairc, G. (2020a). School leaders working towards inclusive schools (Chapter 4). In C. Boyle, J. Anderson, A. Page, & S. Mavropoulou (Eds.), *Inclusive education: Global issues and controversies* (Vol. 45). Series: Studies in inclusive education. Netherlands: Sense/Brill.

Mac Ruairc, G. (2020b). That's enough about me: Exploring leaders' identities in schools in challenging circumstances. In R. Niesche, & A. Heffernan (Eds.), *Theorising identity and subjectivity in educational leadership research*. London: Routledge.

Mac Ruairc, G., Ottensen, E., & Precey, R. (Eds.). (2013). *Leadership for inclusive education: Values, vision and voices*. Sense Publishers.

Mathé, N. E. H. (2020). Preparing to teach democracy: Student teachers' perceptions of the 'democracy cake' as a set of teaching materials in social science education. *Journal of Social Science Education*, *19*(3), 66–85.

Mathé, N. E. H., & Elstad, E. (2018). Students' perceptions of citizenship preparation in social studies: The role of instruction and students' interests. *Journal of Social Science Education*, *17*(3), 74–86.

McGhee, H. (2021). *The sum of us: What racism costs everyone and how we can prosper together* (1st ed.). One World.

McGillicuddy, D., & Machowska-Kosciak, M. (2021). Children's right to belong? – the psychosocial impact of pedagogy and peer interaction on minority ethnic children's negotiation of academic and social identities in school. *Education Sciences*, *11*(8).

Meléndez-Luces, J., & Couto-Cantero, P. (2021). Engaging ethnic-diverse students: A research based on culturally responsive teaching for roma-gypsy students. *Education Sciences*, *11*(11)

Meyer, J. H., & Land, R. (2005). Threshold concepts and troublesome knowledge (2): Epistemological considerations and a conceptual framework for teaching and learning. *Higher Education*, *49*(3), 373–388.

Morales-Doyle, D. (2019). There is no equity in a vacuum: On the importance of historical, political, and moral considerations in science education. *Cultural Studies of Science Education*, *14*(2), 485–491.

Moss, J., O'Mara, J., & McCandless, T. (2017). School leadership and intercultural understanding: School foyers as situated spaces for doing diversity. *International Journal of Inclusive Education*, *21*(9), 956–973.

Mullen, C. A., & Robertson, K. C. (2021). Theorizing about identity politics in education and school leadership. In C. A. Mullen (Eds.), *Handbook of social justice interventions in education*. Springer International Handbooks of Education. Cham: Springer.
Murray, J. J., Snoddon, K., De Meulder, M., & Underwood, K. (2020). Intersectional inclusion for deaf learners: Moving beyond General Comment no. 4 on Article 24 of the United Nations Convention on the Rights of Persons with Disabilities. *International Journal of Inclusive Education*, *24*(7), 691–705.
Nihill, M., & Mac Ruairc, G. (2026). A model to enable professional learning for transformative school leadership. In M. Heinz, M. J. Rodríguez-Entrena, & G. Mac Ruairc (Eds.), *Professional learning for diversity, equity and democracy: Big ideas for better schools* (pp. 47–62). London: Routledge.
Nikolaou, G., Kaloyirou, C., & Spyropoulou, A. (2019). Bullying and ethnic diversity: Investigating their relation in the school setting. *Intercultural Education*, *30*(4), 335–350.
OECD. (2023). *Equity and inclusion in education: Finding strength through diversity*. Paris: OECD Publishing. https://doi.org/10.1787/e9072e21-en.
Parra, S. L., Bakker, C., & van Liere, L. (2021). Practicing democracy in the playground: Turning political conflict into educational friction. *Journal of Curriculum Studies*, *53*(1), 32–46.
Patterson, A. D. (2019). Equity in groupwork: The social process of creating justice in a science classroom. *Cultural Studies of Science Education*, *14*(2), 361–381.
Payne, K. A., Adair, J. K., Colegrove, K. S. S., Lee, S., Falkner, A., McManus, M., & Sachdeva, S. (2020). Reconceptualizing civic education for young children: Recognizing embodied civic action. *Education, Citizenship and Social Justice*, *15*(1), 35–46.
Raphael, J., & Allard, A. C. (2013). Positioning people with intellectual disabilities as the experts: Enhancing pre-service teachers competencies in teaching for diversity. *International Journal of Inclusive Education*, *17*(2), 205–221.
Roberts, L. S., Wong, L. S., & Ebejer, M. (2025). Culturally responsive teaching (CRT) and critical race theory (CRT): When is CRT not CRT? *Journal of Cases in Educational Leadership*, *28*(1), 90–105.
Rodriguez, A. J., & Morrison, D. (2019). Expanding and enacting transformative meanings of equity, diversity and social justice in science education. *Cultural Studies of Science Education*, *14*(2), 265–281.
Rodríguez-Izquierdo, R. M. (2018). Researching the links between social-emotional learning and intercultural education: Strategies for enacting a culturally relevant teaching. *Intercultural Education*, *29*(5–6), 609–623.
Roegman, R., Reagan, E., Goodwin, A. L., Lee, C. C., & Vernikoff, L. (2021). Reimagining social justice-oriented teacher preparation in current sociopolitical contexts. *International Journal of Qualitative Studies in Education*, *34*(2), 145–167.
Rose, A. J., Borowski, S. K., Spiekerman, A., & Smith, R. L. (2022). Children's friendships. In P. K. Smith, & C. H. Hart (Eds.), *Handbook of childhood social development*. Wiley Blackman.
Rutkowski, D., Rutkowski, L., & Engel, L. C. (2014). Inclusive schooling: Fostering citizenship among immigrant students in Europe. *Intercultural Education*, *25*(4), 269–282.
Sadowski, M. (Ed.). (2021). *Adolescents at school: Perspectives on youth, identity, and education youth development and education* (3rd ed.). Harvard Education Press.
Safir, S., & Dugan, J. (2021). *Street data: A next-generation model for equity, pedagogy, and school transformation*. Corwin Press.
Sant, E., McDonnell, J., Pashby, K., & Menendez Alvarez-Hevia, D. (2021). Pedagogies of agonistic democracy and citizenship education. *Education, Citizenship and Social Justice*, *16*(3), 227–244.
Schoorman, D. (2024). Waking up to the 'anti-woke' agenda. *Journal of Educational Administration and History*, *56*(4), 404–410.

Scotton, P. (2020). Knowing, understanding, living, dissenting and countering: The educational moment in the enhancement of democratic citizenship. *Studies in Philosophy and Education*, *39*(1), 71–844.
Shevlin, M., Winter, E., & Flynn, P. (2013). Developing inclusive practice: Teacher perceptions of opportunities and constraints in the republic of Ireland. *International Journal of Inclusive Education*, *17*(10), 1119–1133.
Shirley, D., & Hargreaves, A. (2024). *The age of identity: Who do our kids think they are . . . and how do we help them belong?* Corwin Press.
Shultz, L., & Guimaraes-Iosif, R. (2012). Citizenship education and the promise of democracy: A study of UNESCO associated schools in Brazil and Canada. *Education, Citizenship and Social Justice*, *7*(3), 241–254.
Silcox, J. (2022). Youth crime and depictions of youth crime in Canada: Are news depictions purely moral panic? *Canadian Review of Sociology/Revue canadienne de sociologie*, *59*(1), 96–114.
Slee, R. (2010). *The irregular school: Exclusion, schooling and inclusive education.* Foundations and futures of education. London: Routledge.
Syeed, E. (2022). The space beyond equity: A blueprint of radical possibilities in school design. *Educational Policy*, *36*(4), 769–795.
Szostkowski, A., & Upadhyay, B. (2019). Looking forward by looking back: Equity in science education as socially just and morally healing action. *Cultural Studies of Science Education*, *14*(2), 335–353.
Thomas, G., & Macnab, N. (2022). Intersectionality, diversity, community and inclusion: Untangling the knots. *International Journal of Inclusive Education*, *26*(3), 227–244.
Tomlinson, C. A. (2015). Teaching for excellence in academically diverse classrooms. *Society*, *52*(3), 203–209.
Tuters, S. (2015). Conceptualising diversity in a rural school. *International Journal of Inclusive Education*, *19*(7), 685–696.
Uprichard, E. (2008). Children as 'being and becomings': Children, childhood and temporality. *Children & Society*, *22*, 303–313.
Valenzuela, A. (2005). Subtractive schooling, caring relations, and social capital in the schooling of US-Mexican youth. In *Beyond silenced voices: Class, race, and gender in United States schools* (pp. 83–94). New York: State University of New York Press.
Virta, A. (2016). Whose history should be dealt with in a pluricultural context – immigrant adolescents' approach. *Intercultural Education*, *27*(4), 377–387.
Wahrman, H., & Hartaf, H. (2021). Are schools educating toward active citizenship? The internal school struggle between contradictory citizenship models. *Education, Citizenship and Social Justice*, *16*(1), 3–16.
Warren, S. (2016). The trouble of 'living with others': Language, community and the politics of belonging. *Policy Futures in Education*, *14*(4), 452–465.
Waterson, R. A., & Moffa, E. D. (2016). Citizenship education for proactive democratic life in rural communities. *Education, Citizenship and Social Justice*, *11*(3), 213–230.
Willard, Z. A. (2024). Ambivalent surveillance: Teaching in the times of anti-woke. *Communication and Critical/Cultural Studies*, *22*(1), 67–84.
Wunsch, N., & Chiru, M. (2024). Supranational responses to democratic backsliding: Norm contestation and discursive polarisation in the European Parliament. *Journal of European Public Policy*, *32*(2), 392–416.

4

A MODEL TO ENABLE PROFESSIONAL LEARNING FOR TRANSFORMATIVE SCHOOL LEADERSHIP

Mary Nihill and Gerry Mac Ruairc

Introduction

Professional learning for school leaders is a key pillar in achieving high-quality educational experiences and outcomes in schools (Guerriero & Deligiannidi, 2020). While it does not guarantee these outcomes, an absence of good professional learning leaves leadership vulnerable to ineffective models of practice and, ultimate, untimely burn-out. The development of leadership practice that is required to explicitly work with the concept trilogy of diversity, equity and democracy necessitates a specific type of professional learning. The core concern of this chapter is to further illuminate how leadership learning can contribute to the creation of more proactive and transformative practices in relation to diversity, equity and democracy in schools. Specifically, the chapter will explore how leaders can be enabled to mediate the complexities of addressing these topics in a way that creates schools that are more supportive of diversity and more inclusive as places of learning.

Recently, a professional learning model for school leaders in the broadest sense was developed in the Republic of Ireland (see later in the chapter). The model drew on extant literature related to different models of professional development components and content to ensure sustainable professional learning outcomes. Some empirical work was also carried out in Ireland and Scotland to refine the efficacy and inform the final design of the model. The professional learning model takes a holistic perspective on leadership development and integrates a range of macro-, meso- and micro-perspectives. It has, therefore, the potential to provide an integrative framework within which to explore how best to support school leaders in developing an effective approach to dealing with complex and contentious concepts and ideas

DOI: 10.4324/9781032629292-5

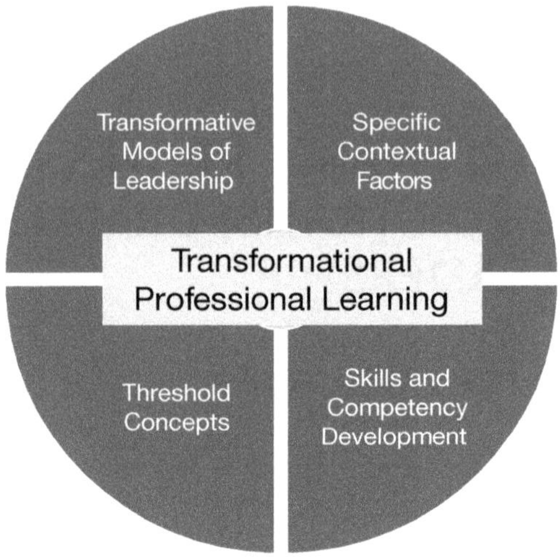

FIGURE 4.1 Foundational principles in professional learning for transformative outcomes

in their leadership work in schools. The key factors, concepts and principles underpinning the professional learning model include (see Figure 4.1):

1. A focus on the more transformative approaches to school leadership, that is, the approach to leadership is one that focuses on ensuring transformative, equity-driven and inclusive outcomes for all in our schools.
2. The development of particular skills and competences to enable effective leadership with respect to diversity contexts in schools, and the leadership of equitable and democratic responses in practice within schools.
3. The value of working with threshold concepts or troublesome knowledge in the context of professional learning.
4. Recognition of factors that shape and frame different national/regional contexts within which schools operate.

The literature related to school leadership is vast and often inconclusive with considerable evidence that many constructs proposed by emerging leadership models may not necessarily be new, leading to an inevitable concern about construct proliferation (i.e. the abundance of models with different names that tap into the same ideas) (Bormann & Rowold, 2018). There is, however, a long-established body of leadership scholarship, with strong roots in social justice perspectives, that has shaped an understanding of leadership that seeks to work towards transformative outcomes for all (Shields, 2021; Leithwood, 2021; Gümüş et al., 2020;

Carrington et al., 2024). In this chapter, we draw on, and take as a point of departure, this body of scholarship, thereby harnessing the fundamental alignment between these transformative perspectives and the work on diversity, equity and democracy in schools. This is to distinguish what is required here from the many forms of professional learning that have a tendency to focus on the operational and informational (Netolicky, 2020) aspects of the role of leaders, forefronting issues such as the financial, legal or human resource domains of school leadership (e.g. Desimone & Garet, 2015; Darling-Hammond et al., 2017; Markussen-Brown et al., 2017; Netolicky, 2020). While it is vital that professional learning attends to these dimensions of the role, it is also important that leaders are supported in their conceptual growth with regard to the complex domains of diversity, equity and democracy. Essentially, work in these areas will always be deeply connected with the identity of the school leader, and a recognition of this is essential for professional growth (see Netolicky, 2020, for an explication of the role professional identities play in professional learning). The type of professional learning required here needs to focus on enabling leaders to lead learning, understanding and appreciation of these areas within school communities and to manage organisational responses that serve to 'dial up' or explicitly intensify efforts within schools to become more mindful of how these, and other related issues, impact the practices of day-to-day school life.

It is important to recognise the liminal positionality and disruptive potential of explicit action in leadership relating to any or all of these ideas and concepts. It is helpful, therefore, to categorise these issues as 'threshold concepts', which means troublesome in the sense that they often challenge learners' common sense and existing knowledge (Walker et al., 2013). A focus on content of this kind has been part of professional learning, both within and outside the education sphere, for a number of years (Brown & Wisby, 2020; Davies et al., 2024). What is often required in more transformative types of school leadership professional learning is perspectives that challenge established ways of thinking (Poekert & King, 2023). Such challenging work is often viewed as troublesome, and this perception is likely to intensify in the short to medium term due to the rise of anti-diversity discourse emerging from the United States and further amplified by far-right ideologies globally (Chapter 3). Consequently, working with these areas requires the development of a specific set of skills and competencies, often because conversations can elicit deeply affective responses from others that can require 'an uncomfortable, emotional repositioning' (Cousin, 2006, p. 4). This is the work of hearts and minds, dealing with what can also be described as 'wicked problems', and it is not easy work. An appreciation of the power of any professional learning that takes on these ideas is evident when five defining principles of 'threshold concepts' are examined. These principles frame knowledge that is:

- transformative (can result in a significant shift in understanding),
- probably irreversible (difficult to unlearn once you know it; transformation occurs, so it is hard to unknow),
- integrative (reveals the association between various topics – links between recognising diversity and how it is linked to equitable/more democratic practice),
- sometimes bounded (specific to a particular discipline, or manifest in specific ways in different sectors – this is especially true of schools as they carry with them a formative competence with respect to children and young people) (Goldring & Greenfield, 2002),
- potentially troublesome (difficult to grasp, sometimes counter-intuitive) (Meyer & Land, 2003, 2005).

In the Irish context, there are some specific national factors that will impact any professional learning for school leaders. As is the case in many other countries, there is a lack of clarity around what constitutes school leadership, an issue that is often compounded by the unchecked assumption that the term 'school leader' refers to the principal. While there is agreement that school leadership is much broader than this, provision for professional learning and the formulation of leadership policy often default back to this more traditional hierarchical view of leadership in schools. Schools also vary considerably in terms of their wider context, and this has implications for designing professional learning programmes and activities. Darling-Hammond and Bransford (2007) discuss how certain barriers may be very difficult to overcome, given the challenges of particular school contexts. Examples of this include rural school locations or a lack of time due to either an overloaded school curriculum or a school leader with full teaching responsibility in a multi-class classroom, which is a common occurrence in Irish schools.

Professional learning for school leaders

There is some overlap between the core elements of effective professional learning for teachers and those for school leaders. However, Bush (2012) argues that many jurisdictions 'now appreciate that school leadership is a distinct profession, related to, but different from, that of classroom teacher' (Bush, 2012, p. 663). This chapter is focused on foregrounding core elements of effective professional learning for school leaders related to mediating controversial, difficult or troublesome professional conversations. In developing the professional learning model for Ireland, a number of models were explored. Sachs (2011) mapped out key purposes of professional development, including:

1. **Retooling** – which focuses on the development of new skills, where immediate application is the prime objective. This type of professional learning presupposes that the application of new skills will bring about improvement in learning outcomes. Retooling is thus limited to techniques – often as part of implementing policy-directed reforms with new approaches.
2. **Remodelling** – this categorisation builds on previous practice and may focus on the skills needed to engage students or on the enhancement of teacher' pedagogical knowledge. Remodelling also has a focus on reshaping existing skills to address improvements.
3. **Revitalising** – includes the issue of teacher motivation and has a focus on reflective practice in and on action and the development of collaborative networks.
4. **Reimagining** – 'transformative in its intent and practice' (Sachs, 2011, p. 160). This is particularly relevant to the work under consideration in this book, as the type of professional learning required here is premised on reimagining and risk-taking.

Kennedy (2014) identified three broad models of professional development – transmissive, malleable and transformative – and created a strong argument for transformative practice, which will, in turn, lead to improvement in student learning experiences and achievement. Kennedy (2014, p. 693) categorised collaborative professional inquiry models as transformative and described the central characteristic of the model as 'a combination of practices and conditions that support a transformative agenda'. Kennedy's transformative model is akin to Sachs's reimagining category, where, through professional learning, there is a commitment to change and the enhancement of practice. While explicating the need for transformative intentions, her framework also makes the case for the use of each of the different types of professional development. She argues:

> I am not suggesting that all CPD experiences must be transformative in nature, but rather that a transformative purpose, or orientation, will privilege models of CPD, while still acknowledging that some skills may well be best learned or refreshed through more transmissive approaches to learning.
>
> *(Kennedy, 2014, p. 694)*

A critical issue in developing a professional learning model is the positioning of leaders in the model and the degree of agency they can exercise in shaping their learning and subsequent practice. Implicit in Kennedy's framework are the different constructions of professionalism. Sachs' (2016) discussion of professionalism also highlights the way in which policy decisions around the type of professional learning promoted are often based on one of two perspectives. The first is a managerial perspective on professionalism, which focuses on efficiency, compliance and externally imposed accountability. The second is what Sachs calls 'democratic professionalism', which 'positions teachers [and leaders] as change agents' (Sachs, 2016, p. 342).

From this brief consideration of two of the many models that exist in relation to thinking about professional learning, it is clear that, while both models provide a broad view of professional development activity, they would support the type of professional learning required for leaders to make progress with diversity, equity and democracy. Their transformative intent, which could be focused on the types of 'disorienting dilemmas' (Mezirow, 1990) needed for transformational outcomes, provides a strong baseline for the development of a model that explicitly focuses on shaping the work of school leaders. The models also highlight the potential impact of professional learning beyond the individual practitioner, thus spotlighting the importance of the context of the school and the classroom.

While it is reassuring to see that literature on professional learning is strongly aligned with transformation, the achievement of this, in practice, is not in any way guaranteed *just* by the inclusion of transformative objectives in any model. Indeed, the provision of leadership development is a very crowded arena, and the many competing foci and voices lead to the amplification of different priorities at particular times. It could be argued that managerial perspectives arising from neoliberal models of practice have dominated, to a limited degree, nationally (Grummell et al., 2009; Holland et al., 2016). In the international context, the impact has been much more significant. The United Kingdom, the United States, Australia and New Zealand provide very clear examples of systems influenced, often to extreme degrees, by neoliberal reforms (Brown & Wisby, 2020; Ball, 2017; Apple, 2017).

There have long been calls in Ireland for a clear articulation of the essential elements involved in the process of learning to be a school leader. In response, the Irish Centre for School Leadership undertook the task of developing a comprehensive framework. The initiative benefited from collaboration with the Scottish College for Educational Leadership, drawing on their experience in navigating the complex landscape of leadership development across diverse school leadership roles. The Scottish model offered valuable guidance by outlining four interdependent and interconnected elements that form the foundation of effective leadership development: 1) reflection, 2) cognitive development, 3) experiential learning and 4) social learning processes (Forde, 2016, p. 118). The Centre for School Leadership aligned with this broad structure because it resonated with the ambition for professional learning for Irish leaders and potential leaders. From the outset, this model prioritises a more personal, reflective component that explicitly incorporates a commitment to content that could include more conceptual threshold-type concepts. Working things out together as a group of professionals is also core to the Scottish model. This requires the professional learning to model the type of collaborative engagement with topics that emulate what would happen in schools among leaders, teachers and extended school staff. As part of the development work, the Centre for School Leadership held a number of collaborative fora with stakeholder groups involved in Irish education to discuss what the principles and core elements of leadership development provision should be. The focus was on both the development of transformational leadership in Irish schools and the conceptualisation of a leadership continuum. Feedback from these consultative fora included:

- an acknowledgement of the importance of professional development for school leaders at each stage of the continuum,
- concern about the predominance of operational and management content of existing professional development provision,
- the influence of the legacy of culture in some schools and how teachers identify as leaders and
- the need for coherence in the provision of professional development and the development of a shared understanding of the essential components of quality professional development for leadership development.

This feedback and the work with the Scottish College of Educational Leadership (SCEL) led to the development of a model of professional development tailored to the Irish context. While closely aligned with the model developed in Scotland, the Irish model was also influenced by the Irish Teaching Council's framework for teachers' professional learning (Teaching Council, 2016).

One of the important issues pertaining to leadership development in education is that teachers, as they progress along a leadership pathway, are often moving from an expert, or at least highly experienced, position into a novice status. While there are transferable skills between pedagogy and leadership, there is a body of knowledge and a range of understandings, skills and attributes relating to leadership and the process of leading that requires attention and development. Some way of mapping out different leadership roles along a leadership pathway is, therefore, necessary. The Centre for School Leadership proposed a continuum of six leadership roles that exist in the Irish system (CSL, 2021; DE, 2022), including: 1) teacher leadership, 2) middle leadership, 3) aspiring senior leaders, 4) newly appointed senior leaders, 5) established senior leaders and 6) system leaders. The potential to plan and revisit leaders' and potential leaders' learning along this continuum offers opportunities for developing spiral and more in-depth professional learning approaches.

A professional learning model for school leadership developed in the Irish context

The use of a model of professional development that focuses on the development of leadership capacity across the continuum can 1) support providers of leadership development in the design, delivery and evaluation of professional development, 2) provide ways of quality assuring the provision of professional development and 3) serve as a tool for participants in professional learning programmes for leadership to review and reflect on their learning. In addition, the proposed model highlights some of the important characteristics of leadership and leading in school, and it is underpinned by current policy expectations regarding the development of distributed, collaborative and instructional leadership. Finally, the model relates to the context of schools and leadership policy in Ireland. As many of the Department of Education's action *plans* and the overall standards outlined in the 'Looking at Our Schools' (LAOS) quality framework for school *self-evaluations* and leadership development (DES, 2022) position diversity and inclusion as fundamental principles, professional learning programmes focusing on diversity, equity and democracy align well with policies guiding schools as well as with school's local priorities. However, we argue for a more explicit and deliberate emphasis on the foundational threshold concepts underpinning ideas such as diversity, equity and democracy. Developing a deeper conceptual and practical understanding of these principles – across all levels of the education system and throughout the leadership continuum – requires a more intentional and integrated approach than has typically been adopted in professional learning to date.

The model for professional learning for school leadership is illustrated in Figure 4.2. The model's design creates space for integrating conceptual content related to diversity, equity and democracy while also offering school leaders practical guidance on how to engage with these topics. This dual function strengthens the potential for such concepts, and school leaders' deeper understanding of them, to meaningfully influence school culture and operations, supporting progress towards a school experience that truly reflects the commitment to 'transformation for all'.

At the centre of the model is the moral imperative of school leadership (Fullan, 2006, 2015, 2020) – that of improving learning experiences, outcomes and well-being for students and school communities. The two semicircles represent the concept of professionalism as a process that impacts both the person and the practice of the leader. Leadership is conceptualised as an inherently social and relational activity. Hence, personal development, including in relation to the emotional impact of leading, needs to be an important focus of professional learning for school leaders. As 'leader development involves a complex interaction between personal traits, early life experiences and career-related

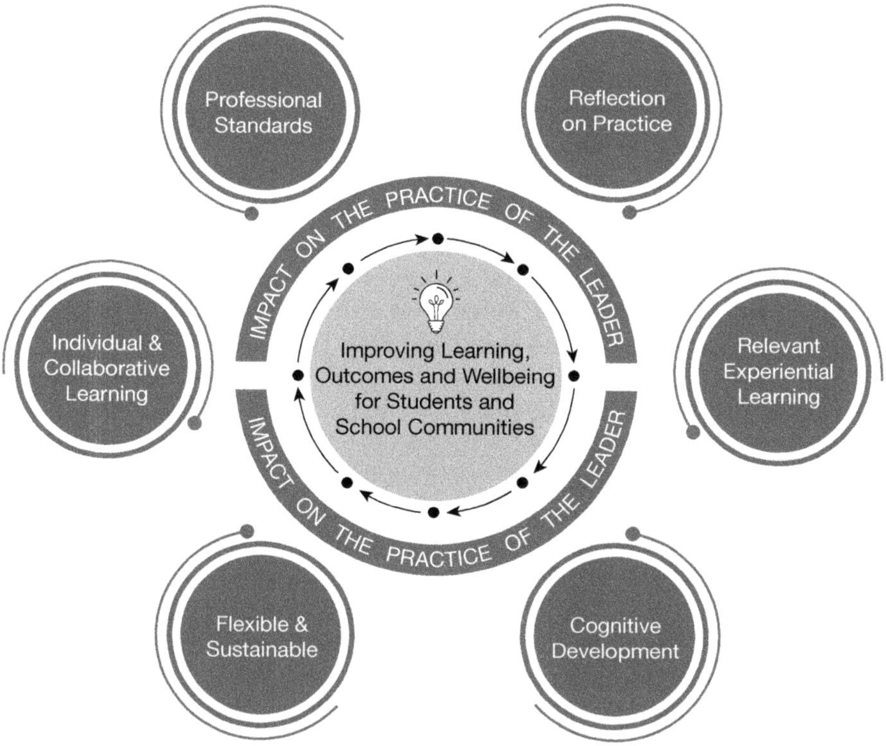

FIGURE 4.2 A model of professional learning for Irish school leaders

Source: Based on CSL 2018

learning opportunities' (McDermott et al., 2011, p. 360), professional learning for leadership must interweave aspects of self-reflection, personal motivation and self-awareness (Brennan & Mac Ruairc, 2019).

There is an increasing body of scholarship that explores how threshold concepts are integrated into professional learning in schools and related professions (Timmermans, 2014; Brown et al., 2021; DES, 2016). This literature explicitly details the potential for threshold concepts to change, not only the learner's knowledge but also their subjectivity, which can, at times, lead to an identity shift. The task of professional learning here is to wrestle with complexity, described by Mezirow (1990) as a 'disorienting dilemma' needed for transformational outcomes. At times, this type of learning can be difficult for teachers and leaders who do always react positively in the liminal learning spaces (Aharonian, 2019; Bjergkilde & Stenner, 2021) that prevail when engaging with these ideas. Additionally, there is a need to appreciate the connections between the personal and the professional spheres of teachers' lives that often go unrecognised (Leitch & Day, 2001), where 'the significance of teachers blurring in- and out-of-school spaces' (Woodard, 2015, p. 37) adds to the complexity of the task of designing professional learning. Because of their categorisation as threshold, troublesome concepts are vital for professional learning. They need to take account of the personal elements of a leader's identity (e.g. gender, culture, beliefs and life experience) because they are deeply embedded, and cannot be separated, from who the leader is professionally (Aharonian, 2019). There is considerable evidence in scholarship that personal epistemologies relating to diversity and inclusion are not always positive, and it is important to take account of this in professional learning because leaders' and teachers' beliefs and attitudes towards diversity influence decision-making in classrooms and how learners are 'seen' (Liang & Zhang, 2009). Challenging deficit views in relation to diversity often requires participants in professional learning to reflect critically on their own identities (Boylan & Woolsey, 2015).

The task, therefore, is complex, and while the model above, by centring students' and leaders' personal (and professional) domains, is potentially well suited to providing the type of experience that leads to high-quality professional learning, it is at the level of content design and competency development that fault lines will most appear. A full appreciation for the design and implementation of professional learning of the types of ideas explored here, including exploring liminality and embracing the threshold nature of the concepts, will need to explicitly underpin professional learning targeting this type of transformative learning.

While all of the domains are important, there is not adequate space in this chapter to explore all of the components. The remainder of the chapter will, therefore, focus on the three domains – reflection on practice, relevant experiential learning and cognitive development – that relate most specifically to the focus of this collection, that is, professional learning for diversity, equity and democracy. The inclusion of each of these areas in the design, development and evaluation of professional learning is essential to achieve the type of transformative, identity-shaping (Netolicky, 2020) outcomes discussed in this collection.

Reflection on practice

Reflective practice is the ability to reflect on actions and to engage in a process of continuous learning and is an inherent component of what it means to be an effective leader. As noted above, this domain is an essential part of working with threshold concepts that are troublesome in the sense that they often challenge learners' common sense and existing knowledge (Walker et al., 2013), require participants to move on from their established ways of thinking and, often, involve 'an uncomfortable, emotional repositioning' (Bolton, 2010, p. 132). The influential work of Donald Schön (1983) distinguished between reflection on action (thinking back through recent events) and reflection in action. The latter type of reflection has increasing relevance for improving the impact of professional learning activities. Schön's (1983) account of reflection in action is of particular interest because it illuminates conditions for changes to practice where reflection stimulates 'reframing', recognising a new way of perceiving or thinking about the professional situation of practice. A recent study by Sæbø and Midtsundstad (2022) illustrates how participants' reflections evolved from descriptive or corrective thinking – how things were or should have been – towards a deeper and more critical examination of the schools' practices.

Relevant experiential learning

Lewis and Williams (1994) define experiential learning as 'learning from experience or learning by doing. Experiential education first immerses learners in an experience and then encourages reflection about the experience to develop new skills, new attitudes, or new ways of thinking' (Lewis & Williams, 1994, p. 5). It, therefore, involves both practice and reflection on that practice, and it can be formal or informal. Kolb (1984, p. 41), in his discussion of adult learning, noted that 'learning is the process whereby knowledge is created through the transformation of experience'. Knowledge results from the combination of grasping and transforming experience (Bohon et al., 2017, p. 164). Reflection can lead to experimentation or new actions, which can, in turn, provide opportunities for further reflection. Greater attention is now paid to experiential professional learning. It is important to note that the effective application of experiential professional learning entails providing space and time for teachers and leaders to enquire into and reflect on their practice. Simply providing experiences without the opportunity for structured reflection on those experiences does not result in learning for the participant. Opportunities for experiential learning through collaborative enquiries and action-based research can play an important role in developing school leaders as reflective practitioners capable of exploring assumptions and trying out new approaches.

Cognitive development

There is a renewed focus on the school leader as a leader of learning (Mac Beath & Dempster, 2009) in professional learning for leadership. Evans (2014, p. 186) associates cognitive development with the 'enhancement of individuals' professionalism'. This type of cognitive development, Evans claims, is closely linked to experiential learning and often constitutes 'mental internalisation processes', which she calls 'micro-level professional development in individuals' (Evans, 2014, p. 188): 'only by breaking down professional development as a cognitive process into such minute singular units of activity do we have any chance of increasing our understanding of how it occurs, by scrutinising those units of activity' (Evans, 2014, p. 187). Cognitive development and knowledge building are, therefore, crucial elements of professional learning.

Theory and research provide alternative lenses through which leaders can explore their practice. Campbell (2003, p. 385) also links professional identity to cognitive learning, arguing that sustaining teacher commitment requires empowering them through inquiry that builds their professional knowledge base. In the Irish context, where a substantial proportion of professional learning for leadership is delivered by practitioners, a system of collaboration between academic researchers and practitioners could yield a richer and more feasible way of ensuring that professional learning is guided by relevant theory and research. Kelchtermans (2021) notes that both practitioners and academics bring expertise with them and that it is important that both types of expertise are included in teams providing professional development. However, similar to other elements of professional learning, Evans (2019) warns that cognitive development is not a quick process; new ideas and ways of thinking may take time to be assimilated into practice and 'in the interim such ideas or perspectives may have been augmented (or diluted) through interaction with a myriad of other (often unrecognisable or unidentifiable) influences on practice' (Evans, 2019, p. 7). Therefore, cognitive development is not simply about building ideas and expecting school leaders to apply these. Instead, it is about building up ideas and exploring – through experiential learning – ways of shaping these in practice.

Concluding comments

There has been considerable research into the elements that contribute to effective professional learning for teachers and school leaders. Rather than relying on a single type of experience or a set of disconnected activities, the model of professional learning presented in this chapter is designed to conceptualise a coherent and integrated range of learning experiences for leadership development. If change and development of leadership practice in schools are to become a reality, professional learning for school leadership needs to incorporate some or all of these elements (as appropriate to the context and objectives of the professional learning activity). With a view to harnessing the fundamental alignment between the potential of this model of professional learning to develop and enhance transformative leadership practices and the work on diversity, equity and democracy in schools, there are some challenges in the

Irish education system that recent research (Nihill, 2024) has identified. These include:

- the need for high-trust models in schools to facilitate genuine collaborative learning,
- placing a greater value on personal development as a core element of leadership professional development,
- a much deeper and sustained engagement between professional learning providers and the holistic and extended imperatives that need to shape and direct professional learning for school leaders and
- the use of LAOS (2022) as an example of a framework that can function as a developmental tool to improve leadership practice that is centred on enhancing a culture of diversity, equity and democracy in schools.

Finally, a focus on both the conceptual and practical dimensions in the design of the course content for school leaders is an essential prerequisite to effective professional learning. Neglecting either dimension impoverishes the other with the result that opportunities for meaningful developments that could enhance how diversity is understood and responded to in our schools are either missed, become perfunctory or are dismissed as unrealistic or inappropriate.

References

Aharonian, N. (2019). Making it count: Teacher learning in liminal spaces. *Professional Development in Education*, *47*(5), 763–779.

Apple, M. W. (2017). What is present and absent in critical analyses of neoliberalism in education. *Peabody Journal of Education*, *92*(1), 148–153.

Ball, S. J. (2017). Laboring to relate: Neoliberalism, embodied policy, and network dynamics. *Peabody Journal of Education*, *92*(1), 29–41.

Bjergkilde, D., & Stenner, P. (2021). Producing and managing continuous change in an educational context: Liminal affective technologies and leadership. *Subjectivity*, *14*(53–72).

Bohon, L. L., McKelvey, S., Rhodes, J. A., & Robnolt, V. J. (2017). Training for content teachers of English language learners: Using experiential learning to improve instruction. *Teacher Development*, *21*(5), 609–634.

Bolton, G. (2010). *Reflective practice: Writing and professional development*. Thousand Oaks, CA: Sage.

Bormann, K. C., & Rowold, J. (2018). Construct proliferation in leadership style research: Reviewing pro and contra arguments. *Organizational Psychology Review*, *8*(2–3), 149–173.

Boylan, M., & Woolsey, I. (2015). Teacher education for social justice: Mapping identity spaces. *Teaching and Teacher Education*, *46*, 62–71.

Brennan, J., & Mac Ruairc, G. (2019). Different worlds: The cadences of context, exploring the emotional terrain of school principals' practice in schools in challenging circumstances. *Educational Management Administration & Leadership*, *47*(1), 129–146.

Brown, A., & Wisby, E. (Eds.). (2020). *Knowledge, policy and practice in education and the struggle for social justice – essays inspired by the work of Geoff Whitty*. London: UCL Press.
Bush, T. (2012). International perspectives on leadership development: Making a difference. *Professional Development in Education*, *38*(4), 663–678.
Campbell, A. (2003). Teachers' research and professional development in England: Some questions, issues and concerns, *Journal of In-Service Education*, *29*(3), 375–388.
Centre for School Leadership. (CSL). (2021). *Learning to be a School Leader in Ireland*. Available at: https://oide.ie/wp-content/uploads/2024/05/Learning-to-be-a-School-Leader-in-Ireland-Downloadable-Publication-1.pdf
Cousin, G. (2006). An introduction to threshold concepts. *Planet*, *17*(1), 4–5. https://doi.org/10.11120/plan.2006.00170004
Darling-Hammond, L., & Bransford, J. (Eds.). (2007). *Preparing teachers for a changing world: What teachers should learn and be able to do*. John Wiley & Sons.
Darling-Hammond, L., Hyler, M. E., & Gardner, M. (2017). *Effective teacher professional development*. Palo Alto, CA: Learning Policy Institute.
Davies, J. P., Gironacci, E., McGowan, S., Nyamapfene, A., Rattray, J., Tierney A. M., & Webb, A. S. (Eds.). (2024). *Threshold concepts in the moment, education futures rethinking theory and practice* (Vol. 77). Netherlands: Brill.
DE. (2022). *Looking at our schools – A quality framework*. Department of Education Inspectorate, Dublin Ireland.
DES. (2016). *Department of education and skills action plan for education 2016–2019*. Department of Education and Skills, Strategy Statement Government Publications, Dublin.
Desimone, L. M., & Garet, M. S. (2015). Best practices in teachers' professional development in the United States. *Psychology, Society, & Education*, *7*(3), 252–263.
Evans, L. (2014). Leadership for professional development and learning: Enhancing our understanding of how teachers develop. *Cambridge Journal of Education*, *44*(2), 179–198.
Evans, L. (2019). Implicit and informal professional development: What it 'looks like,' how it occurs, and why we need to research it. *Professional Development in Education*, *45*(1), 3–18.
Forde, C. (2016). Leadership development. In J. O Brien (Ed.), *School leadership* (3rd ed.). Edinburgh: Dune.
Fullan, M. (2006). The development of transformational leaders for educational decentralization. *Centre for Strategic Education Seminar Series Paper No. 157*.
Fullan, M. (2015). Leadership from the middle: A system strategy. *Education Canada*, *55*(4), 23–26.
Fullan, M. (2020). *Leading in a culture of change*. San Francisco: Jossey-Bass.
Goldring, E., & Greenfield, W. (2002). Understanding the evolving concept of leadership to education: Roles, expectations, and dilemmas. *Yearbook of the National Society for the Study of Education*, *101*, 1–19.
Grummell, B., Devine, D., & Lynch, K. (2009). The care-less manager: Gender, care and new managerialism in higher education. *Gender and Education*, *21*(2), 191–208.
Guerriero, S., & Deligiannidi, D. (2020). The teaching profession and its knowledge base. In *Pedagogical knowledge and the changing nature of the teaching profession*. OECD, February 2017; *Evidence review: The effects of high-quality professional development on teachers and students*. Education Policy Institute (EPI).
Gümüş, S., Arar, K., & Oplatka, I. (2020). Review of international research on school leadership for social justice, equity and diversity. *Journal of Educational Administration and History*, *53*(1), 81–99.

Holland, C., Hughes, J., & Leitch, R. (2016). Neoliberalism and education: Spotlight on Ireland. *Policy Futures in Education*, *14*(8), 1041–1045.
Kelchtermans, G. (2021). Keeping educational research close to practice. *British Educational Research Journal*, *47*(6), 1504–1511.
Kennedy, A. (2014). Understanding continuing professional development: The need for theory to impact on policy and practice. *Professional Development in Education*, *40*(5), 688–697.
Kolb, D. A. (1984). *Experiential learning: Experience as the source of learning and development*. Hemel Hempstead, Herts: Prentice-Hall International.
Leitch, R., & Day, C., (2001). Reflective processes in action: Mapping personal and professional contexts for learning and change. *Journal of In-Service Education*, *27*(2), 237–260.
Leithwood, K. (2021). A review of evidence about equitable school leadership. *Education Sciences*, *11*.
Lewis, L. H., & Williams, C. J. (1994). Experiential learning: Past and present. *New Directions for Adult and Continuing Education*, *62*(1), 5–16.
Liang, X., & Zhang, G. (2009). Indicators to evaluate pre-service teachers' cultural competence. *Evaluation & Research in Education*, *22*(1), 17–31.
Mac Beath, J., & Dempster, N. (2009). *Connecting leadership and learning*. London: Routledge Press.
Markussen-Brown, J., Juhl, C. B., Piasta, S. B., Bleses, D., Højen, A., & Justice, L. M. (2017). The effects of language-and literacy-focused professional development on early educators and children: A best-evidence meta-analysis. *Early Childhood Research Quarterly*, *38*, 97–115.
Mc Dermott, A., Kidney, R., & Flood, P. (2011). Understanding leader development: Learning from leaders. *Leadership & Organization Development Journal*, *32*(4), 358–378.
Meyer, J. H. F., & Land R. (2003). Threshold concepts and troublesome knowledge (1): Linkages to ways of thinking and practising. In C. Rust (Ed.), *Improving Student Learning — Ten Years On*. Oxford: OCSLD.
Meyer, J. H. F., & Land, R. (2005). Threshold concepts and troublesome knowledge (2): Epistemological considerations and a conceptual framework for teaching and learning. *Higher Education*, *49*(3), 373–388.
Mezirow, J. (1990). *Fostering critical reflection in adulthood* (Vol. 366). San Francisco: Jossey-Bass.
Netolicky, D. M. (2020). *Transformational professional learning: Making a difference in schools*. London: Routledge.
Nihill, M. (2024). *Learning to be a school leader in Ireland: Investigating the understanding, use and efficacy of a model of professional learning for the professional development of school leaders in Irish schools* (Doctoral Dissertation) University of Galway.
Poekert, P., & King, F. (2023). Leading professional learning to navigate complexity. *Professional Development in Education*, *49*(6), 953–957.
Sachs, J., (2011). Metaphors for continuing teacher professional development: Skilling or emancipating teachers. In N. Mockler, & J. Sachs (Eds.), *Rethinking educational practice through reflexive inquiry* (pp. 153–168). Dordrecht: Springer.
Sachs, J. (2016). Teacher professionalism: Why are we still talking about it? *Teachers and Teaching*, *22*(4), 413–425.
Sæbø, G. I., & Midtsundstad, J. H. (2022). How can critical reflection be promoted in professional learning communities? Findings from an innovation research project in four schools. *Improving Schools*, *25*(2), 174–186.
Schön, D. (1983). *The reflective practitioner*. London: Temple Smith, London.

Shields, C. M. (2021). Transformative leadership theory: Critical, comprehensive, and activist. In *The Palgrave handbook of educational leadership and management discourse*. Palgrave Macmillan.

Teaching Council. (2016). *Cosán: A framework for teachers' learning*. Teaching Council website.

Timmermans, J. A. (2014). Identifying threshold concepts in the careers of educational developers. *International Journal for Academic Development*, *19*(4), 305–317.

Walker, A., Bryant, D., & Moosung, L. (2013). International patterns in principal preparation: Commonalities and variations in pre-service programmes. *Educational Management, Administration and Leadership*, *41*(4), 405–434.

Woodard, R. (2015). The dialogic interplay of writing and teaching writing: Teacher-writers' talk and textual practices across contexts. *Research in the Teaching of English*, *50*(1), 35–59.

PART TWO

Making it happen – learning from case studies

5

PROFESSIONAL LEARNING WITH SCHOOL LEADERS ON DIVERSITY, EQUITY AND INCLUSION IN IRELAND

Deepening understanding and commitment through safe and honest 'big issue' conversations

Manuela Heinz, Cáitlin Graham, Art O Neachtain, Gerry Mac Ruairc, Sara Gartland, and Claire Whyte

Introduction: Diversity, equity and inclusion in Ireland

Ireland presents a unique context for examining and advancing educational leadership practices for equity and inclusion, as it has been shaped by a complex history of colonisation, emigration and, in recent decades, rapid demographic change. Once a relatively homogeneous nation, Ireland has evolved into a culturally, linguistically and socio-economically diverse society, bringing both new opportunities and pressing challenges to its education system. In this chapter, we – a team of academics, school leaders and teachers – share our experience of collaboratively developing and implementing the 'Diversity and Equity in Our School' professional learning programme for school leadership teams. The initiative aimed to create space for critical, reflective conversations around diversity and equity in education, positioning these not as abstract ideals but as practical and meaningful frameworks for reflection, growth and action. A central goal was to support educational leaders in developing the language, confidence and collegial trust needed to engage honestly and constructively with these complex issues.

No country in Europe has been as profoundly shaped by emigration as Ireland. Since 1800, an estimated ten million people have left the island, including approximately one million during the devastating Great Famine between 1845 and 1852 (Fitzpatrick, 1984). However, the so-called Celtic Tiger period – from the mid-1990s to the early 2000s – marked a significant turning point, as rapid economic growth transformed Ireland from a nation of emigrants into a destination for immigrants. Between 1996 and 2016, the foreign-born population more than doubled. Today, Irish schools reflect this increasing diversity, with students representing around 160 nationalities

DOI: 10.4324/9781032629292-7

(Smyth et al., 2009). This multicultural shift has been further complemented by the growing participation of Ireland's indigenous Traveller community in the education system. At the same time, the inclusion of students with additional educational needs has significantly expanded, driven in part by the partial implementation of the Education for Persons with Special Educational Needs (EPSEN) Act of 2004.

The Irish government has introduced various legislative and policy measures to address the changing school demographics and to promote inclusive education. The 1998 Education Act articulated a commitment to 'inclusive, high-quality education for all students'. This was supported by policies such as the Intercultural Education Strategy (2010–2015), the National Council for Special Education's (NCSE) Inclusive Education Framework (2011) and the Department of Education's Guidelines for Supporting Students with SEN in Mainstream Schools (2017). Additionally, broader legislative frameworks, including the Equal Status Acts (2000–2012) and the Employment Equality Acts (1998–2011), have reinforced efforts to combat discrimination and promote equity in education.

Despite the significant diversification of Ireland's general and school population over the past three decades and the increasing focus on equity in education, its teaching body has remained overwhelmingly homogeneous, creating a notable 'diversity gap' between students and educators (Heinz & Keane, 2018; Heinz et al., 2023). Diversifying the teaching profession has become an international concern, and in Ireland, efforts have been made to address this gap. The Higher Education Authorities' third and fourth National Access Plans (2015–2021 and 2022–2028) included, for the first time, a focus on diversifying teacher education cohorts and supporting equity in initial teacher education, and 5.4 million euros have, to date, been invested in projects to attract and support more individuals from under-represented groups in/to teacher education (Keane et al., 2023).

However, research indicates that while national and local education policies as well as school ethos statements (Travers & King, 2025), ethical standards for teachers (Teaching Council, 2016) and teacher education guidelines (Teaching Council, 2020) are strongly aligned with values of diversity and equity, many teachers feel underprepared to cater effectively to the needs of increasingly diverse classrooms, particularly in areas such as culturally responsive pedagogy (Adebayo & Heinz, 2023; Brown et al., 2024), religious education (Cho & Heinz, 2023) and supporting students with SEN (Rice et al., 2023). Challenges include limited professional learning opportunities focused on equity and inclusion, the persistence of implicit biases, and structural barriers within the education system that hinder the full realisation of inclusive education policies.

The development of the professional learning programme discussed in this chapter formed part of a three-year-long Erasmus+-funded project titled 'Big Ideas for Better Schools' (BIBS), which brought together academics, school leaders and teachers from universities and second-level schools in Ireland, Spain, Norway and Poland.[1] The project aimed to initiate and/or deepen conversations on the 'big issues' of diversity, equity and democracy in schools. The three concepts of diversity, equity and democracy were conceptualised as closely interrelated and, further, connected to a range of other key concepts, including culture, power, identity, justice, inclusion and intersectionality (Heinz et al., 2026). Our core Ireland team was composed of three university-based teacher educators from the University of Galway, all of whom had previously been teachers, one deputy principal and one teacher and subject department lead of civic, social and political education. The three-year project involved several international face-to-face and online events as well as the design of professional learning programmes in the various national contexts.

The Irish partner school, Coláiste an Dóchais (pseudonym), is a co-educational, multidenominational second-level school of over 1100 students, which was established in 2013 and has grown steadily since then. The school leadership team consists of one principal, three deputy principals and over 20 assistant principals, with a total staff of over 120. The school is committed to creating a safe, positive, structured and caring environment, where all students can develop, grow and flourish in a holistic way. It offers a broad curriculum and an exceptional array of co- and extracurricular activities. The Cúnamh class meets the needs of students with moderate general learning disability and autistic spectrum disorders (ASD). There are more than 40 nationalities represented among the student body. The school's mission statement is 'Together We Will Achieve'.

'Diversity and Equity in Our School' – designing a professional learning programme for a school leadership team

Phase 1 – Exploring perspectives of students, teachers and school leaders

As an agreed first step, all national project teams participating in the BIBS project collected survey data from students (aged 14–16) in participating schools to explore their understandings, perspectives and questions regarding diversity, equity and democracy in their schools, their broader lives and their country more generally. To better understand the schools' ethos and work in relation to these issues, interviews were also conducted with school leaders. The professional learning programmes were collaboratively designed by the core national teams and shared with, and peer reviewed by, the international partners during an international meeting.

The analysis of the student data from Ireland (n=36) demonstrated that students related diversity to multiple dimensions – including race, religion, nationality, sexuality, gender, culture, social class and disability/ability. They showed very positive attitudes towards it, appreciating that 'everybody is unique' and that 'diversity broadens experiences and makes life more interesting'. A number of students also felt that diversity and/or 'people living near each other and becoming friends' could prevent 'close-mindedness', 'offending other people' and even 'hate in society'. The vast majority of students (86%) felt that there was diversity in their country with some linking it to globalisation and the economic boom. One student pointed out that we 'need more diversity in positions of power, in the media and in almost every other aspect of society so that everyone's voice is heard'.

Students also demonstrated a strong appreciation for the importance of equity, expressing a range of thoughtful understandings. For some, equity meant 'giving those who are struggling what they need to ensure they have the same opportunities as those who are better off', while others viewed it as a broader social good, stating that 'it improves society and helps reduce inequalities'. One student insightfully reflected that, 'without equity, many people would not be able to live up to their full potential, and the world would miss out on their contributions'. The majority of students (71%) believed that equity exists in Ireland, often pointing to the availability of social welfare benefits and various financial supports, such as higher education grants, as evidence. Similarly, 68% felt that their own school promoted equity, highlighting initiatives like grants for uniforms, books and computers, as well as support for students with learning disabilities and the provision of wheelchair ramps to ensure accessibility. Among the students who assessed equity in their school more negatively, the standout explanation was related to sport, where 'the lads' football gets everything – money, favouritism, trips, bigger celebrations and credit when they win matches, and then the other teams get nothing'.

The interview with one of the school leaders revealed a strong emphasis on cultivating a caring school culture grounded in respect, empathy and kindness towards students. The strong and repeated emphasis on 'just being nice and kind . . . in all your dealings with the kids' was striking, clearly reflecting a core value deeply embedded within the school culture.

> Just be kind. And for us, that's one of our main things . . . just be kind. And that's easy to do. You know, and that's an underlying core thing. You know, as a school, we are kind to students. Be kind, so in a way that's a value that sits at the back of your head that you know, very simple, right? . . . things that can sit at the back there, that are just what you are as a

> person. Your mindset and you know, so that's not hard. The hard bit is putting it down on paper and writing it out. But if you can kind of get to the stage where you're saying to teachers, well look, this is what we are as a school.

The school leader understood equity work as relationship work. Indeed, he argued that 'good teachers are good teachers . . . not necessarily because they know the curriculum content inside out, they're good teachers because they develop good relationships with students, and that's kind of what we try and focus on'.

Phase 2 – Shaping the foundations for our approach with intention and respect

The programme design was led by the academic partners. As we came together to design the programme, we drew on our varied professional and research backgrounds. There was excitement about the possibilities, but also hesitation – we were trying to do something different, and that came with uncertainty. We wanted to create space for thinking, for questioning and for real conversations about theories and concepts of diversity and about equity in practice. We believed that we were stepping onto fertile ground. Given the school's strong commitment to care and respectful relationships, we expected to be met with open minds and hearts. Yet we also felt that a significant deepening of awareness and a recognition and stronger emphasis on issues beyond an existing and predominant focus on care in the school was necessary and possible. We felt some discomfort with the well-intentioned, but somewhat uncritical and narrowly focused, emphasis on care portrayed in terms of individual gestures or interaction. Considering Neary's work (2020), we discussed the ways in which

> power can work through empathy in pedagogical situations to reproduce and exacerbate social injustices and exclusions . . . a focus on empathy can reproduce problematic effects such as the tolerant-tolerated relation, a victimised 'other' at risk, a hierarchy of those deserving of empathy and a focus on the individual that often detracts from the institutionalised workings of inequality.
>
> *(p. 452)*

We talked about research that had demonstrated the persistence of implicit biases among many majority-group teachers (Pit-ten Cate & Glock, 2019), their struggles and insecurities when teaching in diverse settings (Brown et al., 2024) and the fear of getting it wrong or being accused of discrimination (Adebayo & Heinz, 2023). Envisioning the forthcoming professional learning experience, we were honest about the limits of our own expertise. Having spent varying amounts of time away from the classroom and teaching pre-service and in-service teacher cohorts that were, very clearly, much less diverse than contemporary school populations, we really could not claim to have all the answers. Our frank discussions during the preparatory phase demonstrated to us not only how complex issues related to diversity and equity were but also how little we knew, if we were honest, about the everyday experiences and challenges teachers were navigating. This was an important and humbling experience, which hit us much more strongly than would be the case in our usual work with student teachers, where the case for our expertise could more easily be made. Recognising the limits of our own expertise and experience felt liberating. It motivated us to approach the work with humility, curiosity and a strong commitment to listening and to shared and reciprocal learning.

Phase 3 – Design and implementation of the 'Diversity and Equity in Our School' programme

Participants and objectives

Our programme involved long-term engagement and regular meetings, over three years, with a small group of school leaders. However, given the challenges associated with releasing teachers from their teaching, time with the bigger school leadership team was limited to two professional learning days in the school. The first day focused on conceptualising and exploring the 'big issues' of diversity and equity. The second day focused on the development of interdisciplinary teaching units focusing on the same areas. In this section, we describe and discuss the design and implementation of the first professional learning day. In total, 12 educators – eight members of the school leadership team and four teacher educators – took part in the day. The number of participants was intentionally restricted to a small group to facilitate meaningful engagement and conversations. An overview of the objectives and main activities of the day is provided in Box 5.1.

With time at a premium, we recognised the importance of prioritising three key elements: first, the rapid creation of an open, trusting and reflective environment (setting the right tone); second, the inclusion of concise yet powerful inputs grounded in policy, theory and research to deepen and challenge participants' understandings (threshold concepts); and third, the careful design of meaningful activities to enable individual and collaborative reflection as well as forward-looking action (agency). As time would inevitably pass quickly, we made a deliberate decision to ensure all facilitator input was brief, sharply focused and impactful to allow sufficient time for reflection and conversation.

Setting the tone

In our introduction, we acknowledged the complex and challenging nature of diversity, equity and inclusion issues, as well as our own ongoing struggles with them. We were open about our own limitations as academic partners, somewhat removed from everyday school realities, and showed interest and appreciation for the deep, practice-based expertise of teachers and school leaders. We expressed our wish to create a learning space where we could openly share, reflect and learn about diversity, equity and inclusion *together*. To deliberately shift the focus from uncontestable content knowledge to honest collaborative exploration, we introduced Kalinec-Craig's (2017) 'rights of the learner' – 1) to be confused, 2) to claim a mistake, 3) to speak, listen and be heard, 4) to represent only what makes sense and 5) to change one's mind and offer revised ideas – as guiding principles. This framework underscored our belief in the value of not knowing and the importance of moving beyond binary notions of right and wrong. Upon reflection, we feel that our honesty, along with Kalinec-Craig's (2017) practical and refreshingly simple framework, helped us to foster trust, openness and a genuine curiosity for learning and growth.

Following the introduction, we engaged participants in a 'warm-up' anticipation task. Each participant responded, on post-its, to the prompts: What words come to mind when you think of diversity? In what ways are students/ teachers diverse? Does diversity in the student body impact your practice? These initial thoughts were displayed on a whiteboard and served as a valuable point of reference during later discussions.

Conceptualising and problematising the issues

Following the anticipation task, we, the academic partners, led brief, interactive presentations aimed at conceptualising diversity and equity, drawing on some selected research and policy insights. We focused on key concepts such as dimensions of diversity, conceptualisations of equity, the negative effects of labelling and essentialising, and intersectionality. Drawing on Cerna et al.'s (2019) analytical framework for analysing diversity, equity and inclusion, we positioned these issues within the broader context of education and international policy work – offering school leaders a 'bird's-eye' perspective, which we felt they would find valuable. The framework outlines five key lenses: 1) governance, 2) resourcing, 3) capacity-building, 4) school-level interventions and 5) evaluation and monitoring of diversity in education.

To explore the meanings and connections among diversity, equity and inclusion, we next provided a very brief overview – what we called a 'sprinkle of theories' – to highlight key principles. This included the focus on 'providing support for all students to achieve their full educational potential, including in terms of fostering a sense of belonging, well-being, and self-worth, regardless of personal and social circumstances' (Cerna et al., 2019). We emphasised the distinction between fairness and sameness (Safir & Dugan, 2021), as well as the need for teachers to be attuned to the various dimensions of equity, from 'access' and 'achievement', the most commonly discussed and measured dimensions, to 'identity' and 'power', which are more critical concepts challenging traditional schooling models but often overlooked in policy discussions (Gutiérrez, 2011).

In our preparation, we identified two 'threshold concepts' (Meyer & Land, 2003), which we hoped would trigger deep thinking, rethinking, questioning and introspection: the concept of intersectionality (Crenshaw, 1989) and the self-fulfilling prophecy or Pygmalion effect (Rosenthal & Jacobson, 1992). We chose these concepts and spent more time exploring them, as we hoped this engagement could 'irreversibly transform' how participants 'experience the phenomena, think about themselves and about the world' (Meyer & Land, 2003). To make these theories particularly unforgettable, we decided to introduce each with a short, impactful video. The first video, 'All That We Share' (a Danish TV advert), features people from diverse backgrounds, initially introduced as 'high earners' or 'new Danes', stepping out of their boxes as they answer personal questions about their emotions and experiences. The video opened up a conversation around the concept of identity as far more complex than the labels we often assign to people. This sparked critical reflection on the dangers of labelling, essentialising and stereotyping, which was followed by our introduction of Crenshaw's (1989) critical work on intersectionality and the idea that effects of challenge and/or disadvantage multiply in ways that are not always visible and often not considered.

To introduce research on the Pygmalion effect (Rosenthal & Jacobson, 1992), we chose a video that combined classroom footage from several decades ago with a brief explanation of the experiment and the research findings by the researcher. We considered the datedness of the footage to be particularly powerful, as it allowed us to ask the critical question: Does this still happen today? We were aware of numerous subsequent studies that have confirmed Rosenthal's foundational work, with meta-analyses by Hattie (2023) and Jussim and Harber (2005) demonstrating that teacher expectations consistently influence student achievement, particularly for disadvantaged learners, but we did not discuss this with the participants. Instead, we asked the teachers to reflect, independently and privately, on whether the dynamics uncovered in this experiment continue to influence teaching and student outcomes in classrooms today – in their classrooms, in their school. We felt that this threshold concept allowed us to expand the focus from caring relationships to equitable academic expectations, challenge and support.

While it was not our intention to facilitate a discussion about these theories then and there, but rather to provide food for individual reflection and to create some lasting discomfort that would ensure further thinking, it became clear that the participants wanted to discuss and integrate these concepts in their reflections straight away. When we showed a visual of an intersectionality matrix to illustrate the complexities of learner identities and the multiplicative nature of marginalisation, one school leader excitedly exclaimed, 'this is it, these are our students, I need this'. His follow-up explanation that 'we often see them just as one thing or another' showed a realisation of the single-axis framework that often operates in schools, especially in relation to special educational needs. Another participant, in a later discussion, shared her surprise and pride for a student who had won a creative writing competition, something very few teachers would have expected. And later, when the conversation circled back to teacher expectations, another participant described her persistence in challenging students, explaining (and gesturing) in her own 'teacher language' how she would gently but persistently 'poke her students' to push them on and ask them for more, not letting them get away with medium effort.

Promoting reflection, dialogue and agency

After conceptualising and problematising the 'big issues' of diversity and equity, participants were invited to identify and reflect on concrete equity issues they had encountered in their professional practice. They began with individual reflection, followed by small group sharing, guided by the following prompts:

1. Describe one equity-related classroom situation/interaction that you felt good about. What happened? What did you do? How did the student(s) respond? Why do you feel good about this situation/interaction?
2. Describe one equity-related classroom situation/interaction that you wonder or worry about. What happened? What did you do? How did the student(s) respond? Why do you wonder or worry about this situation/interaction?

These prompts led to candid and thought-provoking discussions about various experiences, including a challenge one teacher faced when teaching 'Of Mice and Men' (Steinbeck, 1937) in English class. The novel was acknowledged as particularly difficult to navigate in secondary classrooms due to the characters' use of racist slurs and misogynistic language. The discussion surfaced real tensions around curriculum choices and sparked a broader conversation within the English department. We discussed the importance of critically evaluating readings in English and other classes, not only in terms of literary merit and/or tradition but also through an equity-focused lens that considered whose voices are represented, what messages are reinforced and how texts might impact different groups of students.

Next, participants were invited to browse a gallery of quotes displayed throughout the library, where the professional learning day was held. The quotes came from student data collected at the start of the project, as well as from participants in other studies, to ensure that a wide range of diversity dimensions was represented. This gallery walk – especially reading what their own students had said about equity in their school – captivated teachers and sparked lively conversations. Many were struck by the clarity and depth of the students' perspectives. One quote, in particular, critiquing the unequal treatment of boys' and girls' sports teams, surprised several teachers and became a moment of reflection. The concern was taken seriously, and the school later addressed the issue. To close the day, we invited teachers to pause and reflect using a set of simple but powerful prompts: *I notice. . . . I wonder. . . . Next steps for me. . . . Next steps for our school. . . .* These prompts supported thoughtful closure and encouraged participants to consider both individual insights and potential actions at the school level.

Methodology: Evaluating the impact of the professional learning programme

To track our experiences and thinking, we, the core team, took notes during and after our planning meetings as well as during and after the professional learning days. All participating school leaders and academics completed brief evaluation surveys at the end of the professional learning days. The members of the academic team additionally met after the professional learning days to share their impressions and reflections, in particular regarding how the days went overall, what stood out as particularly interesting or remarkable and in how far the objectives had been achieved. Recognising that the achievement of some longer-term objectives could not be assessed straight away, we mostly discussed: 1) in how far we succeeded in creating an open, trusting and reflective environment, 2) how the 'threshold concepts' we brought to the discussion were received and 3) whether the activities triggered thoughtful discussions focused on diversity and equity issues. Seven of the eight participating school leaders and all academic partners provided further feedback eight months after the completion of the professional learning programme, as part of a final project evaluation. Finally, 18 months after project completion, the members of the core Ireland team reflected, individually, on the longer-term impact of the professional learning programme.

All written reflections, meeting notes and evaluation responses were reviewed to identify recurring themes and key ideas. A reflective thematic analysis (RTA) approach, as outlined by Braun and Clarke (2022), was followed to explore both the explicit content and the underlying meanings in participants' reflections. This approach was considered appropriate, given its flexibility and its emphasis on the interpretive role of analysts (who were also participants) in the process of meaning-making. One academic partner compiled an overview of all data and carried out initial thematic categorisation, drawing on multiple readings and open, inductive coding during which 14 initial themes emerged: academics' awareness of positionalities, academics' limited knowledge of contemporary classroom realities, student voice as a powerful motivator for professional learning, recognising struggles and mistakes as valuable and normal, carefully selecting threshold concepts to disrupt or deepen thinking, shared ownership of project, shared and reciprocal learning and growth, more authentic connections between research and practice, deeper understanding of complexities of concepts, impact on practice, desire/importance to continue the dialogue, benefits of international exchange, time constraints and questions about longer-term impact.

These initial themes were then reviewed and discussed with a second academic partner, and through reflective dialogue, they were further interrogated, combined and interpreted to extract stronger key messages about participants' professional learning experiences. Collaborative professional identity for equity emerged as a central concept of interest. To deepen our analysis of this central concept, an additional, secondary analysis was conducted, drawing on Fairclough's (2003) discourse analytical principles, focusing on pronoun usage. This helped to identify how participants positioned themselves in relation to others and to the issues of diversity and equity.

Full ethical approval was provided by the University of Galway's research ethics committee prior to data collection, and all participants provided informed consent (teachers, school leaders and parents) and assent (students) before taking part.

Key findings and learning from the project

The programme evaluations and participant reflections indicate that all participants – academics as well as school leaders – enjoyed and perceived their participation in the project to be impactful, with some explaining that they found the exploration of the 'big concepts' (of equity and diversity) 'really interesting', 'fascinating', 'exciting' and/or 'compelling' 'from a professional but also a personal point of view'. The analysis revealed evidence of a more nuanced awareness of the multiple dimensions of diversity and the complexity of equity issues – both in thought and in action. The lack of diversity in the teaching body and the importance of 'consciously embracing diversity to avoid bias' were recognised as important new areas of focus. One school leader reflected on the programme's strong impact, noting how it shaped both their professional practice and understanding of how core values like equity, inclusion and democracy are embedded across school life:

> I felt that the programme had a huge impact on my professional practice and also on my awareness of how school policies and extracurricular activities can contribute to the key concepts being lived in practice, and how the challenges of equity and inclusion/democracy are present throughout all areas of the school.

Reflections written 18 months after the projects' completion also indicated that our initial hope – that exploring a small number of well-chosen 'threshold concepts' might prompt deeper, sustained reflection and lasting shifts in perspective and practice – may indeed have been realised. One teacher, for example, shared the lasting impression of the video on the Pygmalion effect, noting how it continued to shape her professional practice:

> I found one of the videos at the time to be very impactful – portraying students' attainment and achievements based on how their teachers perceive them. I feel that others in the room were equally moved by this, and it is something that has stuck with me in my own teaching practice. I am now more aware of treating all my students with equity, ensuring that I express having high expectations for all my students despite their previous grades or understanding, and to be more aware of my own internal bias.

A strong sense of responsibility towards equity and inclusion emerged consistently across participants' feedback, with many expressing a clear commitment to embedding these values into their everyday practice. As one teacher reflected, 'I believe I am a role model and need to demonstrate positive behaviours and practice in every aspect of the three key themes'. Similarly, a teacher educator remarked that the experience would 'spill over into his teacher education practice', describing a shift towards more student-centred pedagogies: 'I felt compelled to explore ways to incorporate student perspectives more actively in my classroom'.

Collaborating with international colleagues was seen as a major benefit as it deepened global awareness. School leaders valued gaining insights into other education systems and sharing concrete ideas. Many found working with non-native English speakers eye-opening and were struck by how 'topics like diversity, equity and democracy were less openly discussed in some of the other countries'. A US scholar who joined one of our professional learning days as a guest emphasised the importance of our project and noted how contentious and difficult engagement with these issues had become in her country. She reminded us of how fortunate we were to have the opportunity to engage with these matters and urged us not to take this for granted. This experience prompted one participant to recognise the importance of 'realising how far we've come, how far we have to go, but also how far we could go backward'.

Analysis of personal and possessive pronoun use in qualitative evaluation statements and later reflections suggests that participation in the project fostered a stronger sense of shared professional identity, responsibility and accountability among the school leadership team regarding equity and inclusion. We observed an increasing use of collective pronouns such as 'we', 'our' and 'us' when referring to both past and future actions. We felt that this subtle linguistic shift indicated a growing commitment to a shared, or collaborative, awareness and responsibility for addressing issues of diversity and equity. The depth of this shared ownership is reflected in the words of one teacher who was part of the core team: 'The training day felt like official recognition of the work we had been doing for the BIBS programme'. School leaders, teachers and academic partners placed high value on the cross-institutional sharing of experiences, viewing it as a means of fostering 'more authentic connections between research and practice' and of helping 'us all to deepen conversations and effect change'. This collaborative spirit reflects a clear openness to what Zeichner (2010) describes as a 'third space' – a dynamic intersection where practitioner expertise and academic knowledge come together to co-construct meaningful educational insights and innovations.

A growing critical consciousness around the complexity of equity-related challenges – and the need for ongoing reflection and action – was evident throughout the data. Participants acknowledged the nuanced nature of these discussions: 'we all had to acknowledge that these discussions are complex, and while we may not have all the answers, we must keep the conversations open'. Others described the project as 'thought-provoking' and an 'opportunity to question current practices', reinforcing a view of teachers as reflective practitioners and agents of change (Cochran-Smith & Lytle, 2015). One participant shared, 'The project made me even more cognisant of the fact that we should open up conversations on these topics', highlighting a commitment to sustained dialogue. The use of tentative ('the issues are complex') and conscience-driven ('we must keep the conversation going') language suggests a transformational, value-driven approach to learning and leadership.

A key enabler of this shift was, in our view, the cultivation of relational trust and psychological safety, both of which have been emphasised as important promoters of professional learning (Bryk & Scheider, 2002). Throughout the project, we were intentional about acknowledging our respective positionalities and emphasising the 'rights of the learners' (Kalinec-Craig, 2017), to foster an environment where academic and practitioner knowledge could be brought together in the spirit of reciprocal, shared learning. While we had initially planned to prioritise individual (private) reflection time, assuming that it might feel safer, participants from the school leadership team quickly 'felt comfortable sharing their thoughts openly'. As a result, rich discussions emerged, with little actually written down. Many participants remarked on how rare and valuable it was to have dedicated time and space for deep, collective reflection on such complex issues. Our experience, therefore, suggests that when professional learning is grounded in trust and collaboration, common fears can be eased, making reflective dialogue not only possible but also empowering.

Despite the many positives, our experience also revealed challenges – highlighting broader structural constraints that collaborative projects face in advancing equity and inclusion. One of the most significant challenges we faced was the constraint of time. Although Erasmus+ funding provided crucial financial support, enabling schools to invest in resources, offer substitute teaching and create time and space for professional dialogue in Ireland and internationally, the three-year project duration posed a barrier to sustained deep collaboration. Much of our energy was invested in exploring the concepts and in opening up and deepening dialogue. However, this intensive cognitive and reflective work left little room for concrete collective planning and/or implementation of forward-looking actions. The disruption caused by the COVID-19 pandemic naturally amplified these issues, as school closures (and post-closure pressures) interrupted momentum and reduced opportunities to move from theoretical exploration towards practical, sustained change.

Another notable challenge was the relatively homogeneous composition of our group of professionals. As a group of largely like-minded educators, we found comfort and trust in our shared space, which enabled open, reflective conversations. Yet we also recognised that this very trust could limit our perspective, creating blind spots rooted in normative assumptions we might not even recognise. From the outset, we were acutely aware of these risks, particularly the danger of unintentionally 'othering' (Dervin, 2016) marginalised experiences. While we shared quotes from students and drew on research highlighting the experiences of various minoritised and disadvantaged groups to broaden perspectives, one of the academic partners questioned whether the engagement 'could have been more intentionally challenging or even productively uncomfortable'. Looking ahead, we recognise the importance of designing projects that hold space for both trust and constructive challenge. Creating collaborations that engage a range of 'first-hand' perspectives to enrich and, at times, unsettle reflective dialogue may be essential to fostering deeper, more transformative professional learning.

Conclusion and principles for our future collaborative diversity and equity work

The Erasmus+-funded BIBS project aimed to support schools in exploring the 'big issues' of diversity, equity and democracy. In our initial conversations with the school leaders, they expressed a preference for a more explicit focus on diversity and equity, as these concepts aligned with ethos development work going on in the school at the time (ETBI Patrons' Framework on Ethos, 2022). With this in mind, we designed 'Diversity and Equity in Our School'. Our aim was never to deliver a fixed message or promote the one 'right way' of doing things. Instead, we set out to create a reflective, dialogic space where educators could collaboratively engage with complex issues that are often sidelined amid the immediate demands of busy school life. We hoped to prompt subtle but meaningful shifts in what teachers notice, the questions they ask and the assumptions that underpin those questions. Feedback from participants, through both formal evaluations and personal reflections, suggests that such shifts did, in fact, begin to take root.

At the outset, we were uncertain whether teachers would feel comfortable sharing their thoughts on these difficult and sometimes personally confronting topics. As Goodson (1991) and, more recently, Netolicky (2019) have highlighted, classroom practice can be a space of profound vulnerability for teachers. Within this context, even well-intentioned external engagement may feel like an intrusion, triggering anxieties about judgement or loss of professional autonomy. Acknowledging this, we paid careful attention to our respective positionalities, particularly to the limitations of academic expertise in relation to lived, everyday school experiences. Rather than adopt a directive or evaluative stance, we consciously situated the project within a 'third space' (Zeichner, 2010), where the knowledge of practitioners and academics could be shared in mutual recognition.

Professional learning programmes, such as our 'Diversity and Equity in our School', carve out time from the daily rush of school leaders' responsibilities, enabling them to engage more deeply with themes they care about but rarely have time to explore meaningfully. Over time, such programmes may hold the potential to shift collaboration among school leaders, teachers and academics from dialogue to shared responsibility and action for more equitable educational environments. However, our experience highlighted the need for ongoing support – dedicated time, space and financial resources – to ensure sustained engagement and long-term impact.

As we reflect on what we have learned, we are aware that the work of equity and inclusion is ongoing and deeply contextual. Rather than fixed answers or recommendations, we want to share a set of evolving principles – orientations that will shape how we approach future collaborations with schools, educators and communities. We offer these principles not as strict guidelines or universal truths but as emerging insights from our shared experience – open to revision, refinement and development:

1. **Democratic, equal and inclusive partnership.** We aim to build all partnerships on mutual respect and a recognition of the value of diverse forms of knowledge and experience. We hope to create spaces where education practitioners, academics and, in future developments, diverse community voices collaborate as equals – in a shared 'third space' that invites co-construction, rather than hierarchy.

2. **Safe, courageous and collaborative learning.** We strive to cultivate a culture of trust where questioning, uncertainty and discomfort are welcomed as part of deep learning. We see everyone as both learner and contributor and aim to hold space for reflection that encourages vulnerability, curiosity and growth. Rather than seeking quick solutions, we aim to engage in conversations that hold space for multiple perspectives, encourage active listening and allow deep exploration of issues and meaning to emerge collaboratively over time.

3. **Contextual and locally rooted action.** We are committed to grounding professional learning in the lived realities of schools and communities. This means listening carefully to students and teachers, collecting and collaboratively interrogating local data and developing context-specific action. We recognise that meaningful change grows from within.

4. **Critical engagement with research and practice.** We view research as a resource to provide insights, support reflection and provoke new thinking, rather than a set of fixed solutions. We aim to engage critically with theory and practice – surfacing assumptions, exploring threshold concepts and allowing ourselves to be unsettled when necessary.

5. **Globally aware and globally connected outlook.** While rooted in local realities, we aim to remain mindful of the broader forces that shape education. We see our work as part of a wider global dialogue about equity and inclusion and seek to learn from, and contribute to, global conversations about professional learning for diversity and equity in education in thoughtful ways.

To live these principles meaningfully, we recognise the essential need for dedicated time, physical and dialogic space, and financial support. These are not peripheral but central enabling conditions for creating the depth, continuity, and shared ownership required for impactful partnership work.

BOX 5.1 'DIVERSITY AND EQUITY IN OUR SCHOOL': A BRIEF OVERVIEW OF A ONE-DAY PROFESSIONAL LEARNING PROGRAMME

Title: Diversity and Equity in Our School

AIM: Teachers and school leaders explore and discuss concepts of diversity, equity and inclusion in theory and practice.

Objectives

- Explore and expand prior understandings of diversity, equity and inclusion in education.
- Share and collaboratively build on experiences of situations relating to diversity and equity.
- Analyse the effects of various assumptions and biases on educational practice.
- Connect theory and practice by examining student and teacher experiences.
- Identify and plan areas for professional growth related to diversity, equity and inclusion.
- Foster appreciation for diverse perspectives, cultures, identities and experiences in the classroom.

Sample activities for a one-day workshop

1. Welcome and guidelines for discussion – setting the tone

Introductions, share objectives, acknowledge the complex and difficult nature of diversity, equity and inclusion issues.

Introduce the Rights of the Learner (Kalinec-Craig, 2017) as a guideline for discussion.

2. Anticipation tasks

Develop an understanding of what prior knowledge and assumptions the participants have about diversity, equity and inclusion. Link back to ideas shared here during later reflections and discussions.

- *What words come to mind when you think of diversity?*
- *In what ways are students diverse? In what ways are teachers diverse?*
- *Does diversity in the student body impact your practice?*

3. Presentation/facilitator input

Facilitators present and discuss key concepts, including dimensions of diversity, intersectionality and the negative effects of labelling and essentialisation. Connect diversity with equity, define equity, outline relevant national policies and pose thought-provoking questions.

Diversity, equity and inclusion

Lenses for analysing the complex topics of diversity, equity and inclusion across society and the education system and dimensions of diversity (Cerna et al., 2019).

Intersectionality

Intersectionality is the idea that any individual will have overlapping identities along multiple dimensions. Individuals may experience discrimination across multiple dimensions (Crenshaw, 1989).

Labels and risk of essentialisation

Labels can contribute to essentialisation and the perpetuation of negative stereotypes. Gorski (2016) describes essentialism as the act of 'embracing the idea there is some singular and consistent true nature shared among large groups of people'. This is often associated with stereotypes and a failure to acknowledge the complexity of people's full identities.

Equity definitions, dimensions and challenges

Cerna et al. (2019) define equitable education systems as 'those that ensure the achievement of educational potential is not the result of personal and social circumstances, including factors such as gender, ethnic origin, immigrant status, special education needs and giftedness'. Gutiérrez (2011) describes equity as 'fairness not sameness' to distinguish the concept of equity from equality because providing every student with the same supports, unfortunately, does not ensure equitable outcomes.

Gutiérrez (2012) identified four dimensions of equity: 1) access, 2) achievement, 3) identity and 4) power.

4. Sharing experiences task

Participants respond to prompts individually and then share in small groups or with the whole group, depending on group size.

1. *Describe one equity-related classroom situation/interaction that you felt good about. What happened? What did you do? How did the student(s) respond? Why do you feel good about this situation/interaction?*
2. *Describe one equity-related classroom situation/interaction that you wonder or worry about. What happened? What did you do? How did the student(s) respond? Why do you wonder or worry about this situation/interaction?*

5. Gallery walk

Participants browse a gallery of quotes from students at their school related to diversity and equity. They should think about the following questions.

- *Student perceptions: What surprised you? What did not surprise you? Why?*
- *Teacher experience: What connections do you notice between the teacher experiences and the student perceptions?*

6. Final reflection

- *I notice . . .*
- *I wonder . . .*
- *Next steps for me . . .*
- *Next steps for our school . . .*

Recommended readings and resources

Gorski, P. (2014, April 10). *Imagining equity literacy. Learning for Justice.* Retrieved from https://www.learningforjustice.org/magazine/imagining-equity-literacy

Barshay, J. (2018, May 7). 20 judgments a teacher makes in 1 minute and 28 seconds. *The Hechinger Report.* Retrieved from https://hechingerreport.org/20-judgments-a-teacher-makes-in-1-minute-and-28-seconds/

Dugan, J. (2021, March 1). Beware of equity traps and tropes. *Educational Leadership, 78*(6). Retrieved from https://www.ascd.org/el/articles/beware-of-equity-traps-and-tropes

Videos

TEDx Talks. (2013, June 13). *The Pygmalion Effect: Robert Rosenthal's study on the power of positive expectations*[Video]. In Robert Rosenthal (Speaker). YouTube. https://www.youtube.com/watch?v=EjbL7zW-Wig

TV 2. (2017, January 27). *All That We Share* [Video]. In TV 2 (Speaker). YouTube. https://www.youtube.com/watch?v=jD8tjhVO1Tc

TEDx Talks. (c. 2015). *Cultural intelligence: the competitive edge for leaders | Julia Middleton | TEDxEastEnd* [Video]. In J. Middleton (Speaker). YouTube. https://www.youtube.com/watch?v=izeiRjUMau4

Acknowledgement of funding

Erasmus+ project, funded by Léargas (Ireland) 2019-1-IE01-KA201-051528

Note

1 For more information about the 'Big Ideas for Better Schools' project, see Heinz et al., 2026. A more detailed conceptualisation of the three key concepts explored in the project – diversity, equity and democracy – is provided in Mac Ruairc et al., 2026.

References

Adebayo, S. B., & Heinz, M. (2023). 'Teachers should put themselves in their students' shoes': Perspectives of parents from minority-ethnic backgrounds on schooling in Ireland. *International Journal of Inclusive Education*, *28*(13), 3124–3142.

Braun, V., & Clarke, V. (2022). *Thematic analysis: A practical guide*. Sage Publications.

Brown, M., Eaton, P., Heinz, M., Hughes, J., Rowan, A., & O'Hara, J. (2024). Cultural responsivity in teacher education research in action (CRiTERiA)-Government of Ireland Shared Island (SCoTENS) final report. In *Cultural Responsivity in Teacher Education Research CRiTERiA-: Government of Ireland Shared Island, Standing Conference on Teacher Education North and South (SCoTENS) Final Report* (pp. 1–129). Government of Ireland Shared Island.

Bryk, A. S., & Scheider, B. (2002). *Trust in schools: A core resource for improvement*. Russell Sage Foundation.

Cerna, L., Mezzanotte, C., Rutigliano, A., Brussino, O., Santiago, P., Borgonovi, F., & Guthrie, C. (2019). Promoting inclusive education for diverse societies: A conceptual framework. *OECD Education Working Papers No. 260*.

Cho, J., Heinz, M., & Choi, J. (2023). Religious education in Catholic schools in Ireland and South Korea: Complex layers of diversity, policy and teacher agency. *Irish Educational Studies*, *42*(4), 1009–1024.

Cochran-Smith, M., & Lytle, S. L. (2015). *Inquiry as stance: Practitioner research for the next generation*. Teachers College Press.

Crenshaw, K. (1989). Demarginalising the intersection of race and sex: A Black feminist critique of antidiscrimination doctrine, feminist theory and antiracist politics. *University of Chicago Legal Forum*, *1*(8). http://chicagounbound.uchicago.edu/uclf/vol1989/iss1/8 (Accessed: 4 April 2020).

Dervin, F. (2016). Discourses of othering. In F. Dervin (Ed.), *Interculturality in education* (pp. 43–55). London: Palgrave Pivot.

Education and Training Boards Ireland (ETBI). (2022). *ETBI Patrons' framework on ethos*. https://www.etbi.ie/wp-content/uploads/2022/11/ETBI-Patrons-Framework-Digi.pdf?x61602

Fairclough, N. (2003). *Analysing discourse: Textual analysis for social research*. Routledge.
Fitzpatrick, D. (1984). *Irish emigration, 1801–1921*. Dublin: Economic and Social History Society of Ireland.
Gorski, P. (2016). Rethinking the role of "culture" in educational equity: From cultural competence to equity literacy. *Multicultural Perspectives*, *18*(4), 221–226. https://doi.org/10.1080/15210960.2016.1228344
Goodson, I. F. (1991). Sponsoring the teacher's voice: Teachers' lives and teacher development. *Cambridge journal of education*, *21*(1), 35–45.
Gutiérrez, R. (2011). Context matters: How should we conceptualize equity in mathematics education? In *Equity in discourse for mathematics education: Theories, practices, and policies* (pp. 17–33). Dordrecht: Springer Netherlands.
Hattie, J. (2023). *Visible learning: The sequel a synthesis of over 2,100 meta-analyses relating to achievement*. London and New York: Routledge.
Heinz, M., & Keane, E. (2018). Socio-demographic composition of primary initial teacher education entrants in Ireland. *Irish Educational Studies*, *37*(4), 523–543.
Heinz, M., Keane, E., & Mc Daid, R. (2023). Charting pathways toward a more diverse, equitable and inclusive teaching profession. In E. Keane, M. Heinz, & R. Mc Daid (Eds.), *Diversifying the teaching profession: Dimensions, dilemmas and directions for the future* (pp. 226–240). Routledge.
Heinz, M., Mac Ruairc, G., & Rodríguez-Entrena, M. J. (2026). Big ideas for better schools: A transnational professional learning project. In M. Heinz, M. J. Rodríguez-Entrena, & G. Mac Ruairc (Eds.), *Professional learning for diversity, equity and democracy: Big ideas for better schools* (pp. 17–23). Routledge.
Heinz, M., Rodríguez-Entrena, M. J., & Mac Ruairc, G. (2026). School leadership for better futures: Collaborative professional learning *about* and *for* diversity, equity and democracy. In M. Heinz, M. J. Rodríguez-Entrena, & G. Mac Ruairc (Eds.), *Professional learning for diversity, equity and democracy: Big ideas for better schools* (pp. 3–16). Routledge.
Higher Education Authority. (2015a). *National plan for equity of access to higher education 2015–2021*. Dublin: HEA.
Higher Education Authority. (2015b). *National access plan, 2022–2028*. Dublin: HEA.
Jussim, L., & Harber, K. D. (2005). Teacher expectations and self-fulfilling prophecies: Knowns and unknowns, resolved and unresolved controversies. *Personality and Social Psychology Review*, *9*(2), 131–155.
Kalinec-Craig, C. A. (2017). The rights of the learner: A framework for promoting equity through formative assessment in mathematics education. *Democracy and Education*, *25*(2), 5.
Keane, E., Heinz, M., & Mc Daid, R. (2023). Diversity in the teaching profession in Ireland: Tracing research and policy development. In E. Keane, M. Heinz, & R. Mc Daid (Eds.), *Diversifying the teaching profession: Dimensions, dilemmas and directions for the future* (36–53). Routledge.
Mac Ruairc, G., Gartland, S., Heinz, M., & Rodríguez-Entrena, M. J. (2026). Diversity, equity and democracy in school leadership: Troublesome concepts in troubled times. In M. Heinz, M. J. Rodríguez-Entrena, & G. Mac Ruairc (Eds.), *Professional learning for diversity, equity and democracy: Big ideas for better schools* (pp. 24–46). Routledge.
Meyer, J., & Land, R. (2003). Threshold concepts and troublesome knowledge: Linkages to ways of thinking and practising within the disciplines. In C. Rust (Ed.), *Improving student learning – ten years on*. Oxford: OCSLD.
National Council for Special Education (NCSE). (2011). *Inclusive education framework*. Dublin: NCSE.

National Council for Special Education (NCSE). (2017). *Guidelines for supporting students with SEN in mainstream schools*. Dublin: NCSE.
Neary, A. (2020). Critical imaginaries of empathy in teaching and learning about diversity in teacher education. *Teaching Education*, *31*(4), 444–458.
Netolicky, D. M. (2019). *Transformational professional learning: Making a difference in schools*. Routledge.
Pit-ten Cate, I. M., & Glock, S. (2019). Teachers' implicit attitudes toward students from different social groups: A meta-analysis. *Frontiers in Psychology*, *10*, 2832.
Rice, C., Kenny, N., & Connolly, L. (2023). Exploring the attitudes of school staff towards the role of autism classes in inclusive education for autistic students: A qualitative study in Irish primary schools. *Education Sciences*, *13*(9), 889.
Rosenthal, R., & Jacobson, L. (1992). *Pygmalion in the classroom*. New York: Irvington. (Original work published 1968).
Safir, S., & Dugan, J. (2021). *Street data: A next-generation model for equity, pedagogy, and school transformation*. Corwin.
Smyth, E., Darmody, M., McGinnity, F., & Byrne, D. (2009). *Adapting to diversity: Irish schools and newcomer students*. Dublin: ESRI.
Steinbeck, J. (1937). *Of mice and men*. New York: Covici Friede.
Teaching Council. (2016). *Code of professional conduct*. https://www.teachingcouncil.ie/fitness-to-teach/updated-code-of-professional-conduct/
Teaching Council. (2020). *Céim: Standards for initial teacher education*. https://www.teachingcouncil.ie/assets/uploads/2023/08/ceim-standards-for-initial-teacher-education.pdf
Travers, J., & King, F. (2025). Social justice leadership in Irish schools: Conceptualisations, supports and barriers. *Irish Educational Studies*, 1–21.
Zeichner, K. (2010). Rethinking the connections between campus courses and field experiences in college-and university-based teacher education. *Journal of Teacher Education*, *61*(1–2), 89–99.

6

DIVERSITY, EQUITY AND DEMOCRACY

Developing an understanding of complex social phenomena with teachers and students in Poland

Jakub Kołodziejczyk, Joanna Kotlarz, Grzegorz Mazurkiewicz, and Joanna Trzópek-Paszkiewicz

Introduction

Recent global events, such as climate change, demographic changes, growing social inequalities, the COVID-19 pandemic and the war in Ukraine, have contributed to an increase in the diversity of the population in Poland. There are currently approximately 1.43 million foreigners living in Poland, including citizens of Ukraine, Belarus, Germany, Russia, Vietnam, India, Italy, Georgia, China and Great Britain. Most of them come from Ukraine (approximately 64%), followed by Belarus (4%) and Moldova (2%) (Urząd do Spraw Cudzoziemców, 2023). After the outbreak of the war in Ukraine, Poles have been found to have the greatest aversion to Russians and, to a lesser extent, to Belarusians and Roma people. At the same time, the sympathy for Ukrainians has been decreasing (CBOS, 2024). National reports indicate a worryingly high percentage of people (30%) with negative attitudes towards people with disabilities (CBOS, 2017), and most respondents believe that homosexuals should not publicly show their way of life, enter marriage (60%) or adopt children (75%) (CBOS, 2021).

Poland used to have some of the lowest levels of equality-focused legislation and policies in the EU. In the ILGA-Europe ranking, which analyses the level of equality of LGBTI people in Europe, Poland scored only 18 out of 100 points (ILGA-Europe, 2020), and Polish attitudes towards diversity reveal that reluctance towards diversity is most pronounced among the youngest respondents, particularly those aged 18–24 (Kantar Millward Brown, 2017). However, a greater focus needs to be placed on understanding and addressing the beliefs and attitudes of young people towards diversity (Kotlarz, 2023). In the last few years, a few legislative initiatives were implemented, concerning

DOI: 10.4324/9781032629292-8

the alignment of Polish legislation with European legislation on the development and promotion of the principles of diversity, democracy and equality in the educational context. One of them is the National Action Plan for Equal Treatment (2022–2030), which outlines measures to prevent discrimination and to promote equal treatment across various sectors, including education, in line with EU anti-discrimination directives (Kancelaria Prezesa Rady Ministrów, 2022). Since September 2024, schools have been required to implement regulations related to inclusive education, which aims to provide access to support at the earliest possible stage of a child's development, improve the quality of teaching (including educational materials and the employment of specialists), introduce a new approach to assessing individual needs and create diverse vocational education pathways as well as support for people with disabilities in entering the labour market. Additional financial resources have been allocated for this purpose, beyond the standard educational subsidy, enabling real change (Ustawa z dnia 12 maja 2022 r. o zmianie ustawy o systemie oświaty oraz niektórych innych ustaw, 2022). Nevertheless, some school principals report difficulties in implementing inclusive education due to inadequate school infrastructure and overcrowded classrooms.

In EU countries, policies of social inclusion have been pursued for a long time, with the aim of including individuals and groups from all socio-demographic backgrounds in education and wider society, and to counteract exclusion and/or marginalisation of groups or individuals (European Commission, 2023). Promoting equity in diverse societies requires dismantling discrimination, fostering inclusivity and empowering marginalised groups. A core principle in law, economics and social justice, equity seeks to reduce disparities to ensure equal access to resources. Ensuring equity and justice in education and educational policy means equipping every student with cultural and civic competences, as well as the best and most appropriate preparation for making individual choices (Walzer, 2007). In Poland, equal access to education was declared in the Constitution of 1997, which provided for compulsory, free education, school autonomy, power decentralisation, freedom to choose schools other than public ones and the right to establish schools (Article 70 of the Polish Constitution). The principles of free and equal access to education, as well as the prevention of discrimination, appear in all legal acts (Sobas, 2019, p. 82). At the operational level, Poland's schools can use tools such as the Equal Treatment School Code, which supports school staff in developing pedagogical approaches that can shape open and respectful attitudes, respect for social diversity and a culture of dialogue (FRS, 2023). However, according to the 'Equal Treatment at School Report on the Research in Schools and Quantitative Analysis of Educational and Preventive Programmes Report', between 10% and 35% of students feel that they experience unequal treatment. The study underlines the importance of mandatory anti-discrimination education, advocating that such programmes contribute to fostering inclusive attitudes and promoting social equity among students (Bulska et al., 2021).

The relationship between education and democracy is a central theme in many philosophical and educational frameworks. There is a widely shared belief in the importance of democratising education to ensure equity and participation (Męczkowska-Christiansen, 2014), juxtaposed with concerns about the contemporary crisis of democracy, marked by challenges such as declining civic engagement and institutional trust (Bauman, 2009; Iwasiński, 2015). Nussbaum has argued for a renewed emphasis on the humanities in education. Instead of viewing education through the narrow prism of gross national income, it should focus on helping students become true democratic citizens (Nussbaum, 2010).

In a democratic society, different social agents, including parents, peers, teachers and schools, shape the civic and democratic attitudes of students (Maurissen et al., 2018). Schools are the leaven of social life (Dewey, 1966), spaces where students 'meet the world' and where they have the opportunity to develop social competences (Kurczewska, 2006), democratic values and civic attitudes (Fullan, 2010). According to Biesta (2019), there are three aims of education: socialisation, empowerment/agency and knowledge/competences. Schools should prepare students to live in society and to be empathic and active citizens in the future.

In Central and Eastern Europe, this preparation for active participation in a democratic society is particularly important after a long history of Russian occupation (Osler & Starkey, 2006). In Poland, our understanding of civil society is often related to memories of political changes and the emergence of democratic opposition to authorities in the 1980s. Although the events of this time resulted in the revival of the idea of civil society (Kazimierczuk, 2021), a 'poorly developed civic culture remains a significant challenge and source of political instability' (Pietrzyk-Reeves, 2012, p. 232).

Multiple factors impact the process of teaching and learning. Policymakers, educational leaders and teachers plan, design and implement various initiatives to improve learning environments and educational processes, for example, through teacher professional development, innovative pedagogies and reduced class sizes (Hattie, 2008). Teachers' knowledge also plays a key role in quality education, as increased knowledge empowers changes in teaching approaches (Broom, 2015). One of the influential philosophical approaches in thinking about education (and teachers' professional development as well) is constructivism, which emphasises the active role of learners in building their understanding (Woolfolk, 2021). Constructivism is defined as a theory of learning, knowledge and a paradigm guiding contemporary social science research. The fundamental premise of social constructivism is that knowledge is a human construction and that the learner is an active participant in the learning process. Core assumptions are: 1) Learners (people) are active in constructing their own understanding, going further beyond the information they are given. Objects influence perception not through the objective properties of objects but through the properties of the perceiving person's psyche (Bruner, 1973), and 2) social interactions are crucial in the construction of knowledge processes (Bruning et al., 2011).

Learners, as active participants, shape learning through personal goals, strategies and self-esteem (Younger et al., 2021). Their current knowledge shapes future learning trajectories and competencies, drawn from diverse formal and informal sources, including daily life, media, family, peers and school. Teachers must adapt to diverse levels of student knowledge, continuously assessing and diagnosing their knowledge base (Schneider & Stern, 2013).

Understanding diversity, equity and democracy: Overview of a collaborative learning programme

The collaborative professional learning project discussed here formed part of the Erasmus+-funded BIBS project, which brought together academic institutions and school partners from Ireland, Norway, Poland and Spain. The project's overall goal was to deepen educators' conversations about, understanding of, and agency in diversity, equity and democracy through collaborative professional learning (Heinz et al., 2026). In our work with schools, we conceptualised the three concepts of diversity, equity and democracy as closely interrelated and, further, connected to a range of other key concepts, including culture, power, identity, justice, inclusion and intersectionality, each underpinned by a rich body of scholarship, research traditions and philosophical foundations (see Heinz et al., 2026; Mac Ruairc et al., 2026). The professional learning programme developed by project partners in Poland involved academics from Jagiellonian University in Kraków, teachers of history and English and 25 students of the third and fourth grades from one of the secondary schools in Kraków. The school was established in 1897 by members of the Lutheran community. The school building is situated in the very heart of the old town of Kraków. It functioned until the outbreak of the Second World War, when it ceased to exist, only being re-established in 1993. The school has always been open and welcoming to students from different religious and cultural backgrounds, including Catholic, Protestant, Jewish and non-religious. It does not impose any viewpoint and hopes to enable students to develop autonomous attitudes towards life and social phenomena.

The cornerstone of this professional development initiative was our shared understanding of school as a learning community and of the value of collaborative learning to promote individual and organisational capacity. At the heart of our approach was a commitment to shedding our expert roles and adopting a collaborative approach that recognises the values, knowledge and expertise of all community members, engaging them in a cycle of exploration, experimentation and reflection. Through collaborative enquiry, we set out to enrich and deepen the knowledge base of the school (Wald & Castleberry, 2000). The design of the collaborative professional learning programme included three stages: 1) teacher interviews and collaborative professional learning during two online meetings, 2) student workshops during which action research data were collected and 3) educational activities for students and professional development workshops for teachers.

During the first stage, we discussed and explored teachers' experiences with introducing complex societal constructs such as diversity, equity and democracy in their school and classrooms. It was assumed that teacher's beliefs and previous experiences significantly impacted the structure of learning and teaching environments. As beliefs might be strongly held but implicit, debates were organised in the school to openly discuss these issues (O'Brien & Guiney, 2001).

Teachers were asked to answer the question: What are the obstacles to introducing concepts of diversity, equity and democracy during regular classes in your school? Teachers shared that they had no time to discuss these concepts as part of their subject teaching. They mentioned the rigid boundaries between school subjects and the feeling that they should not focus on themes that were not from their 'universe' as defined by the curriculum. Some teachers also shared that they were afraid that speaking about these big issues might be perceived as wasting time. However, the complexity and subjectivity of language emerged as their key concerns. When talking about complex concepts, teachers said they were aware that understandings of them often differed from person to person. That, in turn, could create chaos, which they might not be able to control, and, in this situation, they would feel lost or even ashamed. In teachers' words: 'people can use the same words, but they mean different things to them'. Another teacher said: 'with language we describe the world, and yet language is an obstacle. It is very difficult to communicate, to see similarities, to understand diversity'. Language, some of them argued, 'preserved social memory', but, because different generations use words differently, they see the world differently and, hence, different worlds are created'. Overall, teachers accepted their responsibility to support students in interpreting reality. They felt that they 'needed to help our students to critically think about diversity'.

They envisaged conversations that would raise difficult, contemporary issues, leaving room for all shades and angles, in an atmosphere where no one was afraid of being rejected by the group. Success, to them, essentially meant safety and openness; nobody being 'dragged through the mud' due to their personal views.

During the second stage, students first answered the survey including open-ended questions concerning concepts of diversity, equity and democracy in their personal, school and social lives. After that, they participated in an online workshop (due to the COVID-19 pandemic). During this workshop, the students first practised creating definitions using the example of the term 'unemployment'. Following this introduction, they collaborated to create their own definitions for the key concepts – diversity, equity and democracy. Working in groups of three to four people with their own anonymous survey responses, they highlighted words (phrases) that they felt related to the terms being studied. They then used semantic analysis of concepts (described in further detail in the next section) to analyse the data and to collaboratively create definitions. At the end of the workshop, they reviewed and discussed the definitions.

The *third stage* involved a series of educational activities that were intended to develop students' and teachers' thinking about diversity, equity and democracy. The activities included: 1) local expeditions and field research in the neighbourhood during which students constructed and later presented personal and historical stories, 2) a workshop focused on careful observation and diversity during which participants engaged with various methods of observation and reflected on how their own perspectives differ from those of others and how they influence their observations and interpretations of the world around them and 3) a series of workshops on movies as a vehicle of change focusing, in particular, on the movie 'Blue Eyed' (1996, directed by Bertram Verhaag).

In the following sections, we will zoom in on Stage 2 and the process of meaning-making using collaborative semantic analysis. The objective of the analyses was to provide students with an opportunity to gain insight into how they and their peers understand important concepts in education (diversity, equity and democracy) and to deepen their individual understanding of the complexities of these ideas.

Students make meaning through collaborative semantic analysis

During the workshop in phase 2, students used semantic analysis of concepts to analyse the definitions they had collaboratively created. This method was designed by Regine Robin and her team from the Political Lexicology Centre in Saint-Cloud (Robin, 1980) to

> search for the meaning of a text, sentence, or word through the analysis of all its uses and contexts. It requires continuous work with the text, including the apparent distribution of utterance sequences and the order of speech, to reassemble them in a way that ensures meaningful readability.
>
> *(Robin, 1980, p. 252)*

Students followed the analytical approach, which involves two key analytical steps: first, deconstructing the definitions of democracy, diversity and equality and second, constructing them anew.

Deconstruction involves aligning words and phrases from the analysed texts with the six semantic roles indicated below:

1. *Equivalents* – what are the concepts (diversity, equity and democracy) identified with? What expressions are used to substitute the concept in defined contexts?
2. *Descriptions* – indicating what the concept is like and what its features are like. What is its way of being?
3. *Opposition* – what is the concept opposed to, and what are its opposites?
4. *Associations* – what is the concept associated with? What accompanies it?
5. *Description of the concept's actions* – what does it do? What effects does it produce?
6. *Description of actions towards the concept* – what actions are taken towards them?

Assigning specific expressions to individual categories is not easy and sometimes requires a grammatical transformation that considers the function of the concept that is the object of interest, which ultimately allows for qualification for the appropriate category (Kłosiński, 1994; Dudkiewicz, 2006).

The next step, the *reconstruction* of the meaning, or a set of meanings, entailed the

> construction (in accordance with the rules of grammar) of one or several declarative sentences that would act as definitions. All elements of these sentences, apart from connectors, must belong to the set that constitutes the semantic field of the concept under consideration.
>
> *(Kłosiński, 1994, p. 155)*

Therefore, creating a definition involves arranging and connecting expressions extracted from the original definitions during the analysis, ensuring the logical coherence of the reconstructed definition. To ensure that all categories of the semantic field are captured during this process, students followed the prescribed sentence pattern illustrated below (Kłosiński, 1994, p. 155):

> THE SUBJECT MATTER OF THE FIELD (examined impression) . . ., THAT IS (in other words) equivalent . . ., THAT IS . . . (definitions) . . ., CONTRARY TO (oppositions) . . ., WHICH THEY ARE ASSOCIATED WITH (associations) . . ., WHICH CAUSES (action of the subject) . . ., TOWARDS WHOM (actions towards the subject)

The final collaborative analysis, using semantic analysis of concepts, allowed us to deeply interrogate the complexities of the constructs of diversity, equity and democracy, taking into consideration existing literature as well as definitions created by all students and discussions between teachers and students. The discussions among students unfolding during this process of analysis and the resulting definitions (semantic fields) provided teachers with new and deep insight into their students' understandings of the concepts of diversity, equity and democracy, which, later, served as foundations for designing future activities and lessons.

Reconstructions offering deep insights into students' perspectives on diversity, equity and democracy

Diversity

The semantic field that emerged from the analysis of the data describing students' perceptions of the concept of diversity (see Table 6.1) was unbalanced in terms of the number of expressions that refer to the various analytical categories. There was a complete lack of statements that could be categorised as 'descriptions'. Two statements were assigned to the function of 'opposition', and two functioned as 'actions towards the subject'. A greater number of statements were found in the category of 'equivalents', and most belonged to the categories of the 'subject's action' and 'associations'.

TABLE 6.1 Semantic field of the concept 'diversity'

Equivalents *Dissimilarity, uniqueness, exceptionality, distinctness.*	Descriptions None.
Oppositions *Monotony; LGBT-free zone and all that nasty gutter*	Associations *Various views, beliefs, interests, customs, traditions, cultures, languages, skin colours, religions and sexual orientations.*
Actions of the subject *intrigues, diversifies life, allows you to get to know people and understand their views, allows you to expand your views, allows you to look at life from their [other people's] perspectives, diversifies our experiences and encourages reflection.*	Actions towards the subject *Be open-minded and be tolerant.*

Following deconstruction and using the prescribed sentence pattern, the following definition was created from the extracted expressions.

> Diversity, that is, *distinctness, uniqueness, exceptionality, otherness as opposed to monotony, LGBT-free zones and all this nasty gutter, which involves varying views, beliefs, interests, customs, traditions, cultures, languages, skin colours, religions, sexual orientation, which intrigues, diversifies life, allows you to meet people and understand their views, expand your own views, allows you to look at life from their* [other people's] *perspectives, diversifies our experiences, and encourages reflection, towards which it is necessary to be open-minded and tolerant.*

This rich reconstructed definition of the concept of diversity illustrates a complex network of associations with numerous spaces where young people encounter diversity, as well as positive perceptions regarding the impact of diversity on their lives. The teachers involved in the project recognised and discussed that students had multiple opportunities to experience diversity and that, in working with students, they can build on the various benefits students perceive regarding diversity while also supporting and encouraging them to explore further benefits.

Equity

For equity, the extracted expressions were evenly distributed among the individual categories (see Table 6.2). The fewest statements referred to 'actions

TABLE 6.2 Semantic field of the concept 'equity'

Equivalents *Justice, the same rights regardless of gender, skin colour and origin; everyone is equal; good treatment*	**Definitions** *fair treatment without judgement, equal opportunities, equality is necessary, equal treatment, equal opportunities for all, being equal with others*
Oppositions *unnecessary divisions, inequalities, discrimination and treating [people] as if they were inferior, as if they did not deserve anything; privileges, hatred and oppression due to skin colour, ethnicity and appearance*	**Associations** *Compliance with established rules, social justice, there are no better or worse people, everyone is treated equally, caring, respecting other people and basic human rights*
Actions of the subject *There are no hurt people, happy people, people feel safe, dignified and comfortable*	**Actions towards the subject** *One should try and contribute to becoming a better society; if equality is violated, it must be repaired; we are all responsible for social justice.*

towards the subject' (three) and 'equivalents' and 'actions of the subject' (four each), while the largest number of statements were classified as 'oppositions' (seven).

The following definition was reconstructed from the extracted expressions:

> Equity *means justice, the same rights regardless of gender, skin colour, and origin, good treatment is something necessary, it is fair treatment without judgment, equal opportunities for everyone and equal treatment, being equal with others, as opposed to unnecessary divisions, inequalities, discrimination, oppression, treating [people] as if they were inferior, as if they deserved nothing, privileges, and hatred, which involves basic human rights, social justice, observing the established rules, caring for and respecting other people, which causes that there are no disadvantaged people, they feel safe, dignified, and comfortable, they are happier, for which we are all responsible, and we should make an effort, if equality is violated, to repair it.*

In the reconstructed definition, what deserves attention is the social function of this value, which is the basis for creating a community and enhancing social well-being. The analysis of equity in the context of moral development (Kohlberg, 1981) indicates that students comprehend equity at a higher, more advanced level, focusing on concepts such as the social contract. Future activities with this group could aim to develop and apply universal principles that are more abstract and transcend existing laws and rules.

Democracy

The semantic field of emergence during the analysis of students' understandings of the concept of *democracy* was the most diverse (see Table 6.3). The number of 'descriptions', 'associations' and 'actions of the subject' was much larger than was the case for the other categories. The list of expressions assigned to individual categories is presented below:

TABLE 6.3 Semantic field of the concept of 'democracy'

Equivalents	Definitions
Exerting influence	*The best form of government; the greatest social, political and economic opportunities; taking everyone's opinion into account; considering the wishes and respecting all opinions; respecting minorities' opinions; following majority rule; the ability to express one's opinion without any fear of consequences; and the need to respect the principles of a democratic and equal society*

(*Continued*)

TABLE 6.3 (Continued)

Oppositions *Authoritarianism and totalitarianism*	**Associations** *legal provisions, constitution and European law; democratic elections; indirect democracy; close connection with justice; crisis of democracy; a democratic country; healthy democracy; and utopian democracy*
Actions of the subject *People are treated in the same way; brings benefits to the country; satisfaction with the country; enables equal access to public debate; helps people to be heard and represent all people; maintains balance in society; decides what the majority wants; gives a sense of security; the basis for human growth; and protects people by law/constitution*	**Actions towards the subject** *defend democracy* and [ensure] *independent courts*

The large number of expressions and the diversity of content in relation to the term 'democracy' made it impossible to create one logically coherent definition. The reconstruction led to the creation of five qualitatively different definitions of the term democracy.

Democracy is *the best form of government, as opposed to authoritarianism and totalitarianism, which is closely related to justice, compliance with the provisions of law, constitution and European law, which* causes *that everyone has basic human rights, people are treated the same way, and they are protected by law/constitution, for which independent courts should be ensured.*

Democracy is *the best form of government, which brings the greatest social, political and economic opportunities, which brings benefits to the country and satisfaction with the country.*

Democracy is *taking everyone's opinion into account, considering the wishes and respecting all opinions, which involves respecting the opinions of minorities, allows equal access to public debate, helps people to be heard and represent all people and maintains a balance in society that must be defended.*

Democracy, that is, *exerting influence, is acting according to the majority rule, which involves democratic elections and indirect democracy, which decides what the majority wants.*

Democracy is *the ability to express one's own opinion without any fear of consequences, which involves the need to comply with the principles of a democratic and equal society, which protects people by law/constitution and gives a sense of security and the basis for human growth.*

The reconstructed definitions of democracy reveal significant qualitative differences in how the subject is described. The first definition highlights the issue of compliance with the law in a democracy. The second definition points to the conditions created by democracy for the development of society on various levels and the satisfaction derived from it. The third definition pays attention to respecting all opinions and considering the perspective of minorities, which ensures balance in society. The fourth emphasises the influence of the majority on the decisions made, and the fifth underlines the security climate created by democracy as an essential factor for human development.

While these definitions are qualitatively different, they are not contradictory but rather complement each other. They also point to potential tensions that may exist between different ways of understanding the term, the best example of which is the emphasis on exerting influence by the majority, on the one hand, and the need to take the opinion of the minority into account, on the other hand. When designing future classes for this group of students, teachers can utilise the identified tensions between different aspects of understanding the term 'democracy' to choose, design and/or prepare debates, texts or case studies.

Conclusions and recommendations

Our experience has highlighted the value of collaboratively and deeply analysing students' perspectives on complex social constructs as a vital component of constructivist learning. The activities resulted in rich professional development experiences for participating teachers that we are hoping will shape future pedagogical approaches. The teachers who participated in the project recognised their responsibility to help students develop critical thinking skills. They also saw the value of constructivist approaches to teaching and learning about diversity, equity and democracy. They felt that they had succeeded in creating an environment where students could communicate safely and discuss difficult issues openly and where no one felt rejected due to their personal views.

Students understand diversity in multiple ways, ranging from easily visible, external characteristics of people to appreciating what we can learn by observing others' behaviours in various situations. It is encouraging to see that the adolescents who participated in this study perceived diversity as a positive phenomenon, a 'window' that arouses curiosity to learn and understand their surrounding world. The students saw justice as the basis for the functioning of society, the creation of a community, and of societal well-being. The most complex and multidimensional construct was democracy. This is likely related to the current political situation in Poland and the daily experiences of young people. Definitions emphasised qualitatively different, complementary aspects: compliance with the law, respect for minority opinions and the influence of the majority on decisions. Equally important were the consequences of democracy: creating conditions for human development, ensuring social peace and gaining satisfaction.

Connecting these concepts, diversity embodies the varied backgrounds and perspectives within a democratic society, emphasising the need for open-mindedness and tolerance to embrace this variety. Equity serves as the foundation for a democratic society, ensuring fairness, justice and equal treatment for all, aligning with the principles of democracy. Democracy thrives on diversity and equity, respecting and incorporating various opinions, protecting individual rights and maintaining a balanced society, thus fostering an environment where diversity is valued, and equity is upheld for all members. The variety and complexity of the reconstructed definitions of diversity, equity and democracy highlight the breadth and depth of students' knowledge (constructs) and thought and, with this, the value and potential of student voice and collaboration in learning, teaching and pedagogical decision-making. The project has clearly demonstrated, to teachers as well as researchers, the importance and benefits of appreciatively looking at students as knowers, who need teachers to accompany them and inspire them to intersubjective exchange. 'Finding out what others think or feel' (Bruner, 2006) and connecting teaching approaches and learning experiences to students' existing knowledge and beliefs (Woolfolk, 2021) emerged as a profound and inspiring insight from this project.

In traditional classrooms, materials are often not connected to students' knowledge; they are presented as disconnected pieces of information, without understanding and discussing how and why. Authorities are presented as indisputable sources of knowledge, but knowledge is socially constructed and requires critical thinking. Learning requires engaging students in their own learning processes, not just in completing tasks (Sawyer, 2006). It is, therefore, important to create a safe space where students can discuss, exchange views and experience different perspectives, together with teachers as guides.

Based on our experience, we make the following recommendations for professional learning:

- Encourage learners to share their current knowledge and perspectives on the discussed issues. This is essential for integrating every new topic into existing cognitive structures.
- When introducing theoretical concepts, it is crucial to relate them to the real world of our students and to the knowledge that they already possess.

Ignoring this connection is not an option, as students do not exist in isolation; our classroom and the outside world are interconnected.
- Add inclusive training to professional learning. This will help create a more inclusive and tolerant environment.
- Design learning activities that incorporate participatory approaches that allow individuals to voice their opinions, participate in decision-making processes and understand democratic principles through practice.
- Talk to other teachers about supporting diversity, equity and democracy. Try to find cross-subject issues.
- Create a supportive network for teaching and learning with your colleagues. Appreciate the perspectives of other teachers to encourage collaboration in the classroom and school.

The development of professional learning programmes for teachers in Poland should focus on diversity, equity and democratic values. It is important to ensure equal opportunities for all participants. Programmes should value and take advantage of the cultural, linguistic and social diversity of participants. This will ensure that teachers are better prepared to work in diverse school environments. Teachers should be encouraged to engage in open and constructive discussions and support students in developing civic skills.

Acknowledgement of funding

Erasmus+ project, funded by Léargas (Ireland) 2019-1-IE01-KA201-051528

References

Bauman, Z. (2009). *Konsumowanie życia*. Kraków: Wydawnictwo Uniwersytetu Jagiellońskiego.
Biesta, G. (2019). What kind of society does the school need? Redefining the democratic work of education in impatient time. *Studies Philosophy and Education*, *38*, 657–668.
Broom, C. (2015). Empowering students: Pedagogy that benefits educators and learners. *Citizenship, Social and Economics Education*, *14*(2), 79–86. https://doi.org/10.1177/2047173415597142
Bruner, J. (1973). *Beyond the information given: Studies in the psychology of knowing*. New York, NY: Norton.
Bruner, J. (2006). *Kultura edukacji*. Kraków: Universitas.
Bruning, R. H., Schraw, G. J., & Norby, M. M. (2011). *Cognitive psychology and instruction* (5th ed.). Boston, MA: Pearson.
Bulska, D., Skrodzka, M., Smulczyk, M., & Winiewski, M. (2021). *Równe traktowanie w szkole. Raport z badania w szkołach oraz analiza ilościowa programów wychowawczo – profilaktycznych*. Warszawa: Biuletyn Rzecznika Praw Obywatelskich.
CBOS. (2017). *Niepełnosprawni wśród nas. Komunikat z badań*. https://cbos.pl/SPISKOM.POL/2017/K_169_17.PDF (Accessed: 21 September 2023).

CBOS. (2021). *Stosunek Polaków do osób homoseksualnych. Komunikat z badań.* https://www.cbos.pl/SPISKOM.POL/2021/K_121_21.PDF (Accessed: 21 September 2023).
CBOS. (2024). *Stosunek Polaków do innych narodów. Komunikat z badań.* https://www.cbos.pl/SPISKOM.POL/2024/K_025_24.PDF (Accessed: 15 December 2024).
Dewey, J. (1966). *Democracy and education.* Toronto: Collier-Macmillan Canada Ltd.
Dudkiewicz, M. (2006). Zastosowanie analizy pola semantycznego i analizy 'gloss' dla zaprezentowania sposobu postrzegania świata społecznego. *Przegląd Socjologii Jakościowej*, 2(1), 33–52. https://doi.org/10.18778/1733-8069.2.1.03
European Commission. (2023). *Social protection & social inclusion.* https://ec.europa.eu/social/main.jsp?langId=en&catId=750 (Accessed: 11 June 2023).
FRS (Fundacja na rzecz Rozwoju Różnorodności Społecznej). (2023). https://frs.org.pl/szkoly/ (Accessed: 11 June 2023).
Fullan, M. (2010). *All systems go: The change imperative for whole system reform.* Thousand Oaks: Corwin, a SAGE Company.
Hattie, J. (2008). *Visible learning: A synthesis of over 800 meta-analyses relating to achievement* (1st ed.). London: Routledge.
Heinz, M., Mac Ruairc, G., & Rodríguez-Entrena, M. J. (2026). Big Ideas for better schools: A transnational professional learning project. In M. Heinz, M. J. Rodríguez-Entrena, & G. Mac Ruairc (Eds.), *Professional learning for diversity, equity and democracy: Big ideas for better schools* (pp. 17–23). Routledge.
Heinz, M., Rodríguez-Entrena, M. J., & Mac Ruairc, G. (2026). School leadership for better futures: Collaborative professional learning *about* and *for* diversity, equity and democracy. In M. Heinz, M. J. Rodríguez-Entrena, & G. Mac Ruairc (Eds.), *Professional learning for diversity, equity and democracy: Big ideas for better schools* (pp. 3–16). Routledge.
ILGA-Europe. (2020). *Annual review of the human rights situation of lesbian, gay, bisexual, trans, and intersex people in Europe and Central Asia.* https://www.ilga-europe.org/report/annual-review-2020/ (Accessed: 12 July 2023).
Iwasiński, Ł. (2015). Społeczeństwo konsumpcyjne w ujęciu Zygmunta Baumana. *Kultura I Społeczeństwo*, *59*(4), 3–22. https://doi.org/10.35757/KiS.2015.59.4.1
Kancelaria Prezesa Rady Ministrów. (2022). *Krajowy Program Działań na rzecz Równego Traktowania na lata 2022–2030.* https://www.gov.pl/web/rownetraktowanie/krajowy-program-dzialan-na-rzecz-rownego-traktowania-na-lata-2022-2030 (Accessed: 3 May 2025).
Kantar Millward Brown. (2017). *Obecność tolerancji dla różnorodności w społeczeństwie polskim 2017 roku.* Report 2017, Kantar, Millward Brown. https://odpowiedzialnybiznes.pl/karta-roznorodnosci/aktualnosci-karta/zbadano-otwartosc-polakow-wobec-roznorodnosci/#_ftnref1 (Accessed: 3 May 2025).
Kazimierczuk, M. (2021). Ewolucja pojęcia idei społeczeństwa obywatelskiego. In M. Kazimierczuk, & R. Kania (Eds.), *Społeczeństwo obywatelskie. Historia. Teoria. Praktyka* (pp. 14–33). Warszawa: Wydawnictwo Difin.
Kłosiński, M. (1994). Semantyczna analiza pojęć 'bezrobocie' i 'bezrobotny' ('bezrobotni') w wypowiedziach prasowych. *Kultura i Społeczeństwo*, *38*(3), 151–162.
Kohlberg, L. (1981). *The philosophy of moral development: Moral stages and the idea of justice.* New York: Harper & Row.
Kotlarz, J. (2023). *Wyzwania zarządzania edukacyjnego w warunkach różnorodności* (Ph.D. Dissertation) Jagiellonian University in Krakow.
Kurczewska, J. (2006). Lokalne społeczeństwo obywatelskie (dwie możliwości interpretacyjne). In W. B. Jałowiecki, & W. Łukowski (Eds.), *Społeczności lokalne. Teraźniejszość i przyszłość.* Warszawa: Wydawnictwo Naukowe Scholar.

Mac Ruairc, G., Gartland, S., Heinz, M., & Rodríguez-Entrena, M. J. (2026). Diversity, equity and democracy in school leadership: Troublesome concepts in troubled times. In M. Heinz, M. J. Rodríguez-Entrena, & G. Mac Ruairc (Eds.), *Professional learning for diversity, equity and democracy: Big ideas for better schools* (pp. 24–46). Routledge.

Maurissen, L., Claes, E., & Barber, C. (2018). Deliberation in citizenship education: How the school context contributes to the development of an open classroom climate. *Social Psychology of Education*, 951–972. https://doi.org/10.1007/s11218-018-9449-7

Męczkowska-Christiansen, A. (2014). Edukacja dla demokracji jako demokracja w edukacji: wokół podstawowych pojęć. In K. Gawlicz, P. Rudnicki, M. Starnawski, & T. Tokarz (Eds.), *Demokracja i edukacja: dylematy, diagnozy, doświadczenia* (pp. 13–25). Wrocław: Wydawnictwo Naukowe Dolnośląskiej Szkoły Wyższej.

Nussbaum, M. (2010). *Not for profit: Why does democracy need the humanities?* New Jersey: Princeton University Press.

O'Brien, T., & Guiney, D. (2001). *Differentiation in teaching and learning: Principles and practice*. London and New York: Bloomsbury Publishing.

Osler, A., & Starkey, H. (2006, December). Education for democratic citizenship: A review of research, policy, and practice 1995–2005. *Research Papers in Education*, *21*(4), 433–466. https://https://doi.org/10.1080/02671520600942438

Pietrzyk-Reeves, D. (2012). *Idea społeczeństwa obywatelskiego*. Toruń: Wydawnictwo Naukowe Uniwersytetu Mikołaja Kopernika.

Robin, R. (1980). Badanie pól semantycznych. Doświadczenia Ośrodka Leksykologii Politycznej w Saint-Cloud. In M. Głowiński (Ed.), *Język i społeczeństwo* (pp. 205–282). Warszawa: Czytelnik.

Sawyer, R. K. (2006). Introduction: The new science of learningin. In R. K. Sawyer (Ed.), *The Cambridge handbook of: The learning sciences* (pp. 1–16). Cambridge University Press.

Schneider, M., & Stern, E. (2013). Uczenie się z perspektywy poznawczej: dziesięć najważniejszych odkryć. In H. Dumont, D. I. Dumont, & F. Benavides (Eds.), *Istota uczenia się. Wykorzystanie wyników badan w praktyce*. Warszawa: Wolters Kluwer Polska SA.

Sobas, M. (2019). Zasada równego traktowania w odniesieniu do dostępu do edukacji ucznia z niepełnosprawnością – wprowadzenie do problematyki. *Roczniki Administracji i Prawa*, (19), 67–88.

Urząd do Spraw Cudzoziemców. (2023). *Obywatele Ukrainy w Polsce – aktualne dane migracyjne – Urząd do Spraw Cudzoziemców – Portal Gov.pl*. https://www.gov.pl/web/udsc/obywatele-ukrainy-w-polsce-aktualne-dane-migracyjne (Accessed: 26 July 2023).

Ustawa z dnia 12 maja 2022 r. o zmianie ustawy o systemie oświaty oraz niektórych innych ustaw (Dz.U. 2022 poz. 1116). https://isap.sejm.gov.pl/isap.nsf/download.xsp/WDU20220001116/T/D20221116L.pdf (Accessed: 3 May 2025).

Wald, P. J., & Castleberry, M. S. (Eds.). (2000). *Educators as learners: Creating a professional learning community in your school*. Alexandria, VA: ASCD.

Walzer, M. (2007). *Sfery sprawiedliwości. Obrona pluralizmu i równości*. Warszawa: Wydawnictwo Uniwersytetu Warszawskiego.

Woolfolk, A. (2021). *Educational psychology* (14th ed.). Pearson Education Limited.

Younger, K., Branstiter, C., & Bobkowski, P. (2021). From passive participants to active learners. *Journal of New Librarianship*, 6(1). https://doi.org/10.33011/newlibs/10/12

7

WHAT IS DEMOCRACY? RECOGNISING DIVERSE PERSPECTIVES AND BUILDING SHARED UNDERSTANDINGS WITH SCHOOL LEADERS IN SPAIN THROUGH A PROFESSIONAL LEARNING EXPERIENCE

María Jesús Rodríguez-Entrena, Antonio Portela Pruaño, María del Carmen Maldonado López, Francisco Alfonso Hernández López, and Abraham Bernárdez-Gómez

Introduction

In the context of social conflict, fear and violence based on religious and cultural differences, it is imperative to cultivate a sense of global citizenship and foster democratic values and responsibility in young people (Rodríguez-Entrena et al., 2022). Consequently, the pressing challenge for educational institutions is to develop innovative approaches that integrate democratic and civic values into the academic curriculum (Andolina & Conklin, 2021). This work requires a deliberate prioritising of this type of focus that is either on par with or above the current focus on traditional cognitive content. This imperative aligns with the policies of many international organisations, which emphasise the development of cognitive, social and emotional competencies as a central goal of education. The objective is to equip young people with the skills required for active, engaged citizenship in democratic societies (Council of Europe, 2017; UNESCO, 2020). To meet these objectives, it is crucial to focus on the role and preparation of teachers who develop their competencies to facilitate social change and education for citizenship and democratic culture (EURYDICE, 2012; González-Valencia et al., 2024; Massip & Santisteban, 2020; UNESCO, 2018).

Spanish education legislation includes an explicit focus on preparing students for the exercise of active and democratic citizenship. For example, Organic Law 3/2020 of 29 December, which amends Organic Law 2/2006

DOI: 10.4324/9781032629292-9

of 3 May on Education (known as LOMLOE), states in its preamble that education must be the driving force to promote democratic coexistence and respect for individual differences, to encourage solidarity and avoid discrimination, with the fundamental aim of achieving social cohesion. Spanish education policy sees education as a means of guaranteeing the exercise of democratic, responsible, free and critical citizenship, which is essential for the construction of advanced, dynamic and just societies. Thus, among the principles and objectives of education in Spain, it is explicitly stated (LOMLOE) that the aim is to achieve quality education for all pupils without discrimination of any kind, to work for justice that guarantees equal opportunities, to educate for coexistence, respect for human rights, peaceful resolution of conflicts and non-violence in all areas of life, and to foster a critical spirit and preparation for the exercise of active citizenship. It also includes citizenship among the eight key competences, and among the pedagogical principles, it recommends promoting gender equality and mutual respect in all areas of the curriculum.

The degree of interest in schools in preparing young people for the exercise of democracy and active citizenship has resulted in the development of a new subject on the school curriculum called 'Education in civic and ethic values' (see Estellés et al. (2023) and Moreno-Vera (2025) for a review of the debate in Spain on curricular areas focusing on this type of content). This new subject is compulsory for all primary and secondary school pupils and places greater emphasis on aspects such as human rights, global citizenship, equality between men and women, respect for diversity and the culture of peace. There are doubts as to whether the approach to competences established in the new regulations will be sufficiently developed, partly because of the difficulties in assessing everything related to competences linked to attitudes and values (López Ruipérez, 2022). Despite the advantages of the model, the cognitive part of the curriculum continues to be given more weight than these more transversal, loosely framed areas for development, and this, together with the difficulties in assessing attitudes and values, carries the risk of less attention being paid to the development of attitudes and values in schools and classrooms. Another risk comes from the teachers, who are overloaded with tasks and also feel a strong 'curricular pressure', which is more acute in secondary education, where they feel the need to cover all the basic knowledge and competences of the curriculum of each subject. The pressure to cover the 'core curriculum' reduces time for teaching the content oriented to values. Specialised subject teachers do not feel responsible for this 'values-oriented' type of content, so it might not be treated rigorously or at all.

These pressures can be considerable and can really impact how other core priorities are 'fitted in' to the school experience. This has very particular implications for work with areas like democracy in classrooms. Despite the impetus given by education policy to the issue of democratic values and citizenship education, the application of these values and principles in the daily life of schools is not without controversy and difficulties. Research has shown that when values education is embedded in specific subjects, what happens is that values are learned from a theoretical point of view, but they may not be put into practice (Díaz Barriga, 2006), or there may even be a contradiction between what is presented in theory and what they experience in their daily lives in the classroom, at school or in their immediate context. Values education requires not only theoretical knowledge but also opportunities for students to live and practise these values both inside and outside the classroom (Díaz Barriga, 2006; Sáez Rosenkraz et al., 2017; Fielding, 2012). In the words of Dewey (1916), if the school wants to educate in democracy, it must be a laboratory of democracy.

Three distinct types of threats that hinder the development of critical and democratic citizenship in secondary school classrooms can be identified. First, the influence of neoliberal policies pushes teachers to prioritise covering the prescribed core curriculum, focusing primarily on delivering basic knowledge and content, often at the expense of fostering critical thinking and civic engagement (García-Pérez & González-Lamas, 2023). Second, there is a lack of motivation and conviction among teachers to integrate these topics into their instruction. Many educators, being specialists in subjects such as mathematics, language or chemistry, struggle to see how citizenship and democratic principles can be meaningfully incorporated into their subject areas (Estellés et al., 2021). Finally, teachers often lack the necessary pedagogical training – in both their initial and ongoing professional development – required to effectively educate students in citizenship and democracy. As a result, they feel unprepared to take on this critical role (Romijn et al., 2021; Sant et al., 2024). To address these challenges to students' civic and democratic education, the focus must be on schools and on training, both for teachers and for the school itself as a learning organisation. Schools have become the epicentre of improvement and the context for training and innovation (Bolívar & Domingo, 2024), but to achieve positive results, the educational institution must be well managed. Meaningful collaboration is essential, as school improvement cannot be achieved on the basis of individual, unconnected experiences, however well-intentioned and positive they may be.

The European BIBS project, which supported the development of the 'Democracy in Our School' professional learning experience and in which teachers, leaders and academics from four European countries (Spain, Norway, Ireland and Poland) were involved, had two key objectives. First, it aimed to enhance the professional development of teachers and school leaders by equipping them with the knowledge, attitudes and skills to address 'big issues' such as diversity, equity and democracy. Second, it sought to develop and implement subject-specific classroom interventions, integrating these topics into the curriculum. The goal was to prepare students to live democratically in an increasingly diverse society.[1]

The following sections present the secondary school where the experience described in this case study took place. Thereafter, the professional learning experience designed for teachers and school leaders is described and discussed, including specific activities developed with educators and their subsequent implementation in second-level classrooms. Finally, conclusions are drawn from the experience, highlighting lessons learned and offering recommendations for those interested in developing a similar experience in their context.

The school's 'case study' and the context

The participating school is a medium-sized public secondary school located in the Region of Murcia, in south-eastern Spain. This school is held in high regard within the local community and attracts students primarily on the basis of its academic achievements.

This school is primarily concerned with providing secondary education, including lower and upper secondary education and Baccalaureate (Bachillerato). Compulsory lower secondary education commences at the age of 12 and concludes four years later. The curriculum is comprehensive in nature, though it becomes increasingly differentiated as students progress. In addition, the Bachillerato is academically oriented and non-compulsory. It typically commences at the age of 16 and spans two academic years. The educational offer of the school is complemented by a basic vocational training programme, known as Ciclo Formativo de Grado Básico, which is designed for students aged 15 who wish to develop skills for specific work activities while simultaneously completing their training in the skills required for compulsory secondary education.

The school is confronted with significant and complex challenges, which justify its participation in the project. The city in which the school is situated has a population of around 22,000. Approximately 20% of the population is foreign (Centro Regional de Estadística de Murcia [Murcia Regional Statistics Centre], 2024). The population is heterogeneous in terms of its origins, with individuals hailing from a range of regions across Europe and beyond, including Latin America, Africa and Asia. Nearly half of this foreign population is of Moroccan nationality. The school's 70 or so teachers are responsible for the education of just over 700 pupils, who are ethnically and culturally diverse. However, the diversity of the student body extends beyond this. The school also caters for students from lower socio-economic backgrounds and those with learning disabilities and other SEN.

A significant aspect of this school is its dedication to providing a quality education developed over a lengthy period of time, during which the institution has engaged in a process of self-evaluation and quality improvement (Portela & Rodríguez-Entrena, 2018). The school has agreed on a structure designed to promote and maintain that process, including a quality committee and a teacher responsible for quality issues. This structure is supported by a well-established quality culture. Interestingly, this emphasis on educational quality is not perceived as antithetical to inclusion. The school identifies itself as an inclusive institution. Its stated mission is particularly illustrative of its commitment to inclusion in addition to quality, and a number of initiatives have been implemented with the aim of promoting diversity, equity and democracy. These include the identification of pupils with educational needs, the use of support teachers in mainstream classes, linguistic support for immigrant pupils who do not speak Spanish, the so-called curricular diversification programmes, which introduce curricular modifications for pupils who have difficulties in progressing through compulsory secondary education, measures to prevent absenteeism and dropping out of school, the involvement of pupils in community service tasks and the development of social commitment among school members in general.

Eleven teachers took part in the project, several of whom occupied leadership and management roles within the school. This enabled the subsequent dissemination of the experience among colleagues in their respective departments. The participants in the experience were the head teacher, the quality coordinator (English teacher), the head of studies (mathematics teacher), two geography and history teachers, two philosophy teachers, one Latin and Greek teacher, two English teachers and one ethical values teacher.

Professional learning experience

Project design and implementation of 'Democracy in Our School'

In designing the 'Democracy in Our School' professional learning experience for teachers and school leaders, we followed two principles (Kemmis et al., 2014): First, we considered and recognised the capacity and importance for teachers working in the partner school to participate actively in all aspects of the research process. Second, we designed an action research project in collaboration (university–school) with teacher participants to allow them to effect change, and hopefully improvement, in their own professional practice and context.

The critical participatory action research approach allows practitioners to continuously question and improve their methods in response to a changing environment. In particular, the five key elements developed by Kemmis et al. (2014) underpinned our collaborative and action-oriented professional learning approach:

1. ‘Understanding from within’ allows practitioners to understand and develop how practices are carried out from within the traditions that inform and guide them.
2. ‘Shared language’ facilitates practitioners speaking a common language, using shared interpretive categories and engaging in critical debates related to the practice being investigated.
3. ‘Participation in action’ creates the conditions for practitioners to participate in and develop the forms of action and interaction that constitute the practice.
4. ‘Development of communities of practice’ enables practitioners to develop and engage in communities of practice where the practice is carried out, both in a specific site and in the broader professional context.
5. ‘Transformation of practice’ empowers practitioners to transform their practice to adapt to changing times by addressing irrational practices, tackling unsustainable practices and combating unjust practices.

Project objectives

Training modules, designated ‘action learning sets’, were devised with and for teachers using an active and participatory methodology. The modules balanced conceptual exploration of civic principles with a range of more practical school-based applications. The objectives of the module were:

1. To examine the participants’ existing conceptions of citizenship and democracy in their everyday actions.
2. To expand participants’ understanding of the theoretical and practical aspects of democracy.
3. To identify teaching methods, resources and assessment tools that can facilitate the promotion of democracy in the classroom.
4. To encourage teachers to promote competencies for a democratic culture through teaching practices.
5. To encourage teachers to develop the habit of evaluating whether their teaching practices support the promotion of democracy.
6. To facilitate the translation of theoretical democratic values into practical applications in the classroom and school.
7. To provide a list of key resources for extending democratic competence in teaching practices.
8. To contribute to the establishment of safe learning environments that foster respect for diversity, freedom of expression, intercultural dialogue, student decision-making, active participation and related democratic values.

To provide the reader with a clear understanding of the professional learning experience undertaken, Table 7.1 offers a synthesised overview of the entire process, including the different phases, the activities carried out and the participants involved at each stage. Each of these phases will be further developed and discussed throughout the chapter.

TABLE 7.1 Outline of the collaborative professional learning programme

Phase	*Activity carried out*	*Participants*
Level 1: Initial reflection	• Online questionnaire to students aged 13–14 years to explore their conceptions of diversity, equity and democracy '3 big issues'. • Online questionnaire to teachers and school leaders of the school about their conception of democracy. • Interviews with teachers and school leaders to collect examples of democratic participation in school. • Reflection and analysis of responses to identify democratic perceptions and experiences in the school environment.	• 11 teachers and school leaders (six interviews). • 84 students in the third year of compulsory education (236 questionnaires in total about the three 'big issues').
Level 2: Exploration	• Collaborative online professional learning experience with the project countries: Norway, Ireland and Poland. • Application (face to face) of action learning sets (material prepared to broaden teachers' conception of democracy, establish a common language and visualise change). Teacher educators (university) and teachers and school leaders (school) worked collaboratively.	• 11 teachers and school leaders. • Three teacher educators from the University of Murcia.
Level 3: Deep reflection	• Review of the official curriculum to analyse the presence of democratic and citizenship aspects. • Rethink and reflect on the practices that are being implemented in the school/classroom with respect to democracy. • Rethink school/classroom practices to make them more democratic, inclusive and equitable. • Design of training units (democratic project-based learning) by the teaching staff, integrating curricular content from different subjects (philosophy, geography and history, English and mathematics) together with content for citizenship and democracy in the same project.	• 11 teachers and school leaders.

(*Continued*)

TABLE 7.1 (Continued)

Phase	*Activity carried out*	*Participants*
Level 4: Follow-up actions	• Implementation in classes with students of the training units on democracy, designed using the active methodology of project-based learning. The materials and activities used were very varied, with a focus on the active role of students and the promotion of reflection on democracy. An example can be seen in Box 7.2 of this chapter. • Questionnaire to the teaching staff to collect their assessment of their collaborative professional learning experience (university–school) (see Figure 7.3).	• 11 teachers and school leaders. • 33 students.

Project design

The training programme commenced with a conceptual introduction, after which four levels of approximation to the concept of democratic citizenship and its application in classroom work with students were developed (see Figure 7.1). Throughout this process, the implementation of the actions in the classroom, in the last level of the model, was subject to reflection and monitoring. As the Council of Europe has observed, the competences for a democratic culture approach would remain a mere theory without properly educated and trained teachers. Indeed, it is the teachers themselves who are best placed to implement it in the field (2018, p. 76).

FIGURE 7.1 Four-level structure of the training activities approach

Development of the training sessions and working material

The sequence of actions undertaken with the school's teaching staff and pupils over the course of the two-year project is outlined below:

Level 1. Initial reflection

1. The initial data collection was conducted through questionnaires and interviews with pupils and teachers, respectively, in order to ascertain their initial conceptions of democracy, equality and equity.
2. A reflective process involving teachers and leaders was developed, drawing on insights from surveys and interviews conducted with pupils and staff.

Level 2. Exploration

3. Online training was conducted with the participation of head teachers and teachers from other partner countries involved in the project, namely Norway, Ireland and Poland.
4. The utilisation of didactic material, including readings, TED Talks and videos, to facilitate the conceptualisation of democracy through self-directed learning.
5. The development of the 'action learning sets' with the teaching staff in the school itself was followed by a final evaluation questionnaire on the training.

Level 3. Deepened reflection

6. An analysis of the official curriculum of each subject was conducted to ascertain the explicit presence of democratic and citizenship aspects within the curriculum. Where appropriate, the possibility of incorporating subject matter from each subject into the curriculum was also explored.
7. The teaching staff of the different subjects (English, mathematics, geography and history, etc.) planned and designed a 'democratic project-based learning programme' for the development of democratic competence with the students in the classroom.

Level 4. Follow-up actions

8. The implementation of democratic project-based learning in the classroom with the students.
9. Final evaluation of the experience by the students and teachers was conducted.

Activities and materials

Below are presented some of the activities and materials used during the training sessions. There were four levels/stages in the implementation of the professional learning sessions (see Figure 7.1).

Level 1 – Initial reflection

Initially, data on the concept of 'democracy' were collected from students, teachers and school leaders. Students completed an online questionnaire, while teachers and leaders participated in both semi-structured interviews and a questionnaire. In relation to the data collected, students from the three classes of 13–14-year-olds were invited to voluntarily and anonymously participate in an online questionnaire, in which they were asked to provide their understanding of the concepts of democracy, diversity and equity as defined by their respective schools. The respondents demonstrated a lack of clarity and consistency in their understanding of the concepts of diversity and equity. In some cases, the two concepts were used interchangeably, indicating a lack of distinction between them. However, with regard to the concept of democracy, there is a notable degree of consensus among the student respondents in relation to their understanding that democracy is inextricably linked to the capacity to make decisions. Furthermore, the students provided illustrative examples of their experience of democracy within the school context. They described their role as class representatives, which afforded them the opportunity to influence decision-making at the school level and to communicate directly with the management team at any time. This access was perceived as a means of being heard, listened to, valued and considered. The school's commitment to transparency and community engagement is evident in the students' explicit recognition of the factors that contribute to their perception of a democratic environment within the school and in their daily lives. According to preliminary data collected from the students at the school at the beginning of the project, there was already a notable prevalence of democratic principles and active student participation in the school's democratic processes.

In terms of teacher responses, the headmaster acknowledges that, despite efforts to make the school democratic, the current educational policy limits the extent to which democracy can be fully realised in Spanish schools. However, he also recognises that the impending regulatory change the new law and the new subject will contribute to improving this situation.

Throughout the project, a series of seminars were conducted with the participation of school leaders and teachers from the schools, as well as teacher educators from the university. Further details about the overall structure implemented in the schools are outlined below.

Seminar details

The structure of the inaugural training session on the concept of democracy was based on the teachers' existing knowledge and understanding of the subject matter. In order to investigate the democracy concept and foster the initial reflection, the first activity was developed in three stages:

Stage 1: The session commenced with the reading out of the anonymised definitions of democracy that each teacher had provided in the initial questionnaire.

Stage 2: Based on the individual definitions, the participants were required to agree on a new definition in pairs, which they then presented to the larger group.

Stage 3: A joint definition of the concept was subsequently arrived at. Thereafter, following the preceding discussion in smaller groups, a consensus was reached on a unanimous definition of the concept.

This activity served to stimulate interest in democracy and active citizenship, to foster unity and involvement within the group and to establish a shared vocabulary at the outset of our collaborative endeavours. Subsequently, a series of activities were devised to address the concept that the research team identified as requiring further development. The materials and activities developed for teachers were structured across three progressive levels: an introduction, anticipation exercises and further exploration, guiding learners from foundational concepts to more complex and in-depth understanding. The activity first presented educators' responses to three key inquiries: the terminology they associate with the concept of democracy, their interpretation of its definition and their proposed strategies for implementing democratic principles within educational institutions.

The educators' conceptualisation of democracy revealed key themes. The words most commonly associated with democracy in descending order were 'people', 'freedom', 'citizenship', 'participation' and 'public interest'. Additionally, 'choice' and 'power' were frequently referenced in definitions of democracy. Teachers described democracy as a process where citizens elect political leaders and representatives, engage in public affairs and uphold the majority's power over elite dominance. They emphasised collective agreement and decision-making as foundational. When reflecting on democracy within educational contexts, educators outlined practices of participatory governance. This included decision-making roles for various groups such as the school assembly, staff and Pedagogical Coordination Committee (it is a formal body composed of the school principal, department heads and the guidance counsellor. It is responsible for coordinating teaching and learning processes across various subject areas), each tasked with specific functions and empowered to vote on key issues.

The teachers' responses highlight the importance of teamwork and interdisciplinary collaboration as integral to democratic practices within educational institutions. It emphasises the reinstated governing role of the School Council under the LOMLOE framework, which offers a promising avenue for managing schools democratically. However, challenges persist, such as the unequal representation of various sectors of the educational community relative to their actual population size. Key democratic principles are also underscored through their answers, including the right of students, families and staff to actively participate in school governance, the inclusion of diverse voices in decision-making processes and consensus-based approaches to resolving issues. Despite striving for collective agreement, disparities in representation reflect ongoing obstacles to achieving a fully participatory democracy.

In educational practice, teachers recognise that they can model democracy by engaging students, families and staff in collaborative and transparent governance, fostering a culture of inclusivity and shared responsibility. The insights provided underline the need to balance theoretical ideals of democracy with practical implementation.

Level 2 – Exploration

Another training session included in the implementation of the 'action learning sets' comprised the presentation of the Reference Framework of Competences for Democratic Culture (Figure 7.2). This framework defines democratic culture as 'the capacity to mobilise and use relevant psychological resources (i.e. values, attitudes, skills, knowledge and/or understanding) to respond effectively and appropriately to the demands, challenges and opportunities that arise in democratic situations'. (Council of Europe, 2018, p. 32). The framework identifies a total of 20 competences, which are ascribed to four areas: values, attitudes, skills and knowledge. There are three value competences, six attitude competences, eight skill competences and three knowledge and critical understanding competences. Furthermore, the framework includes descriptions of the aforementioned competences, as well as guidance on their implementation and assessment.

The objective of this activity was twofold: firstly, to provide training for teachers in the context of the competences for democratic culture, and secondly, to facilitate the acquisition of the previously mentioned competences. In addition, based on the four areas in which the framework is structured (values, skills, knowledge and critical understanding), the objective was to encourage reflection and analysis of the school in question (see Table 7.2). The activity objective was to facilitate the development of a self-assessment

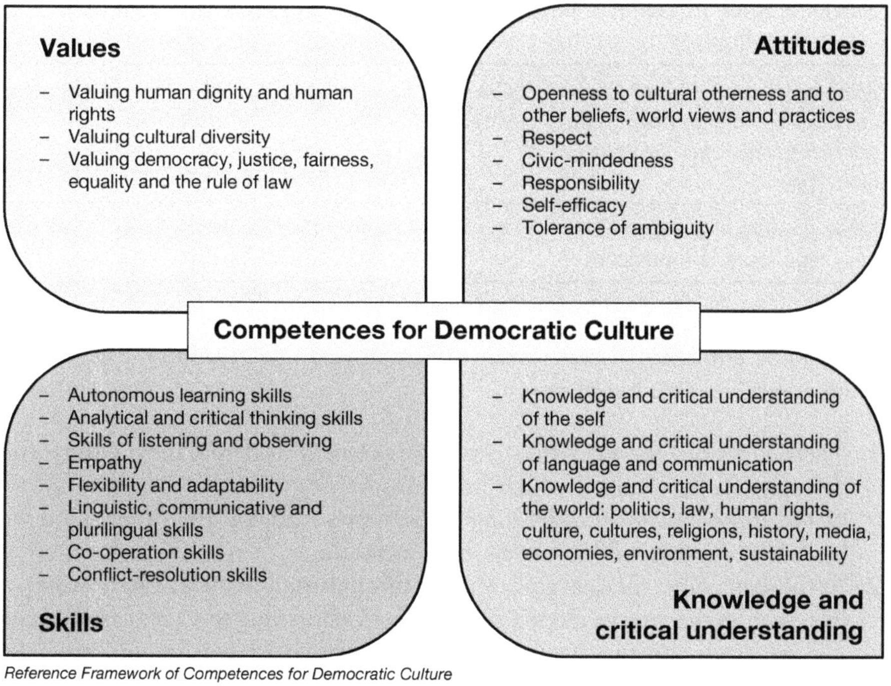

FIGURE 7.2 Framework of Competences for Democratic Culture

(Council of Europe, 2018, p. 38).

of the implementation of democratic culture practices within the context of their respective educational institutions. The training activity enabled a response to be made to the initial key element mentioned in the critical action research: 'Understanding from within'. This enabled a clear identification of the school's position regarding its activities in relation to active citizenship and democracy. Moreover, the assessment of which aspects of competence for democratic culture are most neglected by the school automatically connects to the fifth element of the critical action research: 'transformation of practice'. The term 'transformation of practice' was also introduced and exemplified by the teachers. By identifying the gaps, the teaching team was able to conceptualise potential activities and initiatives to address these shortcomings. The following table (Table 7.2) presents the material of the activity provided to teachers to facilitate analysis and reflection on their own school practices.

Additionally, the educators were requested to identify the actions they believe the institution is undertaking, whether intentionally or unintentionally, to facilitate democratic processes. Also, the participants were requested to identify the requisite conditions for the implementation of a comprehensive

TABLE 7.2 Axes to facilitate reflection and analysis on democratic competences in schools

Analyse which competences are considered significant and are being developed in your institution.	*The most developed in my school*	*The least developed in my school*
Most significant competences		
Less significant competences		

democratic educational programme. In response to this question, the participants identified two big ideas:

1. There is a need for activities to raise awareness of democracy, equity and diversity in the school, which help, on the one hand, to be more aware of the importance of addressing these issues and, on the other hand, to launch new practical initiatives in the school.
2. At the same time, they pointed out that through analysis and reflection activities, such as the one developed with the 'action learning sets', critical thinking is reinforced, and they facilitate the identification of policies and practices that may not be aligned with the development of true human values.

This activity allowed the management team, together with the participating teachers, to analyse the current situation of the school in terms of democracy, and the following conclusions were drawn:

- At the school level: The school was very democratic in its operation, partly due to its quality system: There was participation from all educational sectors, all proposals for improvement contributed by a member were analysed, different collaborative work commissions were established, and that brought improvements to the operation of the school, as well as the system of surveys that were carried out annually for all educational sectors. In short, in terms of the functioning and organisation of the centre, democracy was quite developed.
- At the classroom level: It was detected that there was no planning to work on democracy in a transversal way in the curriculum and that everything that was done was done autonomously by each subject, but without any global planning as a school or in a collegial way among the teachers.

This analysis made it possible for the group to move towards the design of an improvement plan in the school, where the objective was to improve the work of democracy in the classrooms with the students in a transversal way and with joint planning by the teachers.

The training activities were conducted using an experiential and participatory methodology and were accompanied by a learning dossier that included the templates of the activities and a variety of resources and materials (written, audiovisual, etc.) organised by ascending difficulty. The learning dossier included introductory texts on democratic citizenship and more advanced works on the subject, as well as practical materials, links to websites, etc., showcasing exemplary educational institutions that effectively cultivate democratic competencies. All these materials offered valuable insights and inspiration for enhancing the quality of education in these institutions.

Level 3 – Classroom exploration

In the structure of four levels in which the professional development programme for teachers and leaders was designed (see Figure 7.1), once the initial reflection phase (Level 1) was advanced to the exploration phase (Level 2) (explained in the previous sections), progress was made to the level of deepened reflection (Level 3) and follow-up actions (Level 4), which are the levels presented in this section and the next.

In the deepened reflection phase (Level 3), two activities were mainly developed: 1) an exhaustive analysis of the curriculum and the different curricular areas to identify the presence of aspects related to democracy and citizenship or to explore the possibilities of introducing them and 2) the design of materials to educate students on how to live together in a diverse and democratic society, which was later implemented in the classrooms with the students (Level 4).

A democratic project-based learning approach was designed by the teacher collaboratively and implemented in the classes of philosophy, geography and history, English and mathematics. Each teacher planned a training unit with content from their respective subject curriculum, integrating the core principles of democracy and citizenship. To facilitate the planning of the training units, a common template was designed (Figure 7.3), which included the basic aspects of the planning: title, key concepts, objectives, competences, duration, material and implementation. The template concluded with various activities aimed at facilitating the students' critical reflection on the work sessions and identifying what they had learnt with respect to democratic and civic aspects. The pupils gained insight into how different subject areas could offer diverse approaches to exploring the concept of democracy while also contributing to a shared, unified project. It is therefore essential that students are afforded the opportunity to pose questions and engage in critical thinking while simultaneously developing respect for diversity (Council of Europe, 2017, p. 34).

The democratic project-based learning initiative was developed with the same cohort of pupils who had participated in the initial surveys at the project's outset. To address democracy as a holistic and cross-cutting issue, it was conducted concurrently across four academic disciplines, with the aim of fostering a comprehensive understanding of democratic principles that transcended the boundaries of a single subject. Box 7.1 provides the example of a template that was applied for the design of the project in all the subjects involved.

BOX 7.1 EXAMPLE OF A TEMPLATE

TITLE
PEDAGOGICAL/THEMATIC AREA
LEVEL OF DIFFICULTY
SUBJECTS/Curricular Areas
RANGE OF STUDENTS' AGE
DURATION
KEY CONCEPT/S & SKILL/S ADDRESSED
PURPOSE AND OBJECTIVES
RESOURCES REQUIRED
IMPLEMENTATION/METHODOLOGY/ACTIVITIES (Step 1, Step 2, Step 3)
DEBRIEFING/REFLECTION ON LEARNING

A summary of an example training unit designed within the subject of English, with the common axis of democracy, is presented below (Box 7.2).

BOX 7.2 EXAMPLE OF A TRAINING UNIT

English as a First Foreign Language. Timing: 5 or 6 x 45-minute sessions

Concepts: The key concepts of the activity were to develop an understanding of the state of democracy around the world in 2022. This involved analysing the democracy scores assigned to different countries, identifying those with the highest and lowest levels of democracy and exploring the institutions and practices that characterise contemporary democratic systems.

Objectives: The aim of this activity is for students to become familiar with the most and least democratic countries around the world. As part of the learning process, they will acquire context-specific vocabulary and explore socio-cultural and sociolinguistic aspects related to social conventions and language registers. Students will also compare and contrast customs, institutions and rituals across different societies while reflecting on values, norms and beliefs that may differ from their own.

Implementation/methodology

The implementation of the democratic project-based learning approach involved the use of an active, student-centred methodology that emphasised cooperative learning, dialogue, critical reflection and structured debate. The pedagogical focus was on fostering respect for diversity, promoting democratic coexistence and instilling core values that underpin peaceful living within a shared society.

1. **Grouping structure**: Students were divided into a maximum of ten groups, ideally comprising four students each to ensure meaningful collaboration and equitable participation.
2. **Materials required**: Laptops or tablets (one to two devices per group were sufficient) and Internet access for research and use of digital tools (e.g. Canva).
3. **Session breakdown:**

   a. Article reading: Students began by reading the article 'Democracy Countries 2022' from World Population Review (https://worldpopulationreview.com/country-rankings/democracy-countries).
   b. Initial group discussion: Each group was prompted with the question: 'What do you think are the "must-have" ingredients of a democracy?' Their ideas were collected and listed collaboratively on the board to form a class-wide definition.
   c. Democracy index analysis: Groups were directed to the 'Democracy Score' section of the article to identify and write down the Top 10 and Bottom 10 countries in terms of democratic ranking: Top 10 democratic countries: Norway, Iceland, Sweden, New Zealand, Canada, Finland, Denmark, Ireland, Australia and the Netherlands. Bottom 10 countries: North Korea, DR Congo, Central African Republic, Syria, Chad, Turkmenistan, Laos, Equatorial Guinea, Tajikistan and Libya.
   d. WebQuest activity: Each group selected one Top 10 and one Bottom 10 country. They conducted a guided web-based inquiry to identify: 'Reasons why their selected country is democratic or anti-democratic', backed by evidence from credible sources (e.g. governance structures, electoral systems, civil liberties and media freedom).
   e. Output – digital poster or mini presentation: Using Canva or similar tools, groups created a visual poster or short presentation comparing their countries. The product highlighted both 'democratic reasons why' and 'anti-democratic reasons why' and included examples, relevant data and cited sources.
   f. Presentation and reflection: Each group presented their findings to the class, followed by a brief Q&A and peer feedback session to promote critical engagement, comparison and reflection on the global state of democracy.

After completing this unit, the teacher encouraged students to reflect on key questions related to democracy and civic engagement and generated a joint debate in the classroom, arguing the answers to each question. These may include: *Do you think your country is democratic enough? How do you participate in this democratic society? What else can be done to improve democracy? Can you identify examples of democracy in your everyday life? Do you believe our society is fair? What are the main differences between your country and those you have read about?* These questions aim to foster critical thinking, personal connection to the topic and a deeper understanding of democratic values and practices across different cultural contexts.

Through the type of holistic projects to work on democracy and the activities and methodology shown in the example above, students were able to not only learn the concepts of democracy but also experience, live and feel it, which is the most effective way of developing democratic and civic competences. Through the implementation of this project, the school improved the approach to democracy in the classrooms because, although the students lived democracy through their active participation in the school, there was no clear treatment of democracy within the curriculum developed in the classrooms.

Level 4 – Professional learning experiences

The last level of the professional learning programme (Level 4) included a final evaluation. A questionnaire was given to the teachers to find out their opinion regarding the training received.

The questionnaire was designed online through the survey tool of the University of Murcia. It was structured with 22 closed multiple-choice questions with a Likert scale of 1 to 5 ranging from strongly disagree to strongly agree, and five open questions aimed at identifying their takeaways from learning, the aspects on which they have reflected the most and the impact of the training on their professional practice. The questions in the questionnaire can be seen in Figure 7.3.

Most of the teachers' responses are at Levels 4 and 5 of the Likert scale, which shows a high degree of satisfaction with the experience of professional learning about democracy in schools (x = 4,7).

Regarding the open questions, we are going to highlight the following ideas expressed by the teachers in their answers:

The professional learning experience allowed teachers to delve into the concept of democracy in an engaging and dynamic manner. Contributions from educators in varied roles within the same institution enriched the discussion, broadening perspectives beyond the limited scope often encountered in daily educational practices. A noteworthy aspect that they mention was the integration of democratic principles into the curriculum, which transcended specific subject areas, fostering a holistic understanding.

UNIVERSIDAD DE
MURCIA

BIBS - Teacher Post-Action Learning Set Questionnaire

	1	2	3	4	5
The methadology used in the training session was adequate					×
There was enough time for reflection and dialogue					×
The training was useful					×
The expected goals were clear to me					×
I have found the training interesting					×
The facilitators/experts were knowledgeable					×
The delivery of the training was engaging					×
I participated actively in the training					×
I had the opportunity to learn from colleagues					×
The materials shared with us are useful for me as a teacher					×
The training has made me think about the topic of democracy in new ways					×
My knowledge of democracy, diversity and equity has increased					×
I would like to learn more about the topics we discussed					×
The training was relevant for me as teacher					×
I gained new knowledge and skills that I can implement in my professional practice					×
The topics we discussed are important for teachers					×
I believe the training was useful for our school					×
I plan to use some of the ideas from the training in my teaching					×
I think that understanding of democracy, diversity and equity is important for teachers					×
The training will help us to further develop practices in our school					×
I would recommend the training to other teachers					×
The training sessions were adequate in terms of time devoted to activities					×

FIGURE 7.3 Example of a questionnaire for the assessment of the training experience

A key highlight of the experience was the exchange of ideas and perspectives among colleagues. This collaborative dialogue enabled meaningful debates on democracy, addressing potential challenges such as disenchantment or scepticism about its application. Reflective discussions reinforced the importance of democracy within the academic community, emphasising its role in nurturing genuine human values and ethical socialisation.

The training also introduced participants to fresh perspectives on democracy, particularly the evolving concept of freedom, which resonated strongly with educators. Teachers appreciated the opportunity to reconsider absolute notions and explore the relative nature of concepts like democracy and equality. This deeper understanding encouraged a novel approach to student participation and democratic practices in the classroom (Fielding, 2012).

All opinions can be summarised in that it has been interesting to reflect on how democracy affects the organisation of the school in a transversal way, both in the daily functioning and in the decision-making that is carried out, and how this should be taken to the classroom, not only at the organisational level but also within the curriculum of the different subjects.

Connecting this professional learning experience with what the literature says, we can claim that the experience of participants in this type of training is characterised by a process of transformation, as is expected when working with threshold concepts (Mac Ruairc, 2026), whereby schools become professional learning communities. This is achieved through a collaborative approach between teacher educators and schools, which entails the reflection and improvement of educational practices. As Bolívar (2017) outlines, professional learning communities are characterised by a shared vision and common goals, distributed leadership, individual and collective learning, strengthened networks among community members, trust and shared responsibility.

Lessons learned, recommendations and conclusions

To cultivate truly democratic schools, it is essential that democracy is not only taught but also experienced within the school environment (Fielding, 2012). This begins with teachers becoming aware of the importance of addressing democratic values in education and having training to be able to put them into practice. It also requires them to take action at both the school and classroom levels, creating spaces where democratic principles are practised, modelled and lived. Only in such contexts can students meaningfully engage with values like pluralism, freedom of choice and respect for diversity, ultimately becoming democratic individuals in practice – not just in theory.

As has become evident throughout this chapter, education for democracy is not an easy task. Transforming schools into more democratic spaces where tolerance can be increased, facilitating the construction of a democratic, participatory and responsible citizenship, requires school leaders, teachers and students to work together and to generate opportunities for learning together through dialogue and honest engagement (Rodríguez-Entrena et al., 2023). But, to reach this point, it is necessary for educational policies not only to highlight the importance and need to train in democracy but also to offer a clear work approach at the curricular, pedagogical and organisational levels, as well as the teacher training necessary to achieve this objective (Sant et al., 2024). In this way, it would contribute to reducing the gap between what, in theory, should be education for democracy and the reality faced by teachers in schools and classrooms (Sant et al., 2024).

There is general agreement that incorporating democracy education into the school system is crucial for shaping citizens who understand and uphold democratic principles and practices (De Groot & Lo, 2021; Fernandes et al., 2023). The challenge is to move towards the construction of schools where students can learn and practise democratic principles and values and a 'radical democracy' can be experienced (Fielding, 2012). It is necessary to emphasise the need to seek ways to encourage leaders and teachers to develop critical perspectives, ask questions, be innovative and creative and contribute to school improvement (Rodríguez-Entrena et al., 2023). After the experience presented in this chapter, we can offer some recommendations and insights in this regard:

In order to improve teaching and offer students a better learning experience, schools must create opportunities, spaces and times to investigate their own practice, to promote teacher collaboration, to innovate and to create moments for sharing and exchanging experiences (Álvarez-Hevia et al., 2023). In this regard, the role of school principals and middle leaders is crucial for promoting profound democracy and enabling legitimate change within schools. At the same time, legislative changes can be used as an opportunity and an impulse to self-evaluate schools, propose change and implement innovations, those linked not only to the new legislative scenario but also to the rest of the identified needs. In this way, taking advantage of the curricular revision favoured by the LOMLOE, after analysing the specific curriculum of each subject, it can be concluded that it allows incorporating and working on the concept of democracy in an integrated manner, without the need for any parallel activity to address knowledge and democratic attitudes, values and behaviours. These contents can be addressed jointly with the curricular content of each of the subjects: mathematics, language, English, philosophy or history. Likewise, the application of the project-based learning methodology, applying cross-curricular material that grouped different subjects (mathematics, history, English, etc.) under the backbone of democracy, has made it possible not only the theoretical understanding of the concepts but also the practical involvement of the student. The experience has allowed the student to reflect, become aware and learn about issues as relevant as democracy and inclusion.

On the other hand, university–school collaboration and the application of a critical participatory action research model have been two great allies throughout the process of reflection and improvement of the school practices: helping to establish a common language and vision, analysing reality, creating a scenario for collaborative work and learning, and enabling professionals to develop and participate in communities of practice where they have the opportunity to change their own practices. It is also necessary to highlight some of the conditions necessary for the development of formative experiences of professional learning and university–school collaboration:

- The existence of a transformational leadership that facilitates collaboration and the creation of a learning community oriented towards change and continuous improvement, with a strong commitment to social justice.
- The establishment of priorities and working methods based on the school's own context and data, through a bottom-up approach that promotes participation and responsiveness to their real needs.
- The motivation, commitment and involvement of teachers in collaborative experiences of professional learning.
- The provision of time, space and resources that support teachers in reflecting on and redesigning their teaching practices, guided by a critical participatory action research model that facilitates the creation of a common language and begins with an analysis of the school reality through data.
- The establishment of the organisational conditions in the school to promote the sustainability of the improvements made.
- The creation of a system of recognition and visibility of successful practices.

Teachers are the most important agents in charge of carrying out critical democratic citizenship training in the classroom. Therefore, their awareness, involvement and training in the subject and working collaboratively have been essential elements for ensuring its successful integration into the disciplinary curriculum and student learning.

Note

1 For more information about the BIBS project, see Heinz et al. (2026). A more detailed conceptualisation of the three key concepts explored in the project – diversity, equity and democracy – is provided in Mac Ruairc et al. (2026).

References

Álvarez-Hevia, D. M., Hidalgo, N., Martín, R. C., & Lizana, I. (2023). Beyond liberal discourse: Teachers' conceptions of democracy and education in England and Spain. *Education, Citizenship and Social Justice*, *19*(3), 381–398. https://doi.org/10.1177/17461979231162066

Andolina, M. W., & Conklin, H. G. (2021). Cultivating empathic listening in democratic education. *Theory & Research in Social Education*, *49*(3), 390–417. https://doi.org/10.1080/00933104.2021.1893240

Bolívar, A. (2017). El mejoramiento de la escuela: líneas actuales de investigación. *Revista Portuguesa de Pedagogía*, *51*(2), 5–27. https://doi.org/10.14195/1647-8614_51-2_1

Bolívar, A., & Domingo, J. (2024). *Comunidades de práctica profesional y mejora de los aprendizajes*. Graó.

Centro Regional de Estadística de Murcia. (2024). https://econet.carm.es/municipios-en-cifras

Council of Europe. (2017). *Learning to live together: Council of Europe report on the state of citizenship and human rights education in Europe*. Council of Europe.

Council of Europe. (2018). *Reference framework of competences for democratic culture*. Council of Europe. Vol. 1. Context, concepts and model. Author. https://rm.coe.int/prems-008318-gbr-2508-reference-framework-ofcompetences-vol-1-8573-co/16807bc66c

De Groot, I., & Lo, J. C. (2021). The democratic school experiences framework: A tool for the design and self-assessment of democratic experiences in formal education. *Education, Citizenship and Social Justice*, *16*(3), 211–226. https://doi.org/10.1177/1746197920971810

Dewey, J. (1916). *Democracy and education: An introduction to the philosophy of education*. Macmillan Publishing.

Díaz Barriga, Á. (2006). La educación en valores: Avatares del currículum formal, oculto y los temas transversales. *Revista Electrónica de Investigación Educativa*, *8*(1), 1–15.

Estellés, M., Amo, F. J., & Romero, J. (2021). The consensus on citizenship education purposes in teacher education. *Social Sciences*, *10*(5), 164. https://doi.org/10.3390/socsci10050164

Estellés, M., Oliveira, A., & Castellví, J. (2023). National curricula and citizenship education in populist times: The cases of Brazil and Spain. *Compare: A Journal of Comparative and International Education*, *54*(6), 1002–1020. https://doi.org/10.1080/03057925.2023.2170167

EURYDICE. (2012). *Citizenship education in Europe*. European Commission.

Fernandes, P., Belavi, G., Figueiredo, C., & Ciganda, M. B. (2023). Percepciones docentes sobre prácticas democráticas en centros educativos de Portugal y España. *Profesorado. Revista de Currículum y Formación del Profesorado*, *27*(2), 195–213. https://doi.org/10.30827/profesorado.v27i2.22852

Fielding, M. (2012). Beyond student voice: Patterns of partnership and the demands of deep democracy. *Revista de Educación*, *359*, 45–65. DOI:10.4438/1988-592X-RE-2012-359-195

García-Pérez, D., & González-Lamas, J. (2023). Student participation: Between the twilight of the liberal model of democracy and the rise of neoliberal policies. *Pedagogy, Culture & Society*, *33*(1), 225–245. https://doi.org/10.1080/14681366.2023.2243318

González-Valencia, G., González-Monfort, N., Redó, N. A., & Fernández, A. S. (2024). Competencias de cultura democrática del Consejo de Europa: Cómo se interpreta desde la formación del profesorado. *Acta Scientiarum: Education*, *46*(1). https://doi.org/10.4025/actascieduc.v46i1.68046

Heinz, M., Mac Ruairc, G., & Rodríguez-Entrena, M. J. (2026). Big ideas for better schools: A transnational professional learning project. In M. Heinz, M. J. Rodríguez-Entrena, & G. Mac Ruairc (Eds.), *Professional learning for diversity, equity and democracy: Big ideas for better schools* (pp. 17–23). Routledge.

Kemmis, S., McTaggart, R., & Nixon, R. (2014). *The action research planner: Doing critical participatory action research*. Springer.

Ley Orgánica 3/2020, de 29 de diciembre, por la que se modifica la Ley Orgánica 2/2006, de 3 de mayo, de Educación. (2020, 30 de diciembre). *Boletín Oficial del Estado*, *340*, 122868–122953. https://www.boe.es/eli/es/lo/2020/12/29/3

López Rupérez, F. (2022). El enfoque del currículo por competencias: Un análisis de la LOMLOE. *Revista Española de Pedagogía*, *80*(281), 55–68. https://doi.org/10.22550/REP80-1-2022-05

Mac Ruairc, G., Gartland, S., Heinz, M., & Rodríguez-Entrena, M. J. (2026). Diversity, equity and democracy in school leadership: Troublesome concepts in troubled times. In M. Heinz, M. J. Rodríguez-Entrena, & G. Mac Ruairc (Eds.), *Professional learning for diversity, equity and democracy: Big ideas for better schools* (pp. 24–46). Routledge.

Massip, M., & Santisteban, A. (2020). La educación para la ciudadanía democrática en Europa. *Revista Espaço do Currículo*, *13*(2). https://doi.org/10.22478/ufpb.1983-1579.2020v13n2.51513

Moreno-Vera, J. R. (2025). Democratic consciousness' discourses in history education: The Spanish curriculum. *Citizenship: Social and Economics Education*, *24*(1), 102–117. https://doi.org/10.1177/14788047251318279

Portela, A., & Rodríguez Entrena, M. J. (2018). Exploring a journey in school evaluation: A Spanish secondary school. In E. Ottesen, & F. Stephens (Eds.), *School evaluation with a purpose: Challenges and alternatives* (pp. 42–52). Routledge. https://doi.org/10.4324/9780815376484

Rodríguez-Entrena, M. J., Heinz, M., & Mac Ruairc, G. (2023). *School leaders and teachers leading 'big conversations' with students about democracy at school: Líderes escolares y profesorado liderando conversaciones con el alumnado sobre democracia en los centros educativos* (pp. 265–370). IV Congreso Internacional Liderazgo y Mejora de la Educación (IV CILME). Universidad de Sevilla.

Rodríguez-Entrena, M. J., Portela, A., & Bernárdez-Gómez, A. (2022). Democracy at school: What students think about it? *I Congresso Internacional Escola, Identidade e Democracia*. Universidade de Porto.

Romijn, B. R., Slot, P. L., & Leseman, P. P. (2021). Increasing teachers' intercultural competences in teacher preparation programs and through professional development: A review. *Teaching and Teacher Education*, *98*, 103236. https://doi.org/10.1016/j.tate.2020.103236

Sáez-Rosenkranz, I., Bellati, I., & Mayoral, D. (2017). La formación ciudadana en la educación secundaria obligatoria en Cataluña: Análisis del concepto de ciudadanía en el currículum. *International Journal of Sociology of Education*, *6*(1), 110–131. https://doi.org/10.17583/rise.2017.2471

Sant, E., Weinberg, J., & Thiel, J. (2024). Fail to plan, plan to fail: Are education policies in England helping teachers to deliver on the promise of democracy? *British Educational Research Journal*, *50*(4), 1831–1856. https://doi.org/10.1002/berj.4001

UNESCO. (2018). *Preparing teachers for global citizenship education: A template*. UNESCO. https://unesdoc.unesco.org/ark:/48223/pf0000265452

UNESCO. (2020). *Education for sustainable development: A roadmap*. Transforming Our World: The 2030 Agenda for Sustainable Development. https://doi.org/10.54675/YFRE1448

8

DEMOCRACY AS A CENTRAL VALUE IN A NATIONAL CURRICULUM

Working with school leaders and teachers to connect values with practice in Norway

Eli Ottesen, Ruth Jensen, Bård Halvorsen and Pia Merethe Vinje

Introduction

Across the world, democracies are under pressure. The OECD calls for actions to meet challenges of political polarisation, the spread of disinformation and the rise of populism (OECD, 2025, p. 3). Schools have long been seen as sites for nurturing democracy (Andersson, 2019; Biesta, 2015; Dewey, 2016). However, there seems to be controversy concerning what could be effective approaches for democracy education. For example, Apple (2018) argues that

> there is an ongoing contest over different versions of 'democracy'. 'Thick' understandings of democracy that seek to provide full collective participation in the search for the common good and the creation of critical citizens are up against 'thin' market-oriented versions of consumer choice, possessive individualism, and an education that is valued largely as a tool for meeting a set of limited economic needs as defined by the powerful.
>
> *(pp. 4–5)*

In Norway, the national curricula for primary and secondary education and training were revised in 2020. In the revised curricula, democracy education was strengthened both within the syllabus for civic studies and as a general concern for education, which is formulated in the object clause of the Education Act and in the core curriculum (Borgebund & Børhaug, 2023). Education and 'Bildung' form a twin mission for Norwegian schools. In the core curriculum, Bildung is defined as a lifelong process that has 'the individual's all-round development, intellectual freedom, independence, responsibility, and compassion for others as its goal' (The Norwegian Directorate for

DOI: 10.4324/9781032629292-10

Education and Training, 2025a, June). Bildung may refer to education aiming at supporting pupils' efforts to understand more of the world (Hopmann, 1999). Larsen et al. (2022, p. 118) argue that 'there is a continual risk of reconfiguring democracy as an economic concept in Norwegian policy documents'. The argument relates to economic rationality, building on new public management (NPM) and ideas focusing on aims and results, which threaten to undermine the long-term value-based focus of democracy education and Bildung. However, one of the central principles of the national curriculum in Norway is the integration of values into teaching and learning across subjects. For example, it is argued that pupils must develop knowledge and basic skills regarding democracy. The common core curriculum (2025a) in Norway indicates how such knowledge connects to opportunities for participation in society, based on and promoted through respect and the endorsement of fundamental democratic values, 'such as mutual respect, tolerance, individual freedom of faith and speech, and free elections'. Schools are seen as places that can foster values, allowing pupils to learn about democracy and experience democracy in practice.

The Norwegian project, 'Democracy in Education: Connecting Curriculum Values with Practice in Schools', formed part of the Erasmus+-funded BIBS project, which brought together academic institutions and school partners from Ireland, Norway, Poland and Spain. The BIBS project's overall goal was to deepen educators' conversations about, understanding of, and agency in diversity, equity and democracy through collaborative professional learning (Heinz et al., 2026). The three concepts of diversity, equity and democracy were conceptualised as closely interrelated and, further, connected to a range of other key concepts, including culture, power, identity, justice, inclusion and intersectionality (see Heinz et al., 2026). The choice of which key concept to choose in each country's national professional learning programme was led by the school partners, and, in the case of Norway, the concept of democracy was chosen as the core focus and entry point (Mac Ruairc et al., 2026). Full ethical approval for the overall BIBS project was granted by the University of Galway, Ireland, Research Ethics Committee.

'Democracy in Education: Connecting Curriculum Values with Practice in Schools' was designed to work with the core curricula together with school leaders and teachers in a rural school. In line with how we, as researchers, understood democracy education in Norway's overall core curriculum, we applied a three-part approach to teaching and learning – teaching and learning *about*, *for* and *through* democracy (Stray, 2014). Education *about* democracy refers to the development of intellectual competences, including knowledge about democracy. It entails learning about rights and duties, government and politics (Stray & Sætra, 2017, p. 4). As emphasised by Stray and Sætra, 'students must also be prepared to serve as democratic citizens and develop a democratic identity. This approach is characterised as the introduction of community values and attitudes' (p. 4). Teaching and learning *for* democracy are conceptualised as education for democratic participation, and it involves working with values and attitudes. In addition, the authors argue that there is a need for education *through* democratic participation, including through pupil democracy, pupil voice and pupil activism. Accordingly, pupils need to develop knowledge, skills, values and attitudes that will enable them to take a critical stance towards social injustice, rights violations, stereotypes and similar processes that disrupt the democratic process. In addition, pupils must be able to examine their own perceptions and assumptions critically. The three-part approach may be at odds with the neoliberal ideas that have dominated policy discourses in many countries and that impacted Norway's educational reform of 2006. This reform incorporated new performance measurements, standards and accountability processes (e.g. Møller & Skedsmo, 2013). The increased emphasis on outcomes may have shifted towards an increased focus on education *about* democracy. Norwegian policy regulations are mandatory, but school professionals find that they are open to interpretation and translation (Larsen & Mathé, 2023).

The concepts of 'democracy' and 'democracy education' are contested in policy and practice (Skaaning, 2021; Møller et al., 2010). Professional learning communities are, therefore, vital arenas for making sense of them. Teachers need to develop their understanding of what it implies that the curriculum defines democracy education as an overarching value and interdisciplinary theme as well as a principle for learning, development and Bildung for all pupils in the common core curriculum (The Norwegian Directorate for Education and Training, 2025a, June) in Norway. Our interpretation of the texts in the core curriculum is that pupils need to experience participation in everyday democratic processes. This entails taking part in decision-making in school, being listened to and exerting real influence on issues that are important to them. Experiencing democracy in these ways may encourage pupils to embrace democratic ideals and develop their understanding of democracy as an ideal for government (Furberg et al., 2023). However, tensions may emerge between the long-term 'Bildung discourse', evident in the values-based expectations implicit in the core curriculum, and the more instrumental competence-based focus of subject curricula. The competence aims in various subjects are connected to the interdisciplinary topic of *democracy and citizenship*. It seems that teachers mainly teach about democracy by helping pupils obtain knowledge and encouraging them to think critically about democratic issues. Learning through democratic participation has been less evident (Borgebund & Børhaug, 2023; Sætra & Stray, 2019). For example, based on empirical observation of 15 teachers in three schools and the analysis of their planning documents, Furberg et al. (2023) show that the competence aims selected for democracy as an interdisciplinary theme primarily focused on education *about* and *for* democracy. The 'through democracy' dimension seemed highly dependent on individual teachers' understanding and priorities. Collaboration between teachers to tease out the meanings of democracy and how these should be addressed within and across subjects is therefore essential.

Brandon School, which constitutes the case of the present study, is in a rural area in central southern Norway. The municipality has 2,500 inhabitants residing in the municipal centre and smaller hamlets. Brandon School encompasses primary and lower secondary education, and their motto is 'respect, responsibility and care'. At the time of the study, the school had nearly 200 pupils aged 6–15 years. As is the case in most rural areas in Norway, until the 1990s, the municipality consisted of a population that was culturally homogeneous. However, in recent years, the municipality has received and settled many refugees from several countries, and the school's pupil population is now diverse with pupils from close to 40 nationalities. The teachers, however, are all of Norwegian origin. The staff included approximately 40 school leaders, teachers and assistants in the primary and secondary lower schools. We presumed that the recent change from a homogeneous to a diverse pupil population would turn out favourably to our intentions to involve teachers in exploring democracy as a concept and democratic education. Since the Norwegian educational authority expected all schools to realise the overall curriculum, and Brandon School had a diverse pupil population, the school became an important case. The general expectation of the project was to support and challenge the school leaders and teachers at Brandon School in the process of enacting the value of democracy and participation. The specific aim was to support the school leaders in professional development aimed at unpacking national values of democracy.

All staff and school leaders at Brandon School participated in parts of the project, while six lower secondary teachers were the main participants because democracy is more explicitly taught in lower secondary than in primary school. Five workshops were conducted. Based on initial discussions with the leadership team, it was agreed that the professional learning initiative needed to be aligned with the staff's work on the forthcoming renewed curriculum reform (LK20). As already mentioned, the mandated change in the new curriculum provides a renewed focus on the value base of education. As one teacher stated while being interviewed, 'the link between the values [in the renewed curriculum] was really – like hands in a glove – because it's imbued with these issues that we're working on in the project' [BIBS].

In the following sections, we present an overview of the professional learning initiative, contextualising our approach with models of action research and tools for change. We then address big issues for transformation and offer a brief overview of the methodology employed to explore the initiative and the participants' and facilitators' experiences with it. Finally, we present key learning from the project, a conclusion and recommendations.

Design and implementation of a professional learning initiative to connect curriculum values with practice in schools

In this section, we provide a brief introduction to the three models that have partly inspired and guided the structure and content of the professional learning initiative at Brandon School. We then provide an overview of the five workshops that were arranged at the school. Throughout 2020 and 2021, there were intermittent restrictions on travel due to the COVID-19 pandemic, and this impacted opportunities to meet and collaborate. The five workshops, therefore, were delivered both face to face and online. The workshops were stretched over a two-year period, which limited the fluidity of professional learning.

Models of professional learning

The design of the professional learning at Brandon School was inspired by three models – 'responsive' and 'proactive' action research (Schmuck, 2006, pp. 33–34) and 'tools for change' (Fullan & Germain, 2006, p. 6). The three models differ primarily in their sequences of steps. In responsive action research, the process starts with data collection, followed by the analysis, dissemination and identification of necessary changes, refining of practices and recollection of data. Proactive action research begins by listing hopes and concerns, trying new practices and collecting data, before analysing and reflecting on the data to refine the practices. The tools for change model, by contrast, involves starting with beliefs, delving into important aspects, making sense of them, broadening perspectives and engaging in personal reflection to develop future solutions. All three are circular models. They can be used for prescriptive purposes (e.g. designing professional learning) and analytic purposes (e.g. analysing processes). An underlying idea that connects the three models is that 'there is no action without research and no research without action' (Schmuck, 2006, p. 32). All three models indicate recurring processes involving reflection about the past and the present, as well as a focus on future hopes and solutions. In this way, professionals are invited to identify challenges and to act while paying attention to contextual constraints and affordances. An overview of the three models is provided in Table 8.1 below.

While the three models provide 'scaffold' and structure to help plan and carry out professional learning, it is important to align theoretical models with the needs and concerns of staff. Before the first workshop, the school leaders asked their teacher teams: Where are they now in professional development?

TABLE 8.1 Three models of action research: Sequences of steps

Step	*Responsive Action Research (Model 1)*	*Proactive Action Research (Model 2)*	*Tools for Change (Model 3)*
Step 1	Collect data	List hopes and concerns	Get started – begin with beliefs
Step 2	Analyse the data	Try a new practice	Look more deeply – pay attention to what matters
Step 3	Distribute the data and make changes	Collect data	Take action – change the context
Step 4	List hopes and concerns	Check what the data mean	Make sense – build a common language
Step 5	Try a new practice	Reflect on alternative ways to behave	Look wider – learn more
Step 6	Collect data	Fine-tune practices	Personal reflections – future solutions
	(Schmuck, 2006, p. 34)	(Schmuck, 2006, p. 33)	(Fullan & Germain, 2006, p. 6)

Where are they going in professional development? And how would they get there? The many suggestions from the teacher teams included working on more interdisciplinary issues and focusing on the overall curriculum (LK20).

First workshop: Action research – what and how?

The first workshop was used to situate the Norwegian project in the international BIBS project and to present the steps in Model 3 together with examples. As an example of a task provided to the participants, the staff were asked to ponder individually on the following statement: '*Democracy is a central theme for Norwegian schools*'. Next, the staff discussed their reflections in pairs. The purpose of this exercise was to make beliefs and arguments explicit (cf. Step 1, Model 3). To aid the staff in analysing their arguments, we introduced Biesta's (2015, p. 78) framework involving three aims or purposes of education: qualification, socialisation and subjectification. The rationale for using this framework was to help the staff look more deeply and pay attention to what matters (Step 2, Model 3). We challenged pairs of teachers to discuss Biesta's framework. The aim was to contribute to the development of a shared vocabulary (Step 4, Model 3).

In a follow-up conversation with the leadership team, it became evident that the staff found that the workshop's focus was too theoretical. There appeared to be a wish to more explicitly connect the workshop content to the school's primary objective, that is, to the realisation of the new curriculum. Thus, we decided to accommodate this need in further collaborations.

Second workshop: Working with the national curriculum

In the second workshop, the researchers gave a short presentation on the functions of a national curriculum, including the following key ideas: The curriculum reflects society – society's problems become the school's curriculum; the curriculum informs about society's priorities – what knowledge is important; and the curriculum guides the school's teaching (Engelsen, 2003; Gudem, 1990). In particular, the presentation focused on core value concepts from the curriculum: human dignity, identity and cultural diversity, and democracy and participation. This constituted a platform for working individually and in groups with the subject curricula, scrutinising different subjects to identify and discuss how the values were portrayed in different parts of the curriculum (i.e. the core elements, the interdisciplinary topics and basic skills). Finally, the groups used the searchable curricula being developed to identify values as elements of the descriptions of the assessment criteria (competence goals). For an example of a digital curriculum, see the curriculum for social studies (The Norwegian Directorate for Education and Training, 2025b, June). This way of working with the new curricula, along with reflecting on existing practices and concepts, aligned with Steps 4 and 5 of Model 3. The teachers were able to discover the connections between the different parts of the curriculum and how core values were integrated into principles and subjects. One teacher remarked that democracy education 'is introduced as an overarching theme in our teaching practices. It is not just addressed in social science'. The teacher's argument was important because it reflected the interdisciplinary aspect of the overall core curriculum in a Norwegian context.

Before the next session, a questionnaire was developed for pupils to explore their understandings, perspectives and questions in relation to the key issues in BIBS (i.e. diversity, democracy and equity). It was administered by teachers in the lower secondary classes with their pupils (Step 1, Model 1; Step 3, Model 2). The researchers analysed the survey data prior to the next workshop at the school and presented findings from their content analysis at the next BIBS online seminar across the participating countries.

Third workshop: Assumptions and practices in democracy education

Another step in the action research cycle involves practitioners exploring their assumptions, that is, in this case, the teachers' practices, and then checking whether they fit with pupils' opinions and knowledge. After a short introduction about what we know about democracy education from national and international research (Crick, 1998; Sætra & Stray, 2019), the researchers shared findings and data samples from the pupil and teacher surveys conducted at Brandon School. The survey responses indicated that most pupils strongly supported the pupils' council and felt that democracy was, overall, strong in their school. They generally reported high levels of trust in political institutions and positive attitudes towards fulfilling their roles as citizens (e.g. through participation in elections or membership of political parties and unions in the future). Teachers' responses, on the other hand, showed that they wanted to educate *for* democracy mainly by helping pupils acquire (democratic) knowledge and critical thinking skills. Responses aligning with the democracy *through* participation in social practices inside and outside the classroom approach were less prominent in the data. Questionnaire results were shared by the researchers alongside the following quote from West to trigger deeper thinking about what matters (Step 2, Model 3) in democracy education.

> All systems set up to enact democracy are subject to corrupt manipulations, and that is why the public commitment to democratic involvement is so vital. Genuine, robust democracy must be brought to life through democratic individuality, democratic community, and democratic society.
> *(West, 2005, p. 203)*

Following this introduction, teachers were asked to consider the following questions in pairs: *In which situations at your school are pupils taken seriously and given real opportunities to participate and influence areas that are important to them? In which situations are pupils not legitimate participants? Why?*

While the teachers considered themselves to be 'democratic', these questions brought up difficult issues, including how much influence pupils should have, and over what, at what age pupils may be consulted on different issues and the difficulties of giving up part of their professional power. The responses of the pupils who did not believe that the school was democratic filtered into these discussions. While teachers agreed that there was some truth in pupils' criticism that 'although the pupil council might be democratic, the principal nevertheless decided everything', they argued that this did not render the school undemocratic. Other complaints made by some pupils were that their ideas and suggestions were often not taken seriously and that they were forced to 'learn stuff that is not useful'.

Teachers and leaders skimmed through the anonymous pupil data (Step 4, Model 2) and jotted down ideas for topics that could be explored further with both primary and secondary staff. They explored themes arising from the data, selected three issues and discussed how the data could be analysed further and who else should be invited to discuss the results (Step 5, Model 2).

Fourth workshop: Checking data – reflecting on actions

Further data analysis showed that democracy was taken for granted among most pupils. They understood the concept of democracy as an aspect of a country's governance system: the right to vote and to participate in making decisions. Regarding school democracy, the pupils referred to the pupil council and to freedom of speech (they could say what they wanted). While some of the teachers argued that the survey results did not surprise them, there was a realisation that democracy was something that both staff and pupils had taken as given and that by working with this, new perspectives on democracy arise. According to the teachers, working with the survey data increased the pupils' and teachers' curiosity about how the concept could be understood and how democracy might be realised in their school (Step 5, Model 2).

The international BIBS project offered further opportunities for a subgroup of school leaders and teachers who participated in international online and face-to-face meetings and workshops with project partners from Poland, Ireland and Spain. These international experiences 'created curiosity and deeper knowledge about how different kinds of democracy may be presented and practised [across contexts]' (teacher interview).

Fifth workshop: Delving deeper and summing up

In the fifth workshop, the aim was to delve deeper into the aims and practices of democracy education. As an introduction, we used a letter from a survivor of a concentration camp (Ginott, 2025, May) to trigger discussion about the role of knowledge in a democratic society. The core argument was that knowledge is only important if it supports humanity; a separation of knowledge and humanity can result in a tragedy. The researchers referred back to the core values of education and training, as stated in the Education Act (Ministry of Education, June 2025) and the national curriculum in English (D), pointing to the role of knowledge in maintaining, promoting and developing a just society. To broaden teachers' focus, we explored the differences between democracy as a way of living and democracy as a way of governing and among education *about*, *for* and *through* democracy (Stray, 2014) (Step 5, Model 3). These discussions were connected to teachers' professional practice. The teachers were asked to explore *if and how the national curriculum address the multidimensional character of democracy education and what that might imply for their practice* (Stray, 2014). Below, we have listed examples of further recommended readings.

Summarising the experiences

We experienced that it is important to bring in new knowledge when focusing on big issues such as democracy (see the Recommended readings above for some relevant publications) (Box 8.1). It is crucial to work closely with

BOX 8.1 SAMPLE DISCUSSION PROMPTS AND RECOMMENDED READINGS

Prompts for discussion

- *Democracy is a central theme for Norwegian schools. What are your thoughts?*
- *What do we hope for, and what are our concerns? How can we investigate the situation in our school? What will we do about it? (cf. Løver & Postholm, 2016).*
- *In which situations at your school are pupils taken seriously and given real opportunities to participate and influence areas that are important to them? In which situations are pupils not legitimate participants? Why?*
- *Does the national curriculum addressed the multidimensional character of democracy education, and, if so, how? What does this imply for your practice?*
- *How can teachers balance the purposes of education: qualification, socialisation and subjectification (cf. Biesta, 2015)?*

Recommended readings

Biesta, G. and Lawy, R. (2006) 'From teaching citizenship to learning democracy: Overcoming individualism in research, policy and practice', *Cambridge Journal of Education, 36*(1): 63–79.

Fullan, M. and Germain, C.S. (2006) *Learning Places: A Field Guide for Improving the Context of Schooling*. Los Angeles, CA: Corwin Press.

Larsen, E. and Mathé, N.E.H. (2023) 'Teachers' perceptions of their schools' democratic character', *Scandinavian Journal of Educational Research, 67*(2): 327–343.

Schmuck, R.A. (2006) *Practical Action Research for Change.* Los Angeles: CA Corwin Press.

Stray, J.H. (2014) 'Learning and living democracy', A.B. Sterry (ed.). *Global Citizen: Challenges and Responsibility in an Interconnected World*, Leiden, Nederland: Brill, pp. 103–111.

the school leaders in the preparation of the initiative and to debrief at critical points during the training process, as materials and discussions need to be relevant to the teachers and school leaders in the present situation. Connecting the project to the ongoing processes, that is, the renewal of the curriculum, was essential in the Norwegian case. When schools are engaged in many projects at once, there is a need to find a sufficient pace and momentum in the learning processes. The two teachers engaged in international activities reported that they experienced benefits to their teaching by including examples from other contexts in their teaching about democracy. However, how these personal experiences can nurture broader learning across the school community requires further attention.

Exploring experiences and impact: Methodology

Both the researchers and teachers found the workshops inspiring and insightful. A physical gathering was also organised for participants from all partner organisations in Ireland. The participating teachers and researchers from the Norwegian delegation considered this international event particularly useful. They appreciated the plenary presentations about core project issues and the many discussions in multinational groups. In the teacher interview (N=2), the Norwegian teachers emphasised the value of having these group conversations and underscored how they impacted their teaching. They experienced how examples from colleagues in other countries triggered curiosity and a deeper understanding not only among the pupils but also among themselves. In this project, we initially used two models of action research (proactive and responsive action research) and one model of tools for change to trigger interest and to loosely structure the learning journey. However, as the purpose of the Erasmus+ project was not research per se, but rather cooperation and learning among participants across the cohorts, we suggest that it is more appropriate to conceptualise the Norwegian collaborative university–school project as 'action learning' or 'professional learning'. According to Tiller (1999), action learning has many elements in common with action research, but it is more focused on experiential learning. Tiller applies the term 'action learning' to collaborations in which teachers systematically examine their own practice with the intention of improving quality. Notably, he links the term 'action research' to what researchers do when they systematically investigate, analyse and report action learning processes and provide research outputs. In this project, we paid attention to the ongoing feedback from school leaders and teachers to develop and justify activities and to make them relevant for the pupils, which might be conceptualised as action learning. Moreover, we collected interview data from the teachers and materials from the workshops. We conducted a content analysis of the learning materials (e.g. PowerPoint presentations and issues for discussion) and a content analysis of the teacher interview and pupil surveys conducted with students in lower secondary school (democracy n=18 and diversity n=18, age 13–14 and equity n=61, age 13–15). Drawing on the analyses of these varied data sources, our approach might be conceptualised as a mixture of 'action learning' and 'action research'. The model of 'tools for change' has other nuances, which are all relevant to the processes of professional learning being carried out in Norway, such as delving into important aspects, making sense of them, broadening perspectives and engaging in personal reflection to develop future solutions.

We have identified six key learning points from the case of Norway, which are discussed in the next section:

1. Professional learning initiatives need to link with themes that resonate with teachers' and school leaders' perceived needs.
2. Professional learning initiatives should focus on the integration of experience, new knowledge and investigation.
3. The support, engagement and leadership of school leaders are crucial for making the processes relevant to teachers.
4. Sufficient time for collaboration must be set aside.
5. Sufficient pace and momentum are important in the learning process.
6. All staff should gain international experiences, not only the teachers who are most actively involved in the project.

A few contextual issues need to be mentioned, as they may have impacted the learning taking place. The COVID pandemic in 2020 may have had a major impact on the possibility of upholding a continuous collective learning process. Throughout the project period, there were periods of confinement and restrictions on travelling (e.g. from the university to the school). In addition, the school was mandated to carry out school development because of the new curriculum, and initially, the school leadership team and the research team aimed at integrating the BIBS project with the curriculum work. This seemed to be a good fit, as values play a prominent part in the curriculum renewal. However, this also made it difficult to distinguish between regular curriculum work and the project. The teachers had two hours each week to work on school development, and they worked extensively with the so-called competence packages offered by the National Directorate for Teaching and Training. This was ongoing work alongside the project. Curriculum work is a task that pertains to all the teachers in the school, while the project itself was aimed at teachers of the oldest pupils. Moreover, excluding teachers from the project might have been counterproductive to the ethos of the school and to the principle of respect, responsibility and care for all.

Key learning from the project

Clarke and Hollingsworth's model (2002) for professional learning emphasises that effective professional development needs to be flexible and focused on meeting the personal development needs of individual teachers (see also Zhang et al., 2021). This stands in contrast to mandated change, such as the introduction of a new curriculum, as was the case in our project. While the teachers were not uninterested in learning and teaching about democracy, they did not always regard it as a priority, with other pressing needs (e.g. lesson planning, new curricula and addressing pupils' special needs) possibly considered as more pressing.

Teacher workloads are heavy and considered as increasingly 'excessive', 'unrealistic' and 'unsustainable' in the wake of rising accountability measures (Hefferman et al., 2022). Consequently, it is important that schools allocate sufficient time to professional learning initiatives. While teachers in Norway are provided with time for collaboration, this time is often filled with mandated tasks originating from central or regional authorities (Vibe et al., 2009). Our project momentum was often impaired by external demands, as well as the additional challenges of keeping up the work during periods of lockdown and travel restrictions.

Action learning has been criticised for being too focused on here-and-now issues and participants' current knowledge. We suggest that professional learning should provide opportunities for teachers to engage with new concepts and knowledge which may extend and/or contrast with their existing experiences and knowledge. Wells (1999) argues that professional knowledge is developed through the integration of four meaning-making processes: experience, information, knowledge building and understanding. The prior experiences and assumptions of teachers (and pupils) must be activated and explored. New knowledge (or information; cf. Wells, 1999) counteracts the tendency of becoming too near-sighted in the investigation of practices and can help in connecting knowledge and practical experiences in new ways.

Exploratory talk (Mercer, 2008) is necessary to critically explore new knowledge to develop new understanding and, ultimately, new practices. Teachers and pupils who were able to closely connect with our project confirmed that the various activities gave rise to reflection, deeper insights (cf. Model 3) and, to some extent, renewed interest in and experimentation with democracy education. The pupil surveys were particularly useful, showing the importance of gathering data about pupils' knowledge, attitudes and experiences and using these data to trigger deeper and contextualised engagement with values and curriculum and to renew teaching practices about what the data mean (Model 2, Step 4).

Our experience underscored the crucial role of flexible and attentive leadership (Sølvik & Roland, 2022), as school leaders' energy and commitment significantly impact teacher motivation, attention and attitudes towards action learning in school teams (Robinson et al., 2008; Stoll et al., 2006). However, school leaders have vast responsibilities, and when the project initiative is external, like participation in an Erasmus+ project, substantial collaboration is required to embed the project within the school's overarching plans and to clearly define the roles and responsibilities of all participants. In our project, the complexity of the situation, and the blurring of roles and responsibilities of school leaders, subject leaders/teachers and university researchers, posed challenges and resulted, at times, in a piecemeal and fragmentary approach that limited the initiative's impact in terms of the overall school practices.

Conclusion and recommendations

This chapter has briefly summarised Norway's new values-based national curriculum, which provided the trigger and foundation for a professional learning initiative – 'Democracy in Education: Connecting Curriculum Values with Practice in Schools' – which we designed and implemented with school leaders and teachers in a rural school in Norway. We have shown how 'responsive' and 'proactive' action research and 'tools for change' approaches shaped the design and guided the implementation of the professional learning programme, which introduced the participants to new knowledge and involved the collection, analysis and collaborative reflection on data from pupils and teachers. Finally, we have discussed some of our experiences and shared 'learning points' for future work in schools and in school–university partnerships.

In Norway, national education authorities expect that collective professional learning is facilitated at the individual school (The Norwegian Directorate for Education and Training, 2025a) with time allocated for this work. Moreover, there is a long tradition of school–university partnerships (e.g. Blossing et al., 2010; Elstad et al., 2018). Although such partnerships are in operation (and are often founded by central educational authorities), the outcomes have often not been as expected (Møller et al., 2010). Our project did not reveal that the teachers at Brandon School are now experts in dealing with the 'big issue' of democracy and effectively teaching *about*, *for* and *through* democracy in their different subject areas. However, through our work together, we have explored these issues, shared experiences and perspectives, dealt with and overcome challenges. Moreover, both the school staff and the researchers gained experiences that will affect how we design, deliver and engage with future professional learning initiatives.

Although the empirical example is from a Norwegian context, we think that what we have learned has relevance beyond this context. That is because it touches upon issues of professional learning in schools and the responsibilities of school leaders as well as matters of realising national reform initiatives on a local level and various didactics for triggering development and change. Our engagement with the key principles of 'responsive' and 'proactive' action research and 'tools for change' has inspired a focus on the following key questions: *What do we hope for, and what are our concerns? How can we investigate the situation in our school? What will we do about it?* (cf. Løver & Postholm, 2016). All three questions can be operationalised in different ways. The methods chosen for the investigation should consider the school's culture and prior experiences as well as contextual issues, such as current issues, school size and teacher competence.

Working with 'big issues' inevitably presents challenges. Concepts such as diversity, democracy and equity often spark disputes among citizens and between governments and countries. A salient issue is, thus, learning how to live with differences while promoting certain values that are universal in a society, such as human rights. We argue that a promising way of dealing with these challenges is to facilitate arenas for discourse among practitioners based on data, access to new research-based knowledge and what we know about pupils' experiences. In an age of public accountability, education leaders must advocate for the prioritisation of 'big issues', emphasising their importance and ensuring they receive the attention they deserve.

Regarding reflections, sometimes reflection is conceptualised as an exclusively cognitive individual activity. It is not always clear what the relationship is to past, ongoing or future events (Ottesen, 2007). In the context of professional learning, we suggest that reflection needs to be promoted as both an individual activity and a collective activity that connects with people's past engagements, ongoing actions and future hopes and concerns. In this way, it can serve as a discursive tool for conversations with oneself and others. A special characteristic of reflection is its ability to transcend obstacles in the real world and to develop imaginary constructs that, when shared, may lead to deep learning or innovative activities. It allows for the 'low-risk imaginary enactment of practices or understandings' (Ottesen, 2007, p. 6). This, however, warrants a high degree of trust between participants and the courage to try and (potentially) learn from failures. The role of tools for collective learning should not be underestimated; tools can mediate professional learning (Jensen & Møller, 2013).

A project such as BIBS can have an important impact. It brings attention to the purpose of a school and what learning is for: that is, to engage and equip pupils with competences and values. The purpose of schooling, as illustrated by Biesta (2015, p. 28), involves qualification, socialisation and subjectification. Attending to all three functions of education will provide pupils with knowledge, agency and values that give them the potential to participate in and make future worlds that are better for all. The time teachers have for professional learning and cooperation needs to be divided among a range of issues, and there is a danger that 'big issues' may drown in other important concerns. Strong and courageous leadership is required to keep values at the centre of attention.

Acknowledgement of funding

Erasmus+ project, funded by Léargas (Ireland) 2019-1-IE01-KA201-051528

References

Andersson, E. (2019). The school as a public space for democratic experiences: Formal student participation and its political characteristics. *Education, Citizenship and Social Justice*, *14*(2), 149–164.

Apple, M. W. (2018). The struggle for democracy in education. In M. W. Apple, L. Armando, S. Liu, A. Meshulam, & E. Schirmer (Eds.), *The struggle for democracy in education* (pp. 1–19). New York, NY: Routledge.
Biesta, G. (2015). What is education for? On good education, teacher judgement, and educational professionalism. *European Journal of Education, 50*(1), 75–87.
Biesta, G., & Lawy, R. (2006). From teaching citizenship to learning democracy: Overcoming individualism in research, policy and practice. *Cambridge Journal of Education, 36*(1), 63–79.
Blossing, U., Hagen, A., Nyen, T., & Söderström, Å. (2010). *Kunnskapsløftet fra ord til handling: Sluttrapport fra evalueringen av et statligt program for skoleutvikling* [The knowledge promise from words to action: Final report from the evaluation of a state programme for school development], Oslo: Fafo og Karlstads universitet (Fafo-rapport 2001/10: 01. https://www.diva-portal.org/smash/record.jsf?pid=diva2%3A494134&dswid=-7912 (Accessed: 8 May).
Borgebund, H., & Børhaug, K. (2023). Demokratiopplæring gjennom demokratisk erfaring [Democracy education through democratic experience]. *Nordidactica: Journal of Humanities and Social Science Education, 13*(3), 46–65.
Clarke, D., & Hollingsworth, H. (2002). Elaborating a model of teacher professional growth. *Teaching and Teacher Education, 18*(8), 947–967.
Crick, B. (1998). A meditation on democracy. In T. Inoguchi, E. Newman, & J. Keane (Eds.), *The changing nature of democracy* (pp. 255–265). New York, NY: United Nations Publisher.
Dewey, J. (2016). Excerpts from democracy and education (1916). *Schools, 13*(1), 127–139.
Elstad, E., Lejonberg, E., & Christophersen, K. A. (2018). Skolebaserte utviklingsprosjekter på ungdomstrinnet: læreres opplevelser av satsningen Ungdomstrinn i utvikling ['School-based development projects at secondary level: Teachers' experiences of the initiative 'Ungdomstrinn i utvikling']. *Norsk pedagogisk tidsskrift, 102*(3), 271–281.
Engelsen, B. U. (2003). *Ideer som formet vår skole? Læreplanen som idébærer. Et historisk perspektiv* [Ideas that shaped our school? The curriculum as an idea carrier: A historical perspective]. Oslo: Gyldendal Akademisk.
Fullan, M., & Germain, C. S. (2006). *Learning places: A field guide for improving the context of schooling*. Toronto: Corwin Press.
Furberg, A., Rødnes, K. A., Silseth, K., Arnseth, H. C., Kvamme, O. A., Lund, A., . . . & Slungård, K. (2023). Fagfornyelsen i møte med klasseromspraksiser [The curriculum renewal meets classroom practice]. *Eva2020 Report No. 6*. Oslo, Norway: University of Oslo, Faculty of Educational Sciences.
Ginott, H. (2025, May). *So, I am suspicious of education*. https://teachinghistorymatters.com/2012/04/02/so-i-am-suspicious-of-education/ (Accessed: 20 May).
Gudem, B. B. (1990). *Læreplanpraksis og læreplanteori – en innføring* [Curriculum practice and theory of curriculum]: Oslo: Universitetsforlaget.
Heffernan, A., Bright, D., Kim, M., Longmuir, F., & Magyar, B. (2022). 'I cannot sustain the workload and the emotional toll': Reasons behind Australian teachers' intentions to leave the profession. *Australian Journal of Education, 66*(2), 196–209.
Heinz, M., Mac Ruairc, G., & Rodríguez-Entrena, M. J. (2026). Big ideas for better schools: A transnational professional learning project. In M. Heinz, M. J. Rodríguez-Entrena, & G. Mac Ruairc (Eds.), *Professional learning for diversity, equity and democracy: Big ideas for better schools* (pp. 17–23). Routledge.
Heinz, M., Rodríguez-Entrena, M. J., & Mac Ruairc, G. (2026). School leadership for better futures: Collaborative professional learning *about* and *for* diversity, equity and democracy. In M. Heinz, M. J. Rodríguez-Entrena, & G. Mac Ruairc

(Eds.), *Professional learning for diversity, equity and democracy: Big ideas for better schools* (pp. 3–16). Routledge.
Hopmann, S. T. (1999). The curriculum as a standard of public education. *Studies in Philosophy and Education*, *18*(1), 89–105.
Jensen, R., & Møller, J. (2013). School data as mediators in professional development. *Journal of Educational Change*, *14*, 95–112.
Larsen, E., & Mathé, N. E. H. (2023). Teachers' perceptions of their schools' democratic character. *Scandinavian Journal of Educational Research*, *67*(2), 327–343.
Larsen, E., Møller, J., & Jensen, R. (2022). Constructions of professionalism and the democratic mandate in education a discourse analysis of Norwegian public policy documents. *Journal of Education Policy*, *37*(1), 106–125.
Løver, M. E., & Postholm, M. B. (2016). *Ledelse og læreres læring i team* [Leadership and teacher learning in teams]. Oslo: Fagbokforlaget.
Mac Ruairc, G., Gartland, S., Heinz, M., & Rodríguez-Entrena, M. J. (2026). Diversity, equity and democracy in school leadership: Troublesome concepts in troubled times. In M. Heinz, M. J. Rodríguez-Entrena, & G. Mac Ruairc (Eds.), *Professional learning for diversity, equity and democracy: Big ideas for better schools* (pp. 24–46). Routledge.
Mercer, N. (2008). Talk and the development of reasoning and understanding. *Human Development*, *51*(1), 90–100.
Ministry of Education and Research in Norway. (2025, June). *The education act* [Online]. https://lovdata.no/dokument/NL/lov/2023-06-09-30 (Accessed: 8 June).
Møller, J., Ottesen, E., & Hertzberg, F. (2010). Møtet mellom skolens profesjonsforståelse og Kunnskapsløftet som styringsreform Between the school´s professional understanding and the Knowledge Promotion Reform as a governing reform. *Acta Didactica Norge*, *4*(1), 15.
Møller, J., & Skedsmo, G. (2013). Modernising education: New public management reform in the Norwegian education system. *Journal of Educational Administration and History*, *45*(4), 336–353.
The Norwegian Directorate for Education and Training. (2025a). *The core curriculum – values and principles for the primary and secondary education and training.* https://www.udir.no/lk20/overordnet-del/?lang=eng (Accessed: 8 June 2025).
The Norwegian Directorate for Education and Training. (2025b). *The curriculum for social studies.* https://www.udir.no/lk20/saf01-04?lang=eng (Accessed: 8 June 2025).
OECD. (2025). *The OECD reinforcing democracy initiative: Monitoring report – assessing progress and charting the way forward, OECD public governance reviews.* Paris: OECD Publishing. https://doi.org/10.1787/9543bcfb-en
Ottesen, E. (2007). Reflection in teacher education. *Reflective Practice*, *8*(1), 31–46.
Robinson, V. M., Lloyd, C. A., & Rowe, K. J. (2008). The impact of leadership on student outcomes: An analysis of the differential effects of leadership types. *Educational Administration Quarterly*, *44*(5), 635–674.
Sætra, E., & Stray, J. H. (2019). Læreplan og demokrati: Om lærernes bruk av læreplanen i samfunnsfag i et demokratipedagogisk perspektiv [Curriculum and democracy: About teachers' use of the curriculum in social studies from a democratic pedagogical perspective]. *Nordic Journal of Comparative and International Education (NJCIE)*, *3*(1), 3–18.
Schmuck, R. A. (Ed.). (2006). *Practical action research: A collection of articles.* London: Corwin Press.
Skaaning, S. E. (2021). Democracy: Contested concept with a common core. In *Research handbook on democracy and development* (pp. 27–44). Cheltenham: Edward Elgar Publishing.

Sølvik, R. M., & Roland, P. (2022). Teachers' and principals' diverse experiences expand the understanding of how to lead collective professional learning among teachers. *International Journal of Leadership in Education*, 1–24. https://doi.org/10.1080/13603124.2021.2021295
Stoll, L., Bolam, R., McMahon, A., Wallace, M., & Thomas, S. (2006). Professional learning communities: A review of the literature. *Journal of Educational Change*, *7*(4), 221–258.
Stray, J. H. (2014). Learning and living democracy. In A. B. Sterri (Ed.), *Global citizen: Challenges and responsibility in an interconnected world* (pp. 103–111). Brill Sense.
Stray, J. H., & Sætra, E. (2017). Teaching for democracy: Transformative learning theory mediating policy and practice. *Nordisk tidsskrift for pedagogikk og kritikk* [Nordic Journal for Pedagogy and Criticism], *3*(1).
Tiller, T. (1999). *Aksjonslæring: forskende partnerskap i skolen* [Action learning: Collaborative research in school]. Oslo: Cappelen Damm.
Vibe, N., Aamodt, P. O., & LØdding, T. C. (2009). *Å være ungdomsskolelærer i Norge: Resultater fra OECDs internasjonale studie av undervisning og læring (TALIS)* [Norwegian results from the OECDs international study of teaching and learning (TALIS)]. Oslo: NIFU STEP.
Wells, C. G. (1999). *Dialogic inquiry* (Volume 10). Cambridge: Cambridge University Press.
West, C. (2005). *Democracy matters: Winning the fight against imperialism*. London: Penguin.
Zhang, L., Carter, R. A., Zhang, J., Hunt, T. L., Emerling, C. R., Yang, S., & Xu, F. (2021). Teacher perceptions of effective professional development: Insights for design. *Professional Development in Education*, *50*(4), 611–624.

9

EDUCATION FOR CITIZENSHIP UNDER DEMOCRATIC STRAIN

Professional learning for school leaders and teachers in Chile

Camila Jara Ibarra, Macarena Sánchez Bachmann, and Javiera Peña Fredes

Introduction

Over the past two decades, citizenship education has been a central focus of Chile's educational policies, with various curricular adjustments made to address the topic (Cox & Castillo, 2015). Since the end of the military dictatorship and the restoration of democracy in 1990, Chile has seen a significant decline in voter turnout, placing it among the countries with the lowest electoral participation in Latin America (Cox & Corvalán, 2015; Bargsted et al., 2019). By 2015, Chile had 'the largest decline in electoral participation among all the democracies in the world' (Cox & Corvalán, 2015, p. 177). This decline occurred alongside a wave of widespread social mobilisation, culminating in 2019 with the 'social upheaval', which represented the largest protests in Chile in three decades (Donoso & Von Bulow, 2017; Jara Ibarra, 2019). These events had profound socio-political and cultural consequences, leading to a political crisis and the initiation of a constituent process aimed at drafting a new constitution to replace the one imposed during the dictatorship. Moreover, in line with global trends, Chile experienced a rise in populist ideologies, the resurgence of authoritarian ideas and the spread of misinformation and political polarisation (Mignozzetti & Spektor, 2019; Kaltwasser & Van Hauwaert, 2020; Levin et al., 2021).

In response to these challenges, attention shifted to the school system's role in promoting democratic values, managing conflicts peacefully and fostering social cohesion. In 2016, a national law (Law No. 20.911) introduced curricular adjustments for citizenship education. Since then, all schools have been required to develop a CEP to teach democratic values and encourage political participation through actions integrated across the entire institution

DOI: 10.4324/9781032629292-11

and at all grade levels (Ministerio de Educación de Chile, 2016). Additionally, a new citizenship education subject for the final two years of secondary school was introduced and implemented in 2020, coinciding with the major social protests of October 2019 and the subsequent political agreement that initiated the process of drafting a new constitution.

In Latin American countries like Chile, where democratic systems and peaceful electoral processes were re-established only a few decades ago, schools, in addition to being situated in fragile democracies, face significant direct challenges such as political polarisation and distrust towards institutions. As they strive to address social conflicts and handle controversial issues, educators must navigate the complexities of a divided and sceptical society (UNESCO, 2017). Citizenship education teachers, in particular, grapple with disputes and controversies that arise in the public sphere. Compounding this is the fact that many teachers and principals belong to a generation socialised during dictatorial or post-dictatorial periods, where political discussions were often avoided (Jara Ibarra, 2019).

Since 2016, CEPs have been implemented in public schools across Chile. However, despite their widespread adoption, these plans have not fully realised their potential as formative, ambitious and cohesive initiatives for fostering citizenship education (UNDP, 2018; Jara Ibarra et al., 2019; Zúñiga et al., 2020). Many school CEPs tend to prioritise regulatory compliance, such as establishing representative bodies, facilitating participation and conducting elections, over creating meaningful and engaging experiences for students.

Over the past five years, we have conducted research on various aspects of citizenship education aimed at improving its quality. Our focus has included the role of school leadership (Jara Ibarra et al., 2019, 2023), gender gaps and biases (Jara Ibarra et al., 2021), teachers' perspectives, national curriculum guidelines (Cox et al., 2022), managing controversial issues in the classroom (Cox et al., 2023) and the role of leadership in student conflicts and mobilisations (Villalobos et al., 2017; Peña & Sémbler, 2019). Our research involved interviews with teachers, students and families from more than 30 schools, alongside classroom observations and reviews of school materials. Additionally, we conducted surveys with 1,600 high school students and their parents, as well as with 100 history and social sciences teachers.

The research revealed several key findings: First, there is an excessive focus on the citizenship education subject and subject teacher(s), which contradicts the policy's intended transversal and comprehensive nature (Jara Ibarra et al., 2019). Second, there is a significant lack of professional development opportunities, as well as theoretical and practical tools for citizenship education, available for both pre-service and in-service teachers. Additionally, a predominant emphasis on fostering harmonious relationships among students, promoting a positive school climate and cultivating personal values – rather than political literacy and engagement – shapes how CEPs are defined and implemented in schools. This imbalance, which favours the civil dimension over the civic or political dimension of citizenship (Cox et al., 2014), prompted our team to create training opportunities and resources to assist teachers and school leaders in developing more holistic citizenship education programmes.

Drawing on our research findings, we designed the 'Tools for Understanding Citizenship Education' programme, delivered through summer schools and workshops. In total, approximately 500 teachers from various Chilean schools participated in these professional development events. The summer schools were held in person in 2020, with 34 participants, and virtually in 2021 and 2022, with 42 and 21 participants, respectively. Additionally, two two-hour workshops were conducted in 2019, involving 385 teachers and school leaders.

In this chapter, we present and discuss some of the professional learning tools we designed to support teachers and school leaders in: 1) developing comprehensive and transversal CEPs within their schools and 2) deepening their understanding and skills for addressing controversial issues in their classrooms. We will first describe the key objectives, the design and some activities of these professional development initiatives. Following this overview, we outline the methodology used for course evaluations. The chapter concludes with a discussion of the lessons learned and recommendations based on our experience.

These initiatives are valuable in any context, but especially in areas marked by high polarisation and political mobilisation, as seen in Chile in recent years. It is essential for teachers and schools to be equipped with the right tools to strengthen citizenship education, as this will allow them to make a significant contribution during moments of political crisis.

'Tools for Understanding Citizenship Education': Design and implementation of a professional learning programme for teachers and school leaders

The 'Tools for Understanding Citizenship Education' in-service programme comprised ten modules that integrated both theory and practice for citizenship education. Specifically, the theoretical modules concentrated on political and democratic theory, as well as on national and international research evidence in the field. In contrast, the practical modules focused on approaches for planning citizenship education in schools and on pedagogical strategies for addressing controversial issues.

Leveraging conceptual frameworks to enhance understanding and practice

We adapted Kerr's '3 Cs' model (2015) as a theoretical and practical tool to enrich teachers' understanding of citizenship education and to guide critical reflection about the design of CEPs. The '3 Cs' model encompasses three overlapping contexts of the school experience: the curriculum (classroom), school culture (school institution) and the local community (relationship of the school institution with its environment) (Kerr, 2015). In addition, we integrated two dimensions of citizenship: its civil dimension, referring to the structure of shared connections among people, such as close relationships with peers; and its civic dimension, referring to the relationship with distant and different individuals mediated by politics and its institutions (Cox et al., 2014; Schulz et al., 2023). The civil dimension of citizenship can also be understood as the social climate in the school, related to the ways in which students relate respectfully and tolerantly to others. The civic dimension reflects the dimension of politics, that is, the relationships with others who are different, distant and unknown, mediated through structures of social and political organisation and representation, as well as relationships with the state (Schulz et al., 2023). The civic dimension, then, fundamentally, refers to the political organisation of society and the forms and social institutions through which society democratically processes power conflicts. The various elements are illustrated in Figure 9.1.

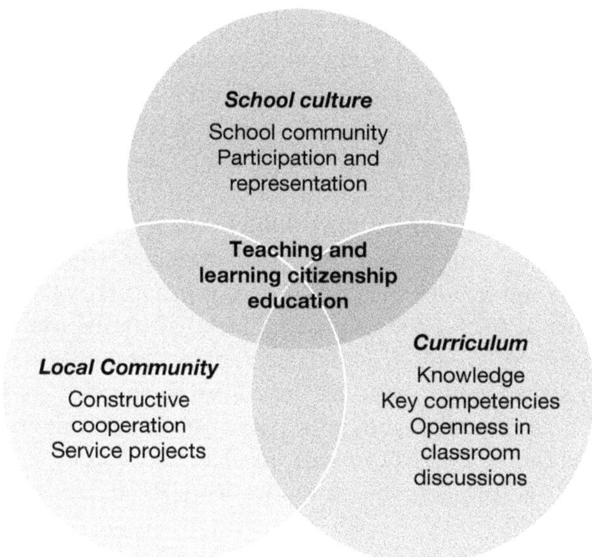

FIGURE 9.1 Contexts and dimensions for the teaching and learning of citizenship (Universidad Diego Portales – UDP & Instituto Unibanco, 2023, p. 27)

Adapted from Kerr (2015).

The 3Cs and two-dimensional conceptual framework of citizenship education were presented to participants as a conceptual and practical tool that can guide both 1) the analysis of existing or current citizenship education practices at their schools and 2) the development of future strategies and practices for democratic citizenship education.

Following the introduction and discussion of the framework, participants were asked to analyse, compare and discuss three CEPs, using the following questions:

- Considering the 'Contexts and Dimensions for the Teaching and Learning of Citizenship' model, on which of the three areas does each of the analysed plans place the main emphasis?
- Considering the distinction between the civic and civil dimensions of citizenship, which of these do you believe prevails in each of these plans?
- Evaluate each of the plans in terms of their coherence and completeness. What, from your perspective, is the main weakness of each one? How could each plan be improved to strengthen students' learning experiences and outcomes?

The CEPs presented were abbreviated versions of real plans, which we had collected through our previous research fieldwork. Participants worked in groups of four to five people and were asked to deliberate, reach an agreement and collectively draft a response to the three questions (60 min). The three key goals for the activity were: 1) to explore the conceptual framework as a tool for the planning and for implementing CEPs, 2) to clarify the different contexts for citizenship education in schools and 3) to promote the design of more coherent, comprehensive and integrated CEPs.

The group discussions were documented, and facilitators provided feedback to each group. Participants then analysed their own CEPs and conducted a similar exercise (30 min), which sparked engaging discussions about strategies for integrating the civic dimension into their teaching. For example, some groups suggested community service projects to link classroom learning with civic engagement. Participants' motivation surged upon discovering this model, which, though theoretical, was appreciated as a highly practical tool that could help them to envision and design more effective and holistic citizenship education. Realising that citizenship education transcends the classroom and involves the school as a whole, participants noted the importance of school leaders' active involvement and commitment.

The discussion emphasised not only the need to involve the entire school community in the task of educating for citizenship but also the importance of ensuring that this education achieves a suitable balance between the political or civic dimension and the civil or interpersonal dimension among students.

Dealing with controversial issues: Recognising fears, understanding responsibilities and exploring pedagogical approaches

A key pedagogical concern and objective of the citizenship education professional development programme is related to the challenging task of dealing with controversial issues in the classroom. Controversial issues are disputes or problems that lack consensus, thus dividing communities, forming identities and involving competing or conflicting explanations and interests (Crick, 1998; Oulton et al., 2004; Johnson & Johnson, 2009; Kerr et al., 2015). Controversial issues are questions that public policy has not been able to resolve, sparking debates that cannot be conclusively settled through evidence or rational bases (Hess, 2004; Oulton et al., 2004; Cooling, 2012).

Our team had previously explored how debating controversial issues is employed as a pedagogical strategy by teachers of citizenship education. Our findings indicated that, while teachers expressed positive attitudes towards it, they rarely employed this strategy in their classrooms (Cox et al., 2023). Indeed, literature from various contexts indicates that discussions of controversial issues are mostly avoided by teachers due to their fear of conflict, accusations of indoctrination, loss of classroom control or student disinterest or apathy (Hess, 2002; Knowles & McCafferty-Wright, 2015; Schuitema et al., 2018). Additional obstacles include time constraints and pressure to cover other curriculum content (Johnson & Johnson, 2009; Schuitema et al., 2018; EuroClio, 2020). Neutrality, along with a rather rigid approach to handling controversy, is often viewed by teachers as the most appropriate strategy in the classroom (Cox et al., 2023). This perspective contrasts with the more adaptive and flexible pedagogical strategies advocated by educational guidelines (Reinhardt, 2016; Pace, 2021; Cox et al., 2023). Worryingly, relevant literature highlighted that such rigid or neutral approaches may not only fall short of their intended goals but could also inadvertently reinforce existing biases within the classroom (Crick, 1998; Huddleston & Kerr, 2017; Pace, 2021).

One of the objectives of our in-service programmes was to address some of the obstacles identified in research. The exercises detailed below were specifically designed to encourage reflection and provide practical support for teachers in handling controversial issues in the classroom. We were particularly mindful of the heightened and complex challenges faced by teachers in Chile, who must implement citizenship education in the context of global political polarisation. To respond to these challenges, we developed a professional learning session aimed at encouraging and supporting participants to: 1) explore conceptual tools to distinguish between controversial and contentious issues, 2) reflect on the strategies teachers use to address controversial topics in the classroom and 3) recognise the importance and formative potential of addressing controversy in fostering citizenship skills and attitudes.

Firstly, we asked participants to reflect and share within a small group their own experiences and views regarding approaching controversy in the classroom and/or school (15–20 min). We proposed the following guiding questions:

- How have you addressed controversial issues in your classroom?
- What pedagogical strategies do you think educators can use when addressing controversy? Would you state any opinion about a controversial issue? What pedagogical strategies have you implemented to reflect on, address or manage your own personal beliefs, opinions or ideological positions when teaching or engaging with controversial or sensitive topics?
- What role do you play as educators in the face of different opinions in the classroom?

Following this initial discussion, participants read about two classroom discussions that we observed during our fieldwork (Box 9.1). They were asked to analyse these cases in small groups, determine whether each one presented a controversial issue and reflect on how they would handle the situation, documenting their responses (15–20 minutes). Afterwards, they shared their analysis and proposed pedagogical approaches with the larger group. The cases were as follows:

BOX 9.1 TWO CASES TO DISCUSS WHAT MAKES AN ISSUE 'CONTROVERSIAL'

What makes an issue controversial?

Case 1: In a class, students raise the issue of lynching or citizen detentions. One group of students argues that this practice (administering physical punishment to a suspected criminal) is justified and necessary since justice and security institutions do not function promptly and efficiently. This sparks a discussion among students.

Case 2: In a class, students raise the issue of the legalisation of marijuana. One group believes that it should be legalised and that it causes less harm than other legal drugs like alcohol and tobacco. Other students agreed with this view.

A controversial issue is a topic without a broad social consensus.

A contentious issue can be resolved through knowledge or shared values. In the latter, teachers are expected to take a clear stance aligned with democratic and human rights principles.

Mislabelling issues – treating controversial ones as settled or vice versa – can either lead to indoctrination or undermine the educator's civic role.

In the plenary session, participants generally agreed that the first case (lynching) was not a true controversial issue and required teacher intervention to affirm legal principles like due process. The second case (marijuana legalisation) was seen as a genuinely controversial topic in society. Most participants felt that teachers should remain neutral, though some noted that health evidence might warrant careful guidance.

Facilitators then helped clarify what defines a controversial issue – a topic without a broad social consensus – and distinguished it from a contentious issue, which can be resolved through knowledge or shared values. In the latter, teachers are expected to take a clear stance aligned with democratic and human rights principles. The session concluded by addressing concerns about indoctrination. Facilitators emphasised that mislabelling issues – treating controversial ones as settled or vice versa – can either lead to indoctrination or undermine the educator's civic role.

To support discussions during the in-service programme and also to enhance teachers' pedagogical competence, we developed and shared a framework and four key strategies for teaching controversial issues (see Table 9.1). The framework synthesises our review of research, academic discussions and pedagogical guidelines for teaching controversial issues (Cox et al., 2023). It demonstrates that there is no single strategy that works in every situation and that remaining neutral is not preferable, regardless of the classroom context. This discussion served as the final part of the activity (30 min), bringing together the participants' analyses and deepening their understanding of how to approach these issues in the classroom.

Our primary goal was to challenge the prevailing notion that teachers must remain neutral in all student discussions. In reality, active intervention is sometimes essential, especially in the context of citizenship education, where guiding discussions and addressing controversial issues can significantly enrich students' understanding and engagement, ultimately fostering the development of more balanced and informed perspectives.

TABLE 9.1 Strategies for teaching controversial issues in the classroom (Cox et al., 2023, p. 6), translated from Spanish by the authors

Classroom context	*Heterogeneous student group*	*Homogeneous (or uninterested) student group*
Students develop solid arguments	a. **Neutral moderator** (Teacher does not argue any position.)	b. **Declared commitment.** (Teacher argues for their own position.)
Students do not develop any argument, or their argumentation is insufficient	c. **Balanced approach** (Teacher argues for different positions in a balanced way.)	d. **Challenger of consensus** (Teacher challenges students' ideas or arguments.)

Exploring experiences and impact: Our approach to programme evaluation

To assess the impact of the professional learning programme, an evaluation was conducted to explore participants' experiences and their assessment of the activities and facilitators. Online feedback questionnaires, containing both closed and open-ended questions related to various aspects of course facilitation, were administered to all participants at the end of the programme. An assessment rubric was developed to gather information on the opinions and experiences of participants (teachers and school leaders), covering three main areas. First, participants were asked about their perceptions of general aspects of the course, including its methodology and format, on a five-point scale of agreement. Second, open-ended responses were collected regarding key learning outcomes that participants identified as a result of the training. Last, participants were invited to suggest areas they believed should be improved or changed. Participation in the evaluation was voluntary, and responses were anonymous. On average, 84% of participants completed the evaluation each year. Responses were systematically analysed and discussed among the facilitation team, allowing for both reflection and course adjustments. In addition, group meetings were held after the course to discuss participants' feedback and to assess the strengths and weaknesses of the programme from the facilitators' perspective.

Overall, throughout the three years in which the 'Tools for Understanding Citizenship Education' course was delivered, participants provided highly positive evaluations of their learning experiences. The content and pedagogical approaches used were particularly well rated. In the most recent edition (2022), 81% of participants agreed or strongly agreed that the course 'changed some of my knowledge or ideas about the topics covered'. Over 90% indicated that the course 'met my initial expectations' and expressed their willingness to recommend it to colleagues. These findings point to a sustained and significant interest in professional learning in the area of citizenship education.

However, a more critical analysis of the evaluation responses also revealed a number of challenges that participants faced, which could limit the long-term impact of the training. A prominent obstacle mentioned by some participants related to time constraints, particularly the difficulty of balancing participation in professional development activities with their existing teaching and administrative responsibilities. In addition, some participants pointed to institutional limitations within their schools, such as a lack of collective spaces for reflection on pedagogical practices or limited support from school leadership to integrate citizenship education into the broader curriculum.

Despite these barriers, some practical strategies were reported by participants and facilitators to address these challenges. For instance, some participants described forming peer support groups within their schools to adapt and implement the course materials collaboratively. Others suggested or initiated small-scale workshops with colleagues to share key ideas from the programme and to contextualise them for their school settings. From the facilitators' side, efforts were proposed to structure the course with asynchronous components and flexible deadlines, allowing participants to engage with the material at their own pace. These adaptations were beneficial for sustaining engagement and ensuring that the training was accessible despite institutional or time-related constraints.

Finally, participants frequently emphasised the need for future iterations of the course to place greater emphasis on the application of theoretical content to classroom practice. While the presentation of research findings was valued, there was a clear call to further bridge the gap between theoretical insights and actionable strategies. Responding to this feedback, future versions of the programme will prioritise the development of practice-oriented tools and collaborative design spaces to support teachers in implementing citizenship education more effectively in diverse school contexts.

Key learnings from the experience

When describing the most valuable learnings, participants frequently noted that the course allowed them to reflect on and incorporate new perspectives regarding civic and political education in their educational communities. The understanding of the teacher's and principal's role in developing and strengthening democratic values and in promoting civic and political participation was highlighted as a key learning outcome.

> This course contributed to my professional work, allowing a new perspective on a very transcendental topic.
>
> *(Participant, 2020)*

> The course as a whole favoured a personal and professional reflection on processes that occur daily in different areas and understanding that civic education is part of life.
>
> *(Participant, 2020)*

> The important role we have as a school in knowing and transmitting the relevant values for the formation of participative citizens.
>
> *(Participant, 2021)*

Participants also emphasised understanding civic education from a broader perspective and with due regard to the importance of balancing civic and civil knowledge and values in citizenship.

> The importance of developing civic and civil development in citizenship education in our educational communities. Continue to improve and use listening as one of the fundamental tools for our citizenship education plans.
>
> *(Participant, 2021)*

In addition, participants highlighted the acquisition of practical tools to develop CEPs, both at the school and in the classroom, as particularly beneficial.

> Techniques to work in school with the Citizenship Education Plan and also in the classroom.
>
> *(Participant, 2021)*

> Acquisition of new tools and knowledge to be used in my teaching practices.
>
> *(Participant, 2022)*

Finally, participants underscored their appreciation for the pedagogical and formative value of addressing current and controversial topics in the classroom within the framework of citizenship education. They emphasised their crucial role as educators in remaining informed about contemporary issues and the importance of fostering reflective discussions that engage and mobilise both students and the wider community in a meaningful manner.

> The importance and need for the active role of teachers in current issues.
>
> *(Participant, 2022)*

> I think the most important thing I learned from the course is the ability to generate instances of sensitivity to our reality through close experiences that encourage community reflection.
>
> *(Participant, 2021)*

> I really liked working on the topic of debate, discussion, and deliberation of ideas.
>
> *(Participant, 2022)*

Overall, many teachers noted that the professional development programme and, in particular, the practical tools motivated them to carry out more effective citizenship education. In the politically polarised and socially mobilised context of Chile, citizenship education faces high expectations. Participants valued the '3Cs' activity for its practical support in developing school-level citizenship education programmes. They also valued the opportunity to reflect on and collaborate with peers, acquiring pedagogical tools to navigate socio-political and cultural conflicts in the classroom. Engaging in discussions with colleagues about addressing controversies that spill over from the public sphere into the school while employing a protective and educational approach was particularly appreciated. However, a certain degree of frustration arose among some participants, as they perceived that the successful implementation of citizenship education would largely depend on school leadership's awareness and active involvement.

From the perspective of the facilitators, a key challenge and area for improvement was the need to better balance research/theoretical modules and practical modules. This requires a concerted effort to translate research findings into meaningful, practical teaching tools for educators. Integrating a facilitator with expertise in didactics or pedagogical tools into the team could help bridge the gap between theoretical insights and actionable strategies. Such an approach would significantly enhance the overall impact of the course, equipping teachers with the essential tools to effectively implement citizenship education in their classrooms.

Conclusion and recommendations

As Kerr (2015) highlights, citizenship education should be seamlessly integrated into the classroom through both curriculum and pedagogical practices. This integration should extend throughout the school by creating spaces for deliberation and participation while also engaging with the community through service activities and educational outings. Together, these interconnected areas and dimensions form a comprehensive model for planning and action in the field of citizenship education.

However, evidence on citizenship education in Chile reveals a concentration of responsibilities within the classroom and a lack of balance between the civic and civil dimensions of citizenship. Furthermore, preparation for democratic participation – both civil and political – lacks a crucial element when the experience of debate and controversy is excluded. Despite its significance, debate on controversial issues is not widely employed as a pedagogical tool (Johnson & Johnson, 2009; Huddleston & Kerr, 2017; Schuitema et al., 2018). In the current socio-political context, the risks and challenges facing the school system are diverse and impact both civic and civil dimensions, affecting the three identified areas of teaching and learning democratic citizenship.

To address these challenges, the teacher professional learning exercises presented here are aimed at equipping educators with practical tools for integrating various school areas in the task of educating for democratic citizenship. These exercises sought to provide resources that emphasise the importance of collaboration among different school sectors to foster an inclusive approach to citizenship education. Additionally, the programme aimed to create a reflective space to underscore the importance of this integration while providing educators with tools to develop specific pedagogical strategies for addressing controversial issues. This approach was designed to empower and motivate teachers to navigate complex topics with greater confidence, particularly in politically polarised contexts like the one recently observed in Chile. Box 9.2 shows a summary of the professional learning exercises.

BOX 9.2 TOOLS FOR UNDERSTANDING CITIZENSHIP EDUCATION: A BRIEF OVERVIEW OF A PROFESSIONAL LEARNING PROGRAMME

Tools for Understanding Citizenship Education

Aim: Teachers and school leaders explore the scope of citizenship education at the classroom and school level.

Objectives

- Deepen understanding of citizenship education, recognising its civic and civil dimensions.
- Share and analyse participants' experiences of citizenship education at their schools.
- Identify opportunities and areas for the development and planning of citizenship education at the school level.
- Recognise the importance of controversial issues for citizenship education.
- Share and reflect upon the challenges of dealing with controversy and build strategies to overcome them.

Activities for a two-hour workshop

1. *Welcome and introduction to citizenship education (30 min)*

Facilitators briefly present some theoretical foundations of citizenship education and its relationship with the historical, institutional and philosophical principles for democracy. Two core ideas about democracy are emphasised:

a. Democracy as an ideal, which is historically built and not the default. Therefore, we have to promote and believe in democracy to teach it.

b. Fundamental principles of democracy are deliberation and participation; the organisation of the state and the rule of law; and policy-making for dealing with public issues.

Facilitators subsequently introduce the concept of citizenship education, starting with its purposes in contemporary school curricula. Emphasis is placed on its focus on interpersonal relationships and school climate, on political and democratic institutions, on contemporary social issues and on the acquisition of political and civic knowledge as well as practical skills and attitudes (Cox et al., 2014; Cox & García, 2021).

Using the '3 Cs' framework (Figure 9.1), facilitators explain the scope of citizenship education: (1) teaching and learning contexts of citizenship education (the curriculum, school culture and the local community) and (2) the civic and civil dimension of citizenship experiences.

Following the presentation, participants reflect on the broad scope of citizenship education and the challenge of teaching the democratic ideal.

2. Group task: Citizenship education at the school level. Analysing citizenship education plans (30 min)

In groups of three to five, participants review the 'Contexts and Dimensions for the Teaching and Learning of Citizenship' model (Figure 9.1). Use the model as a framework to analyse, compare and discuss three CEPs (abbreviated versions of real school plans), considering the following questions:

- On which of the three areas – school culture, curriculum or local community – does each of the CEPs place the main emphasis?
- Which of the two dimensions – the civic or the civil dimensions of citizenship – prevails in each of these plans?
- Evaluate each of the plans in terms of their coherence and completeness. What is their main weakness? How could each plan be improved to strengthen students' learning experiences and outcomes?

3. Group task: Citizenship education in the classroom: Introducing and dealing with controversial issues (30 min)

Facilitators ask participants to reflect and share their own experiences and views regarding approaching controversy in the classroom and/or school in small groups (15–20 min):

- How have you addressed controversial issues in your classroom?
- What pedagogical strategies do you think educators can play when addressing controversy? Would you state any opinion about a controversial issue? What strategies have you taken regarding your own beliefs and opinions?

- What role do you play as educators in the face of different opinions in the classroom?

Participants then read about two classroom discussions. They discuss: 1) whether they present a controversial issue and 2) how they would handle the situation (15–20 minutes). Following these discussions, groups share their analysis and proposed pedagogical approaches with the larger group.

- Case 1: In a class, students raise the issue of lynching or citizen detentions. One group of students argues that this practice (administering physical punishment to a suspected criminal) is justified and necessary since justice and security institutions do not function promptly and efficiently. This sparks a discussion among students.
- Case 2: In a class, students raise the issue of the legalisation of marijuana. One group believes that it should be legalised and that it causes less harm than other legal drugs like alcohol and tobacco. Other students agreed with this view.

At the end of the session, facilitators share and explain in Table 9.1 (Strategies for teaching controversial issues in the classroom), emphasising that there is no single strategy that works in every situation when dealing with classroom discussions.

4. Final reflections and sharing experiences and ideas (20 min)

In the last part of the workshop, facilitators encourage participants to share their views and ideas regarding their own experiences and how their experiences might relate to the concepts and tools presented during the workshop.

Additional resources

Universidad Diego Portales – UDP & Instituto Unibanco (2023) *Liderança educacional para uma cidadania democrática.* Coleção Políticas Públicas em Educação – N° 6. Available at: https://observatoriodeeducacao.institutounibanco.org.br/cedoc/detalhe/lideranca-educacional-para-uma-cidadania-democratica-politicas-publicas-em-educacao-no-6,08fe1285-406d-48fc-966a-9984bdd12936

Kerr, D., Huddleston, T., Papamichael, E., Gannon, M., Djukanovic, B., & Garvín Fernández, R. (2015) *Living with Controversy. Teaching Controversial Issues Through Education for Democratic Citizenship and Human Rights. Training Pack for Teachers.* Council of Europe Publishing. Available at: https://edoc.coe.int/en/human-rights-democratic-citizenship-and-interculturalism/7738-teaching-controversial-issues.html

Huddleston, T. & Kerr, D. (2017) *Managing controversy: developing a strategy for handling controversy and teaching controversial issues in schools.* Strasbourg: Council of Europe Publishing.

The described professional learning sessions achieved high participation and satisfaction rates. Evaluations highlighted their effectiveness in transforming ideas and practices, meeting expectations and providing practical tools for citizenship education. Based on this experience, we, as facilitators of this programme, value the relationship between research and professional learning as an active and mutually beneficial partnership. Our involvement in the professional learning programme has fostered closer ties between education researchers and practitioners, promoting informed engagement and dialogue on both sides. However, we think that our work is still facing the challenge of addressing the gap between theory and practice, as well as between researchers and practitioners. From our experience, one of the most valuable aspects of our professional learning programme was the use of real situations to illustrate the main ideas that we wanted to communicate. If we had more time, we would try to discuss more practical examples and situations with teachers. We think that what made our examples so valuable was that teachers recognised them as situations that they could face in their own practice. In that regard, if anyone were to replicate these activities in different contexts, they would greatly benefit from building their own examples and situations based on local educators' experiences, rather than using some general examples that might not be meaningful for a particular group of practitioners.

In conclusion, we emphasise the need for pre-service and professional training initiatives and tools that support teachers and leaders in enhancing their competencies for the demanding task of educating new generations in the language and rules of democracy. Citizenship education plays a significant role in countering the anti-political tendencies of market culture and individualisation. Within this setting, school leadership can play a crucial role in addressing controversies, managing conflicts and promoting essential skills such as tolerance and peaceful conflict resolution (Journell, 2022; Cox et al., 2023). Only through a committed effort to integrate citizenship education within all aspects of the educational experience can we prepare future citizens to navigate and contribute positively to their democratic societies.

Acknowledgement

This chapter was carried out with the support of the ANID/FONDECYT Initiation Project No. 11221043; FONDECYT regular project No. 1221560; and the Ministry of Education of Chile (Mineduc), through the funding provided to the C-Líder (Center for Educational Leadership).

References

Bargsted, M., Somma, N. M., & Muñoz-Rojas, B. (2019). Participación electoral en Chile. Una aproximación de edad, período y cohorte. *Revista de ciencia política (Santiago)*, *39*(1), 75–98. https://doi.org/10.4067/S0718-090X2019000100075

Cooling, T. (2012). What is a controversial issue? Implications for the treatment of religious beliefs in education. *Journal of Beliefs & Values*, *33*(2), 169–181. https://doi.org/10.1080/13617672.2012.694060

Cox, C., Bascopé, M., Castillo, J. C., Miranda, D., & Bonhomme, M. (2014). *Educación ciudadana en América Latina: Prioridades de los currículos escolares*. https://unesdoc.unesco.org/ark:/48223/pf0000227975

Cox, C., & Castillo, J. C. (Eds.). (2015). *Aprendizaje de la ciudadanía: contextos, experiencias y resultados*. Santiago, Chile: Ediciones Universidad Católica de Chile.

Cox, C., & García, C. (2021). Chile's citizenship education curriculum: Priorities and silences through two decades. *Encounters in Theory and History of Education*, *22*. https://doi.org/10.24908/encounters.v22i0.14991

Cox, C., Jara Ibarra, C., & Sánchez Bachmann, M. (2022). Citizenship education in Chile: Curricular orientations and teachers' beliefs in a context of political crisis and social mobilization. *The Curriculum Journal*, curj.164. https://doi.org/10.1002/curj.164

Cox, C., Jara Ibarra, C., Sánchez Bachmann, M., & Peña Fredes, J. (2023). Asuntos controversiales en la formación para la ciudadanía: criterios y prácticas docentes en la educación media de Chile. *Pensamiento Educativo: Revista de Investigación Educacional Latinoamericana*, *60*(2). https://doi.org/10.7764/PEL.60.2.2023.3

Cox, P., & Corvalán, A. (2015). Participación y desigualdad electoral en Chile. In C. Cox, & J. C. Castillo (Eds.), *Aprendizaje de la ciudadanía: contextos, experiencias y resultados* (pp. 175–206). Ediciones Universidad Católica de Chile. Santiago de Chile.

Crick, B. (Chairman of the advisory group). (1998). *Final report of the Advisory Group on citizenship: Education for citizenship and the teaching of democracy in schools*. London: Qualifications and Curriculum Authority. https://www.teachingcitizenship.org.uk/sites/teachingcitizenship.org.uk/files/6123_crick_report_1998_0.pdf

Donoso, S., & Von Bulow, M. (Eds.). (2017). *Social movements in Chile: Organization, trajectories, and political consequences*. Palgrave Macmillan. https://doi.org/10.1057/978-1-137-60013-4

EuroClio. (2020). *Learning to disagree*. European Commission. https://www.euroclio.eu/wp-content/uploads/2020/02/Learning-to-Disagree-Teachers-Guide-2020.pdf

Hess, D. E. (2002). Discussing controversial public issues in secondary social studies classrooms: Learning from skilled teachers. *Theory & Research in Social Education*, *30*(1), 10–41. https://doi.org/10.1080/00933104.2002.10473177

Hess, D. E. (2004). Controversies about controversial issues in democratic education. *Political Science and Politics*, *37*(2), 257–261. https://doi.org/10.1017/S1049096504004196

Huddleston, T., & Kerr, D. (2017). *Managing controversy: Developing a strategy for handling controversy and teaching controversial issues in schools*. Strasbourg: Council of Europe Publishing.

Jara Ibarra, C. (2019). *(Des)movilización de la sociedad civil chilena: post-trauma, gobernabilidad y neoliberalismo (1990–2010)*. Santiago de Chile: Ariadna Ediciones. https://www.doabooks.org/doab?func=fulltext&uiLanguage=en&rid=43270 (Accessed: 12 January 2022).

Jara Ibarra, C., Sánchez Bachmann, M., & Cox, C. (2019). Liderazgo educativo y formación ciudadana: visión y prácticas de los actores. *Calidad en la Educación*, (51), 350. https://doi.org/10.31619/caledu.n51.687

Jara Ibarra, C., Sánchez Bachmann, M., & Cox, C. (2023). Liderazgo Educativo y Educación Ciudadana: Evidencia del Caso Chileno. *REICE: Revista Iberoamericana sobre Calidad, Eficacia y Cambio en Educación*, *21*(3), 5–22. https://doi.org/10.15366/reice2023.21.3.001

Jara Ibarra, C., Sánchez Bachmann, M., Cox, C., & Montecinos, M. J. (2021). Socialización política y formación ciudadana en el contexto escolar chileno: un análisis desde el enfoque de género. *Calidad en la Educación*, (54), 73–106. https://doi.org/10.31619/caledu.n54.932

Johnson, D. W., & Johnson, R. T. (2009). Energizing learning: The instructional power of conflict. *Educational Researcher*, *38*(1), 37–51. https://doi.org/10.3102/0013189X08330540

Journell, W. (2022). Classroom controversy in the midst of political polarization: The essential role of school administrators. *NASSP Bulletin*, *106*(2), 133–153. https://doi.org/10.1177/01926365221100589

Kaltwasser, C. R., & Van Hauwaert, S. M. (2020). The populist citizen: Empirical evidence from Europe and Latin America. *European Political Science Review*, *12*(1), 1–18.

Kerr, D. (2015). Ciudadanía a nivel nacional, regional e internacional: una revisión de enfoques, investigaciones y debates. In C. Cox, & J. C. Castillo (Eds.), *Aprendizaje de la ciudadanía: Contextos, experiencias y resultados* (pp. 111–141). Santiago, Chile: Ediciones Universidad Católica de Chile.

Kerr, D., Huddleston, T., Papamichael, E., Gannon, M., Djukanovic, B., & Garvín Fernández, R. (2015). *Living with controversy: Teaching controversial issues through education for democratic citizenship and human rights: Training pack for teachers*. Council of Europe Publishing. https://edoc.coe.int/en/human-rights-democratic-citizenship-and-interculturalism/7738-teaching-controversial-issues.html

Knowles, R. T., & McCafferty-Wright, J. (2015). Connecting an open classroom climate to social movement citizenship: A study of 8th graders in Europe using IEA ICCS data. *The Journal of Social Studies Research*, *39*(4), 255–269. https://doi.org/10.1016/j.jssr.2015.03.002

Levin, S. A., Milner, H. V., & Perrings, C. (2021). The dynamics of political polarization. *Proceedings of the National Academy of Sciences*, *118*(50), e2116950118. https://doi.org/10.1073/pnas.2116950118

Mignozzetti, U., & Spektor, M. (2019). Brazil: When political oligarchies limit polarization but fuel populism. In T. Carothers, & A. O'Donohue (Eds.), *Democracies divided: The global challenge of political polarization* (pp. 228–254). Washington: Brookings Institution Press. https://muse.jhu.edu/pub/11/edited_volume/book/67890 (Accessed: 1 August 2023).

Ministerio de Educación de Chile. (2016). *Crea el plan de formación ciudadana para los establecimientos educacionales reconocidos por el Estado*. https://bcn.cl/2f702

Oulton, C., Day, V., Dillon, J., & Grace, M. (2004). Controversial issues: Teachers' attitudes and practices in the context of citizenship education. *Oxford Review of Education*, *30*(4), 489–507.

Pace, J. L. (2021). How can educators prepare for teaching controversial issues? cross-national lessons. *Social Education*, (85), 228–233.

Peña, J., & Sémbler, M. (2019). Movilizaciones estudiantiles y liderazgo directivo: un estudio exploratorio en tres liceos de la Región Metropolitana. *Calidad en la Educación*, (51), 315. https://doi.org/10.31619/caledu.n51.488

Reinhardt, S. (2016). The Beutelsbach consensus. *JSSE – Journal of Social Science Education*, 11–13, 128 kB. https://doi.org/10.4119/UNIBI/JSSE-V15-I2-1523

Schuitema, J., Radstake, H., van de Pol, J., & Veugelers, W. (2018). Guiding classroom discussions for democratic citizenship education. *Educational Studies*, *44*(4), 377–407. https://doi.org/10.1080/03055698.2017.1373629

Schulz, W., Fraillon, J., Losito, B., Agrusti, G., Ainley, J., Damiani, V., & Friedman, T. (2023). *IEA international civic and citizenship education study 2022 assessment framework*. Cham: Springer International Publishing. https://doi.org/10.1007/978-3-031-20113-4

UNDP. (2018). *Estudio sobre la puesta en marcha del Plan de Formación Ciudadana*. Santiago de Chile: United Nation Development Program (UNDP). http://www.ciudadaniayescuela.cl/wp-content/uploads/2018/04/Estudio-puesta-en-marcha-del-Plan-de-Formaci%C3%B3n-Ciudadana.pdf

UNESCO. (2017). *La Formación Inicial Docente en Educación para la Ciudadanía en América Latina: Análisis comparado de seis casos nacionales*. http://bibliotecadigital.mineduc.cl//handle/20.500.12365/2175 (Accessed: 13 October 2023).

Universidad Diego Portales – UDP, & Instituto Unibanco. (2023). *Liderança educacional para uma cidadania democrática. Coleção Políticas Públicas em Educação – N° 6*. https://observatoriodeeducacao.institutounibanco.org.br/cedoc/detalhe/lideranca-educacional-para-uma-cidadania-democratica-politicas-publicas-em-educacao-no-6,08fe1285-406d-48fc-966a-9984bdd12936

Villalobos, C., Peña, J., Aguirre, E., & Guerrero, M. (2017). Liderazgo escolar y conflictos socioeducativos. Un estudio exploratorio en liceos públicos chilenos. *Calidad en la educación*, (47), 81–111. https://doi.org/10.4067/S0718-45652017000200081

Zúñiga, C. G., Ojeda, P., Neira, P., Cortés, T., & Morel, M. J. (2020). Entre la imposición y la necesidad: implementación del Plan de Formación Ciudadana en escuelas chilenas. *Calidad en la Educación*, (52), 135. https://doi.org/10.31619/caledu.n52.767

PART THREE

Review of learning and charting pathways for the future

10

TRANSFORMATIVE PROFESSIONAL LEARNING IN ACTION

Embracing complexity and critical co-inquiry for diversity, equity and democracy

Gerry Mac Ruairc, María Jesús Rodríguez-Entrena, and Manuela Heinz

Reframing leadership learning: Calling out complexities in difficult times

Our primary motivation for compiling this edited collection was our desire (and perceived pressing need) to encourage and support school leaders to engage in more critical conversations with other leaders and teachers on core issues related to the increasing diversity in schools. We hoped that a deeper understanding of diversity would lead to the development of more widely appreciated and deliberate, equitable responses drawing on democratic principles in school policy and action. At the time of developing the proposal for our 'Big Ideas for Better Schools' (BIBS)[1] project, we were aware that focusing on the three complex and interconnected concepts of diversity, equity and democracy was a major and ambitious task. However, we also understood the power, and indeed the necessity, of keeping interrelatedness and interdependencies between the three concepts alive in our conversations.

Diversity has become a highly contested terrain – sometimes, there is a view that the more it is 'seen', the more of it there is to see. It is like a gift that keeps giving. And that is not always viewed positively. In our work, as teacher educators and leadership professional learning providers, we have become keenly aware of a growing discomfort among some leaders in engaging with some of these ideas in a proactive way. In some cases, it was clear from school leaders that opting for surface-type approaches, deployed to 'gloss over' some of the more controversial and challenging aspects of diversity, was part of a survival strategy. A more superficial and compliance-oriented approach is often taken to keep policy developments in schools moving forward without getting bogged down in some of the more contested

DOI: 10.4324/9781032629292-13

issues. Even at a time when resources are (at least in some contexts) plentiful, overseeing a distribution of these resources on the basis of equity, while drawing on democratic principles, can present many challenges for school leadership. A deeper exploration of how diversity and equity manifest (or not) in schools, and how they are understood among staff and students, is often avoided, even though such understanding is an essential prerequisite to ensuring school-wide effective action.

As outlined in Chapter 3, the new world order we now face, where views on diversity and policies that support diversity and equity are challenged by increasingly more vocal individuals and groups, creates a very different dynamic for leaders in schools. In this collection, we argue against this current anti-DEI drive by employing the concept of intersectionality – and of the multiplicities of identities – as a way of arguing for school leadership that is much more knowledgeable with respect to diversity and equity and, in turn, can better support all children and young people to reach their full potential. Current trends are signalling a turning away from diversity – as if this were possible – to a kind of blurring of what it is that makes each person unique by denying the very core of their individuality. What is more disturbing in this turn is the overt denial, by some powerful voices, of inequalities and inequities that have been identified and deliberated on for decades. What we are now seeing are systems that deliberately set out not to support those who are not as equally positioned as the most advantaged in society to avail of the benefits that education generally offers. In the past, there may have been a lack of awareness of the diversity of learners in our schools. Attendance at school was not the norm. Many groups self-selected out of school for a variety of reasons. Ideas about diversity were neither called out nor well understood. Responses to diversity were not developed at any systemic level. However, over time, and as differential outcomes for certain groups in education were identified, responses were put in place. Head Start, in the United States, is a good example of what became a widely used intervention internationally in support of disadvantaged groups (Vinovskis, 1993). These interventions and programmes did not always achieve all they set out to achieve, but they were trying to effect change, not denying the need for it.

As we stand at the moment, we know so much more about diversity. We have much stronger knowledge within educational research and scholarship to guide and shape policy and practice. At a time when we have all this knowledge, some jurisdictions are choosing to shut it down, ignore, or worse, deny what we know and engage in practices that are harmful. The current trend is not just going back; it is deliberately and knowingly going the wrong way. As educators, we cannot follow this misdirection. In this book, we therefore call for a renewed and deeper commitment to understanding and appreciating the complexities of diversity, equity and democracy. We advocate for an alternative approach – one that starts with embracing a more intentional and sustained engagement with the substance of diversity so that the essence of who we are as individuals can be genuinely recognised, nurtured and supported within our schools.

We used the ideas of 'threshold concepts' (Meyer & Land, 2005), 'troublesome knowledge' (Perkins, 1999) and the 'pedagogy of discomfort' (Boler, 1999) as the main frameworks within which to position and consider each of the three interconnected concepts. The purpose of any consideration of diversity, equity and democracy is essentially transformative, particularly when they are so central to informing and framing the work of schools and school leaders. While this is important for all schools, it has a particular resonance for schools located in more marginalised and disadvantaged communities. It can be reasonably said that the more one moves towards the margins, the more necessary it is to problematise and act *on* and *with* these ideas.

Positioning these concepts as troublesome knowledge provides a legitimate basis for calling out their complexity from the outset (Poekert & King, 2023). Simple solutions and 'one size fits all' neatly arranged lists should not be expected here, and this needs to be signalled at the outset. Sometimes in professional learning, this 'calling out' does not happen – efforts are often made to simplify issues, to make things real-life, ready-made and practical at the expense of the conceptual and critical (Salo et al., 2024; Jara Ibarra et al., 2026). This is not what is required here. These 'big issues' require a rethinking of leadership professional learning broadly in line with recent thinking on more sustained, development-oriented, dynamic and open-ended approaches to research and professional learning (Salo et al., 2024; King, 2024). As outlined in (Nihill and Mac Ruairc, 2026), the model developed for use in the Irish context aligns with this type of approach, placing the leader as a person and the leader as a professional at the core of the design of professional learning activities that centre ongoing, sustained dialogic processes rooted in critical inquiry, reflection and ethical responsibility.

Language matters: Making concepts and terminology explicit

Concepts like diversity, equity and democracy are often contested and contextual (Banks, 2015; Crenshaw, 1991). In addition to this, it is the language that describes diversity, in particular, and that functions to call out different identities (Ahmed, 2012; Semião et al., 2023) that can become an impediment to good-quality, collaborative enquiry. In our initial discussions with university colleagues and school leaders, this difficulty with language and terminology was frequently raised. Leaders identified a lack of confidence and an ontological insecurity among themselves and among teachers (Gordon et al., 2021) in relation to how to describe, and by extension, how to discuss, many diversity issues. University colleagues were unsure how discussions about diversity were framed in schools and in classrooms. The pronoun battle in relation to the trans community (MacKinnon, 2014; Zimman, 2017) has become the most recent signifier of some of these language/terminology interfaces, and this controversy has served as a symbol for a broader sense that terminology has gotten so contested that it might be easier to say nothing at all. Changes to language and discourse, often following a period of significant review and consideration within minority groups themselves, do not resonate in the same way outside the group; the use of the word queer, for example, long reclaimed by the gay community (Jagose, 1996; Sedgwick, 2008), continues to be viewed as pejorative by many. The ongoing extensions of the original acronym LGBT to the current LGBTQIA+ have also caused confusion (Thelwall et al., 2022) and, at times, a diminishing appreciation of what the acronym signifies, as sometimes evident in offhand 'whatever the letters are now' statements.

Exploring terminology and the conceptual underpinnings of the areas of focus was part of this project from the outset. Unless the complexity of the concepts was explicated, providing correct terminology would only address the surface level (Freire, 1970). In many ways, explicating concepts and their evolving complexity in professional learning activities with leaders and teachers provides the rationale for why a consideration of terminology is so necessary, and why, as thinking develops and becomes more refined, terminology must alter. Working with a 'rights of the learner' approach (Kalinec-Craig, 2017), especially in the Irish case study (see Heinz et al., 2026), provided a helpful scaffold to address both the complexities of concepts and difficulty with terminology together. Foregrounding the right to make mistakes with words and concepts and the right to reach new and emerging understandings – while at the same time often posing further questions – allowed conversations to happen in more open and authentically educative ways (Biesta, 2010; Mezirow, 2000).

A shared intellectual journey: Theory–practice interdependence, equal status and common goals

Engaging school leaders and teachers with this work was a key concern from the outset. There is a considerable body of scholarship on teachers' resistance to change, particularly when it involves more disruptive types of learning (Sherman & Teemant, 2021). Research shows that due to the increasing complexity of leadership, specialised training and capacity development are required (Jara et al., 2024). Two main engagement factors were identifiable from our work with schools: 1) the importance of a meaningful entry point into the discussion, that is, the hook, and 2) the shared intellectual journey as an effective methodology.

The choice of relevant and context-specific *hooks* – or entry points – played a key role in initiating professional dialogue. We took into account previous research, which indicates that principals value training primarily as a useful tool to address and solve everyday challenges (Jara et al., 2024). In Ireland, the participating school was a relatively new school and was developing its mission statement based on the exact areas of the project. The fit was excellent, and this resulted in 'buy-in' from the school leadership team. In the case of Chile, Norway and Spain, changes in educational policies on democracy and citizenship (CEPs in Chile, a new democratic curriculum in Norway and a new organic law and a new subject in Spain) connected the projects' aims with school leaders' interests. Using the policy change as a starting point helped to spark engagement in 'big issue conversations' among teachers and school leaders because the invitation was perceived as relevant. Faced with policy changes, both school leaders and teachers were motivated to deepen their understanding of its implications, to inform their decisions and support implementation. In Poland, the recent dismantling of some of the democratic structures long fought for and developed following *perestroika* provided a strong rationale for critical engagement with each of the topics.

From the beginning, we envisaged the project as a *shared intellectual journey*. Traditional academic language, typical of research and lecture-based teaching, was not compatible with this vision. The primary objective was to interrogate and transform professional practice, which required exploring alternative ways of exploring theory with those engaged in practical settings. It was necessary to establish the *interdependence* between theory and practice and the value of dialogue between school and university personnel, emphasising the shared goal of professional learning and continuous improvement. On reflection, this was one of the key concerns for academic partners. Lecture-based teaching and any form of 'expert positioning' were deliberately avoided. Instead, the professional learning programmes were grounded in the principle of equal status and mutual recognition of diverse, overlapping and distinct – yet equally valuable and interdependent – forms of expertise. There was no need to avoid the conceptual but rather to find a way of presenting it in ways that were accessible but also provocative. The participating leaders and teachers were very aware and interested in the complexity of the ideas. Once we had found a way in, they were off, and the unravelling of complexity started. For example, in Ireland, the idea of intersectionality generated emotional engagement, sparking learning and rethinking (Zembylas, 2015). The concept powerfully captured the professional interest and curiosity of the participants, whose perceptions shifted as they recognised the dangers of essentialising students or of unintentionally using a single-axis framework approach to supporting them.

Context and concepts matter: One size does *not* fit all

When it comes to addressing controversial issues that generate uncertainty in schools, there is often a call for 'recipes' that can help facilitate the fulfilment of either internal or external mandates. This recipe-type approach can provide cover to the school, as they can be 'seen' to be engaging with areas such as diversity, equity or democracy. As we have argued, these surface-type approaches do little to inform or transform practice. As context is a key factor in engaging with this type of work, it is essential to take it into consideration in each school. It is equally vital to understand context as a system that operates with varying degrees of unpredictability, rarely following any degree of linearity (Rönnström & Skott, 2019). Consequently, it is not feasible to apply a homogeneous or universal approach – 'one size fits all' directives are simply too crude to elicit authentic transformative outcomes. There are, however, patterns of practices that can transfer effectively between contexts, and schools can undoubtedly learn from each other.

The case studies presented in this book have adapted a number of models and concepts and explicated ways in which they can be used to engage teachers in thinking and discussions which are transformative. The methodological frameworks used to design professional learning programmes included collaborative action research, responsive and proactive action research, critical inquiry, the collaborative professional inquiry model and the '3Cs' model (classroom, school–community). All of them have a transformative intentionality in common; that is, they are linked to a commitment to change and improvement of professional practice and to making schools more democratic and inclusive spaces (although it must also be noted that intentionality *alone* does, of course, not produce change). The professional learning experiences presented have also underlined the importance of reciprocal learning and of creating space and time for deeper and sustained interaction. In the Spanish case study, the use of the 'Framework of Competences for Democratic Culture' developed by the Council of Europe (2018) provided a solid theoretical foundation for analysing the specific reality of democratic practices within the school (Entrena-Rodrígues et al., 2026). In Norway, teachers explored the differences between democracy as a way of living and democracy as a way of governing, and among education *about*, *for* and *through* democracy (Stray, 2014; Ottesen et al., 2026). Dialogic explorations of theories and practice *together*, such as in these cases, helped to disrupt hierarchical knowledge structures (Cochran-Smith & Lytle, 1999) and allowed participants to focus on collective knowledge creation (Freire, 1970).

Meaningful collaboration and leading by example: Valuing diverse forms of knowledge

The professional learning programmes presented in this collection were purposefully and collaboratively designed and implemented – school leaders, teachers and teacher educators worked together to enhance understanding of both theoretical frameworks and practical approaches. Professional collaboration is widely recognised as a fundamental factor contributing to effectiveness and overall success (Hargreaves & O'Connor, 2017; OECD, 2014). It is not possible to advance the transformation of school cultures without generating structured spaces for collaboration, where experiences can be shared, pedagogical perspectives can be refined, and future scenarios can be collectively designed. School leaders occupy a central role in strengthening professional collaboration and capacity (Hargreaves & Fullan, 2012; Hitt & Tucker, 2016; Leithwood et al., 2020), as they not only facilitate structural conditions for learning but also act as catalysts for the cultural and pedagogical change required to foster more inclusive and participatory school environments.

Studies on leadership with strong roots in social justice perspectives have shaped an understanding of leadership that seeks to work towards transformative outcomes for all (Leithwood, 2021; Shields, 2022). During the BIBS project, it became clear that having the leader on board is central to engaging with these complex ideas. If school leaders are to engage teachers in conversations that challenge status quo thinking, and if they are to lead schools that support better teacher and student learning (MacKenzie et al., 2023; Shields & Hesbol, 2020), they need to be drivers and agents of the professional learning actions themselves. Our engagement in the project highlighted the critical role of school leaders in actively challenging inequitable school cultures and modelling transformative thinking and action through their example (Shields & Hesbol, 2020).

However, the challenge is not only to promote collaborative learning but also to do it well and sustain it because not all forms of collaboration lead to positive results. To design and implement transformative collaborative professional learning programmes in schools, it is essential to examine what forms of collaboration work best and under which conditions. Based on the experiences presented in this book, we have identified three key factors that contributed to impactful professional learning.

The first key factor was *starting from the data generated in schools*. Sharing data collected through surveys which investigated teachers' and students' understandings, experiences, concerns and aspirations around the three thematic areas – diversity, equity and democracy – helped to anchor the professional learning programmes in the concrete realities of each school. In particular, the incorporation of the students' vision emphasised the value of including the student voice in improvement processes. It activated interest and a cycle of inquiry into how students understood, perceived and lived the principles of diversity, equity and democracy in their schools. Beyond acknowledging the importance of a bottom-up design that emerged from the needs and priorities of each school, this approach fostered greater interest in and ownership of the proposal. Context-specific data, therefore, provided a common ground for reflection and contextualised action, making the inquiry process more meaningful. There was also evidence of instances when these data directly impacted the identification of areas for improvement and action. The 'data-informed' approach, thus, helped to generate collective commitment and shaped reflection on and for improvement of pedagogical practices (Datnow & Park, 2015).

A second factor promoting collaborative learning, related to the *ethics and values* on which the experience was based. The professional learning programmes presented in this collection were based on democratic principles: the principle of social justice, moral purpose and the promotion of culturally responsible educational practices. The equity, diversity and inclusion (EDI) approach underpinned the professional learning experiences as a measure to achieve equity and move towards fostering meaningful inclusion and change across the school contexts (Kelly et al., 2022). Reflection on the reality of schools was necessary to understand and address the root causes of inequality, including the very structures, institutions and processes that shape and sustain inequalities (MacKenzie et al., 2023).

Finally, a third factor was the nurturing of *mutual trust* (social capital) (Hargreaves & Fullan, 2012), *respect and appreciation* of the experiences and opinions of all involved (teacher educators, teachers and school leaders) through equal partnership. Relational trust grew as participants listened to one another and showed personal regard for each other's perspectives, competencies and integrity (Hargreaves & O'Connor, 2017). Collaboration was based on equality, and equal importance was afforded to the practical experience of the leaders and teachers and the theoretical contributions from university personnel. Respect, mutual recognition and genuine interest in all points of view contributed significantly to the creation of 'collaborative professionalism' and authentically shared – and expanded – visions for change (Hargreaves & O'Connor, 2018) with school leaders and teachers as key agents. The experiences presented in this collection have demonstrated that equity in schools can be strengthened through collaborative professional learning and authentic equity literacy (Ainscow, 2020).

Looking forward: Sustaining commitment to critical professional learning

As has been highlighted throughout the chapters of this collection, schools face significant challenges in the current increasingly unstable political and social context, which is marked by increasing polarisation and intolerance towards diversity. International education policies (OECD, 2024; UNESCO, 2016, 2017) and research on school leadership have echoed the need to teach values of democratic citizenship to prepare students to live in a diverse, complex and uncertain society. The vision of school success and leadership has expanded beyond academic performance, standards and international test scores, with a stronger focus on the development of personal, social and economic capabilities, and the promotion of positive values such as justice, equity and active citizenship (Day et al., 2016). In turn, schools and the work of school leaders are becoming increasingly complex, experiencing multiple tensions and an overload threat (Rönnström & Skott, 2019; Day et al., 2016). This collection underscores the critical need to cultivate collaborative professional learning experiences in schools that strengthen the capacity of teachers to respond to these challenges. We have argued – and demonstrated – that this work demands a deepening of school leaders' and teachers' own epistemological understandings so that they are better prepared to nurture and extend their students' knowledge, insight and experiences on and for diversity, equity and democracy. However, this endeavour faces challenges – many of which we have documented throughout our work.

One of the first challenges is to find ways to awaken interest in professional learning around 'big issues', in a context where both teachers and leaders are immersed in a maelstrom of urgent demands (Stray, 2014) and controversy (Cox et al., 2023). In the case studies presented, the starting points have been diverse. However, the initial impetus to activate processes of reflection and improvement and initiate 'the disruption of the system' in schools came from external stimuli, such as the invitation to participate in a European project, collaboration in research or the implementation of a legislative change in the country. These circumstances were configured as valuable opportunities to establish collaborative work dynamics between universities and schools, aimed at creating spaces to rethink educational practice, as well as to plan and implement improvement scenarios. Once the collaboration was established, it was essential to develop the process from a *bottom-up* approach, based on the contextualised analysis of the reality of each centre, and linked to its specific concerns and interests around the major threshold concepts of *diversity, equity and democracy*.

Another challenge identified lies in establishing the necessary conditions so that the attempts at improvement can be sustained over time. Reflection on leadership and sustainability of change is a long-standing concern (Fullan, 2004, 2021). The ability of schools to improve and sustain that improvement over time is closely linked to the presence of leadership capable of generating an improvement-oriented culture. This was precisely the founding intention of the European BIBS project: to contribute to empowering leaders and teachers to make a transformative change in schools towards more democratic and equitable spaces. Through the deep and contextualised understanding of the so-called big issues, the project sought to generate a significant transformation in professional practices, both at institutional levels and in classrooms.

The pivotal role of leadership in strengthening teachers' professional capacity (Day et al., 2016; Hitt & Tucker, 2016; Leithwood et al., 2020) has been clearly established throughout the book. The kind of 'leadership we need' to create the conditions in which more proactive and transformative practices can be developed is leadership guided by values – moral and ethical purpose – and leadership aimed at developing people through the nurturing of individual and group capacities. It is leadership that builds collaborative organisational learning cultures and that awakens the commitment of teachers, students and the community to the need for improvement (Day et al., 2016; Hallinger & Heck, 2010). Last but not least, leadership needs to identify specific needs and apply context-sensitive strategies that are integrated into the school culture itself (Day et al., 2016) and that seek to work towards transformative outcomes for all (Leithwood, 2021; Shields, 2022).

The BIBS project highlighted the critical role of leaders in placing conversations about the 'big issues' at the heart of schoolwork while also promoting quality professional learning opportunities to better prepare teachers to engage in much more deliberative and reflective ways with these areas so that they can better *see* and *know* the students whose learning they need to inspire. The professional learning programmes were, first and foremost, designed to create new spaces for thinking and dialogue. Within these spaces – and grounded in a culture that equitably values the knowledge, experience and perspectives of all participants – school leaders, teachers and teacher educators identified conceptual tensions, worked together to build shared meanings around 'threshold concepts' and co-created new understanding.

Although profound change requires time, dialogue and perseverance, we have seen that it is possible to move towards a more equitable and democratic school if the right conditions for transformative professional learning are cultivated. Professional learning around diversity, equity and democracy is complex. It requires much more than the technical implementation of policies, pedagogical approaches or curricular reforms. It requires a deep commitment to the values that underpin education and to a school's mission. It requires professional learning that generates 'discomfort', challenges established practices that reproduce inequality and encourages critical and ethical thinking.

Acknowledgement

The Erasmus+-funded BIBS project was funded by Léargas (Ireland) 2019-1-IE01-KA201-051528

Note

1 For more information about the BIBS project, see Heinz et al., 2026. A more detailed conceptualisation of the three key concepts explored in the project – diversity, equity and democracy – is provided in Mac Ruairc et al., 2026.

References

Ahmed, S. (2012). *On being included: Racism and diversity in institutional life*. Duke University Press.
Ainscow, M. (2020). Promoting inclusion and equity in education: Lesson from international experiences. *Nordic Journal of Studies in Educational Policy*, *6*(1), 7–16.
Banks, J. A. (2015). *Cultural diversity and education: Foundations, curriculum, and teaching* (6th ed.). Routledge.
Biesta, G. (2010). *Good education in an age of measurement: Ethics, politics, democracy*. Routledge.
Boler, M. (1999). *Feeling power: Emotions and education*. Routledge.
Cochran-Smith, M., & Lytle, S. (1999). Relationships of knowledge and practice: Teacher learning in communities. *Review of Research in Education*, *24*, 249–305.
Council of Europe. (2018). *Reference framework of competences for democratic culture*. Council of Europe. Vol. 1. Context, concepts and model. Author. https://rm.coe.int/prems-008318-gbr-2508-reference-framework-ofcompetences-vol-1-8573-co/16807bc66c
Cox, C., Jara Ibarra, C., Sánchez Bachmann, M., & Peña Fredes, J. (2023). Asuntos controversiales en la formación para la ciudadanía: Criterios y prácticas docentes en la educación media de Chile. *Pensamiento Educativo: Revista de Investigación Educacional Latinoamericana*, *60*(2). https://doi.org/10.7764/PEL.60.2.2023.3
Crenshaw, K. (1991). Mapping the margins: Intersectionality, identity politics, and violence against women of color. *Stanford Law Review*, *43*(6), 1241–1299.
Datnow, A., & Park, V. (2015). Data use for equity. *Educational Leadership*, *72*(5), 49–54.
Day, C., Gu, Q., & Sammons, P. (2016). The impact of leadership on student outcomes: How successful school leaders use transformational and instructional strategies to make a difference. *Educational Administration Quarterly*, *52*(2), 221–258.
Freire, P. (1970). *Pedagogy of the oppressed*. Continuum.
Fullan, M. (2004). *System thinkers in action: Innovation*. DfES with NCSL.
Fullan, M. (2021). *Los impulsores correctos para el éxito de todo el sistema*. Centre for Strategic Education. https://michaelfullan.ca/wp-content/uploads/2021/03/21_Right-Drivers-Spanish-comp.pdf
Gordon, S. R., Yough, M., Finney-Miller, E. A., Mathew, S., Haken-Hughes, A., & Ariati, J. (2021). Faculty perceptions of teaching diversity: Definitions, benefits, drawbacks, and barriers. *Current Psychology*, 1–10.
Hallinger, P., & Heck, R. H. (2010). Collaborative leadership and school improvement: Understanding the impact on school capacity and student learning. *School Leadership and Management*, *30*(20), 95–110.
Hargreaves, A., & Fullan, M. (2012). *Professional capital: Transforming teaching in every school*. Teachers College Press.
Hargreaves, A., & O'Connor, M. T. (2017). Cultures of professional collaboration: Their origins and opponents. *Journal of Professional Capital and Community*, *2*(2), 74–85. https://doi.org/10.1108/JPCC-02-2017-0004
Hargreaves, A., & O'Connor, M. T. (2018). *Collaborative professionalism*. Thousand Oaks: Corwin Press.
Heinz, M., Mac Ruairc, G., & Rodríguez-Entrena, M. J. (2026). Big ideas for better schools: A transnational professional learning project. In M. Heinz, M. J. Rodríguez-Entrena, & G. Mac Ruairc (Eds.), *Professional learning for diversity, equity and democracy: Big ideas for better schools* (pp. 17–23). Routledge.
Heinz, M., Graham, C., O Neachtain, A, Mac Ruairc, G., Gartland, S, & Whyte, C. (2026). Professional learning with school leaders on diversity, equity and inclusion in Ireland: Deepening understanding and commitment through safe and honest 'big issue' conversations. In M. Heinz, M. J. Rodríguez-Entrena, & G. Mac Ruairc

(Eds.), *Professional learning for diversity, equity and democracy: Big ideas for better schools* (pp. 65–86). London: Routledge.
Hitt, D., & Tucker, P. (2016). Systematic review of key leader practices found to influence student achievement: A unified framework. *Review of Educational Research, 86*(2), 531–569.
Jagose, A. (1996). *Queer theory: An introduction.* NYU Press.
Jara, C., Peña, J., & Weinstein, J. (2024). ¿Por qué los directores quieren aprender? Motivaciones, expectativas y necesidades de formación continua desde la perspectiva del liderazgo escolar en Chile. *Perspectiva Educacional, 63*(1), 5–28.
Jara Ibarra, C., Sánchez Bachmann, M., & Peña, J. (2026). Education for citizenship under democratic strain: Professional learning for school leaders and teachers in Chile. In M. Heinz, M. J. Rodríguez-Entrena, & G. Mac Ruairc (Eds.), *Professional learning for diversity, equity and democracy: Big ideas for better schools* (pp. 146–164). London: Routledge.
Kalinec-Craig, C. A. (2017). The rights of the learner: A framework for promoting equity through formative assessment in mathematics education. *Democracy and Education, 25*(2), 5.
Kelly, C., Dansereau, L., Sebring, J., Aubrecht, K., FitzGerald, M., Lee, Y., . . . & Hamilton-Hinch, B. (2022). Intersectionality, health equity, and EDI: What's the difference for health researchers? *International Journal for Equity in Health, 21*(1), 182.
King, F. (2024). Professional learning: A call to criticality, action and reflexivity. *Professional Development in Education, 50*(6), 1053–1055.
Leithwood, K. (2021). A review of evidence about equitable school leadership. *Education Sciences, 11*(8), 377. https://doi.org/10.3390/educsci11080377
Leithwood, K., Harris, A., & Hopkins, D. (2020). Seven strong claims about successful school leadership revisited. *School Leadership & Management, 40*(1), 5–22. https://doi.org/10.1080/13632434.2019.1596077
Mac Ruairc, G., Gartland, S., Heinz, M., & Rodríguez-Entrena, M. J. (2026). Diversity, equity and democracy in school leadership: Troublesome concepts in troubled times. In M. Heinz, M. J. Rodríguez-Entrena, & G. Mac Ruairc (Eds.), *Professional learning for diversity, equity and democracy: Big ideas for better schools* (pp. 24–46). Routledge.
MacKenzie, M., Sensoy, Ö., Johnson, G. F., Sinclair, N., & Weldon, L. (2023). How universities gaslight EDI&I initiatives: Mapping institutional resistance to structural change. *International Journal of Education Policy and Leadership, 19*(1), 1–18. https://doi.org/10.22230/ijepl.2023v19n1a1303
MacKinnon, C. A. (2014). *Gender in constitutional law.* Oxford University Press.
Meyer, J. H. F., & Land, R. (2005). Threshold concepts and troublesome knowledge: Epistemological considerations and a conceptual framework for teaching and learning. *Higher Education, 49*(3), 373–388.
Mezirow, J. (2000). *Learning as transformation: Critical perspectives on a theory in progress.* Jossey-Bass.
Nihill, M., & Mac Ruairc, G. (2026). A model to enable professional learning for transformative school leadership. In M. Heinz, M. J. Rodríguez-Entrena, & G. Mac Ruairc (Eds.), *Professional learning for diversity, equity and democracy: Big ideas for better schools* (pp. 47–62). London: Routledge.
OECD. (2014). *TALIS 2013 results: An international perspective on teaching and learning.* OECD Publishing.
OECD. (2024). *The OECD reinforcing democracy initiative: Monitoring report – assessing progress and charting the way forward.* OECD Publishing. https://www.oecd.org/en/publications/the-oecd-reinforcing-democracy-initiative_9543bcfb-en.html
Ottesen, E., Jensen, R., Halvorsen, B., & Vinje, P. M. (2026). Democracy as a central value in a national curriculum: Working with school leaders and teachers to connect values with practice in Norway. In M. Heinz, M. J. Rodríguez-Entrena,

& G. Mac Ruairc (Eds.), *Professional learning for diversity, equity and democracy: Big ideas for better schools* (pp. 128–145). London: Routledge.
Perkins, D. (1999). The many faces of constructivism. *Educational Leadership*, *57*(3), 6–11.
Poekert, P., & King, F. (2023). Leading professional learning to navigate complexity. *Professional Development in Education*, *49*(6), 953–957.
Rodríguez-Entrena, M. J., Portela Pruaño, A., Maldonado López, M. C., Hernández López, F. A., & Bernárdez-Gómez, A. (2026). What is democracy? Recognising diverse perspectives and building shared understandings with school leaders in Spain through a professional learning experience. In M. Heinz, M. J. Rodríguez-Entrena, & G. Mac Ruairc (Eds.), *Professional learning for diversity, equity and democracy: Big ideas for better schools* (pp. 103–127). London: Routledge.
Rönnström, N., & Skott, P. (2019). Líderes escolares, maestros de la complejidad. En J. Weinstein, & G. Muñoz (Eds.), *Liderazgo en escuelas de alta complejidad sociocultural. Diez Miradas* (pp. 111–152). Ediciones Universidad Diego Portales.
Salo, P., Francisco, S., & Olin Almqvist, A. (2024). Understanding professional learning in and for practice. *Professional Development in Education*, *50*(3), 444–459. https://doi.org/10.1080/19415257.2024.2311108
Sedgwick, E. K. (2008). *Epistemology of the closet*. University of California Press.
Semião, D., Mogarro, M. J., Pinto, F. B., Martins, M. J. D., Santos, N., Sousa, O., . . . & Tinoca, L. (2023). Teachers' perspectives on students' cultural diversity: A systematic literature review. *Education Sciences*, *13*(12), 1215. https://doi.org/10.3390/educsci13121215
Sherman, B., & Teemant, A. (2021). Agency, identity, power: An agentive triad model for teacher action. *Educational Philosophy and Theory*, *54*(9), 1464–1475.
Shields, C. M. (2022). Responding to the UNESCO framework: A transformative approach to educational leadership. *Leading and Managing*, *28*(2), 1–10. https://search.informit.org/doi/10.3316/informit.097849011294250
Shields, C. M., & Hesbol, K. A. (2020). Transformative leadership approaches to inclusion, equity, and social justice. *Journal of School Leadership*, *30*(1), 3–22.
Stray, J. H. (2014). Learning and living democracy. In A. W. T. Hanse, H. Sætra, & S. Ø. Sæther (Eds.), *Global citizen: Challenges and responsibility in an interconnected world* (pp. 103–111). Brill. https://brill.com/downloadpdf/display/book/edcoll/9789462099296/BP000013.xml
Thelwall, M., Devonport, T. J., Makita, M., Russell, K., & Ferguson, L. (2022). Academic LGBTQ+ Terminology 1900–2021: Increasing variety, increasing inclusivity? *Journal of Homosexuality*, *70*(11), 2514–2538. https://doi.org/10.1080/00918369.2022.2070446
UNESCO. (2016). *Education 2030: Incheon declaration and framework for action for the implementation of Sustainable Development Goal 4: Ensure inclusive and equitable quality education and promote lifelong learning opportunities for all.* Author. https://unesdoc.unesco.org/ark:/48223/pf0000245656
UNESCO. (2017). *La Formación Inicial Docente en Educación para la Ciudadanía en América Latina: Análisis comparado de seis casos nacionales*. http://biblioteca-digital.mineduc.cl//handle/20.500.12365/2175
Vinovskis, M. A. (1993). Early childhood education: Then and now. *Daedalus*, *122*(1), 151–176.
Zembylas, M. (2015). Pedagogies of strategic empathy: Navigating through the emotional complexities of anti-racism in higher education. *Teaching in Higher Education*, *20*(2), 113–126.
Zimman, L. (2017). Gender as stylistic bricolage: Transmasculine voices and the relationship between fundamental frequency and /s/. *Language in Society*, *46*(3), 339–370.

INDEX

Note: Page locators in *italic* indicate a figure, and page locators in **bold** indicate a table on the corresponding page.

3Cs model (Kerr) 13, 149–150, 157, 172

academic difference 30
action learning (Norway) 138
action learning sets 108; analysis/reflection activities, development 116; implementation 114
action-oriented professional learning, underpinning 108
action research, models **133**
active citizenship, interest (stimulation) 113
active participation 108
additional educational needs (AEN) 66
agency 70; promotion 73–74
'All That We Share' (video advert) 72
anticipation tasks 81
anti-discrimination education, importance 88–89
anti-diversity discourse/policy, rise (worry) 17–18
associations (semantic role) 93
autistic spectrum disorders (ASD) 67

Bernárdez-Gómez, Abraham 12
bias: avoidance 75; implicit biases, demonstration 69–70; internal bias, awareness 76
'Big Ideas for Better Schools: Professional Learning for Diversity, Equity and Democracy' project (BIBS) 167; background/ 17–18; Erasmus+-funded project 66–67; Erasmus+-funded transnational BIBS project 11; European BIBS project 105–106; findings 75–78; focus 19; integration 139; international BIBS project 136; learning 75–78; objectives 17, 19; philosophy/approach 20–21; programme, training day 77; teacher post-action learning set questionnaire *121*; template, example 118
'big issue' conversations 65
Bildung (Norway) 128–129
Black Lives Matter movement, growth 18
'Blue Eyed' (movie) 92
bounded knowledge 50
Brandon School (Norway): description 131; learning initiative, structure/content 132
Brexit, impact 18
burn-out 47

cancel culture movement 25–26
care, school commitment 69

Central Europe (democratic society), action participation (preparation) 89
children, life-chances 25
Chile: 3Cs model (Kerr) 13, 149–150, 157, 172; citizenship, teaching/learning (contexts/dimensions) *149*; civic dimension 149; civic education, understanding 155; community reflection, encouragement 156; comprehensive/transversal CEPs, development 148; 'Contexts and Dimensions for the Teaching and Learning of Citizenship' model, consideration 150; controversial issues, debate 151; controversy (addressing), pedagogical strategies (educator usage) 152; democratic strain, citizenship education 146; electoral participation 146; experience, learnings 155–157; in-service programmes, objectives 151; issues, controversy (cases) **152**; issues, controversy (clarification) 153; legal principles, affirmation 153; neutrality, teacher viewpoint 151; participative citizens (formation), values (knowledge/transmission) 155; pedagogical approaches, exploration 151–153; personal values, cultivation 148; professional development activities, participation (balancing) 154; professional learning programmes 11, **158–160**; programme evaluation, experiences/impact (exploration) 154–155; reality (sensitivity), instances (generation) 156; research findings, presentation 155; school climate, promotion 148; school leadership, awareness/active involvement 157; school leaders/teachers, professional learning 146; social cohesion, fostering 146–147; teachers, active role (importance/need) 156; teachers/school leaders, professional learning programme (design/implementation) 148–153; 'Tools for Understanding Citizenship Education' 148–153; 'Tools for Understanding Citizenship Education' course, delivery 154
Chile, citizenship education: 3Cs/two-dimensional conceptual framework 150; civic/civil development, importance 156; focus 147–148; implementation 151
Chile, Citizenship Education Plan (CEP): development 146–147; fears (recognition)/responsibilities (understanding) 151–153; public school implementation 147; school definition/implementation 148
Chile, classroom: controversial issues, addressing 152; controversial issues, teaching strategies **153**; opinions, educator role 152
Ciclo Formativo de Grado Básico 106
circular models 132
Citizen Education Plan (CEP) (Chile) 146–148, 151–153
citizenship: interdisciplinary topic 130–131; participant conceptions, examination 108; teaching/learning, contexts/dimensions (Chile) *149*
citizenship education: curricular adjustments 146–147; national plan 9
citizenship education (Chile) 146; understanding, tools **158–160**
civic culture, shaping (Poland) 9
civic education, understanding (Chile) 155
civic engagement, fostering (expense) 105
civic participation, framing 9
classroom: exploration ('Democracy in Our School') 117–120; secondary school classrooms, critical/democratic citizenship (development) 105
climate emergency, intensification 4
cognitive competencies, development 103
cognitive content, focus 103
cognitive development 57–58
collaboration, importance 172–174
collaborative dialogue (Spain) 122
collaborative diversity, principles 79–80
collaborative exploration 71
collaborative learning 80; facilitation, high-trust models (need) 59; programme, overview 90–92; promotion 174
collaborative networks, development 51
collaborative professional identity: emergence 75; underpinning 108
collaborative professional learning 3; programme, outline **109–110**

collaborative semantic analysis, usage 92–94
collaborative work commissions, establishment 116
collaborative work commissions (Spain), establishment 116
collaborative work/learning, scenario (creation) 124
collective agreement, striving 114
collective pronouns, usage (increase) 77
commitment, deepening 65
common core curriculum (Norway) 129
common goals 170–171
common sense 24
Competences for Democratic Culture: framework *115*; Reference Framework 114
complexity, embracing 167
comprehensive/transversal CEPs, development (Chile) 148
concepts: actions, description (semantic role) 93; conceptualisation 7; explicitness 169–170; semantic analysis 92
conflict: management 36–37; resolution 104
conflicting intersectionality 34
consensus-based approaches, diverse voices (inclusion) 114
constructive intersectionality 34
constructivism 89–90
constructs, interrelatedness 29
consultative fora, feedback 53
consumer choice, 'thin' market-oriented versions 128
content knowledge 71
'Contexts and Dimensions for the Teaching and Learning of Citizenship' model (Chile), consideration 150
context-specific hooks (entry points) 170–171
contextual action 80
continuous learning, process 56–57
corrupt manipulations, impact 135
country-specific portfolio reports 21
COVID-19 pandemic: activity disruption 21; disruption 78; impact 18, 92, 139; travel restrictions 132
CPD experiences, transformativeness 51
critical co-inquiry, embracing 167
critical engagement, research/practice (usage) 80
critical intersectionality 34
critical perspectives, development 19
critical professional learning, commitment (sustaining) 174–176
critical thinking: fostering, expense 105; reinforcement 116
cultural difference 30
cultural diversity, core value (focus) 134
culturally responsive pedagogy, development/refinement 28
culture, legacy (influence) 53
curricular diversification programmes 107
curricular pressure, feeling 104
curriculum values/practice connection, professional learning initiative (design/implementation) 132–138

decision-making processes, diverse voices (inclusion) 114
declarative sentences, construction 93
deconstruction, words/phrases (alignment) 93
deficit thinking 32
democracy 35–38, 87; approaches 29; awareness, activities (school need) 116; central value 12–13, 128; challenges, presence 76; characterisation 36; collaborative/deliberative nature 38; collaborative professional learning 3; complexities, understanding/appreciation 168–169; complexity/critical co-inquiry, embracing 167; conceptualisation 6–8, 113; conceptual map *30*; core value, focus 134; definitions, differences 97–98; democratic competence, resources list (providing) 108; Dewey conception, usage 20; education, assumptions/practices (Norway) 134–135; education, concept 130; enactment (system setup), corrupt manipulations (impact) (Norway) 135; identification 103; interdisciplinary topic 130–131; interest, stimulation 113; participant conceptions, examination 108; positioning 35–36; presupposition 36; processes 36–37; professional learning 10–11; promotion (teaching practices support), evaluation

habit (teacher development) 108; promotion (facilitation), teaching methods/resources/assessment tools (identification) 108; radical democracy, experience 123; reconfiguration, risk (Norway) 129; reconstructed definitions 98; school work plan (absence) 116; society basis 18; strain, increase 3–4; student perspective, insights (reconstruction offering) 96–98; term, usage 97; theoretical/ practical aspects, participant understanding (expansion) 108; theoretic democratic values, translation (facilitation) 108; thick understandings 128; undermining 25–26; understanding 90–92; versions, contest 128
democracy concept 67, 90, 92, 112, 123–124, 130, 175; data, collection 112; semantic field **96–97**
'Democracy in Education: Connecting Curriculum Values with Practice in Schools' (Norway) 129
'Democracy in Our School': action learning sets, implementation 114; activities/materials 112; classroom exploration (Level 3) 117–120; Competences for Democratic Culture, framework *115*; deepened reflection (Level 3) 111; democratic educational program, ideas (identification) 115–116; design 107; development 105–106; exploration (Level 2) 111, 114–117; follow-up actions (Level 3) 111; implementation 107–108; initial reflection (Level 1) 111; initial reflection (Level 1), activities/materials 112; lessons, learning 122–124; professional learning experiences (Level 4) 120–122; project design 107–108, 110; project objectives 108–109; recommendations 122–124; reflection, deepening 111; schools, democratic competences (reflection/ analysis facilitation) **116**; seminar details 113–122; seminar details, stages 113; training sessions, development 110–112; training unit, example **118–119**; working material, development 110–112
democratic citizenship: concept, approximation 110; international education policies/research 174–175; visibility 9
democratic collaborative school-university partnership work, understanding/commitment (deepening) 17
democratic community 135
democratic culture: approach, competences 111; competencies (promotion), teaching practices (teacher usage/promotion) 108
democratic educational program, ideas (identification) 115–116
democratic identity, development 129
democratic individuality 135
democratic partnership 80
democratic processes 35–36
democratic professionalism 52
democratic project-based learning approach 117
democratic schools, cultivation 122–123
democratic society 135; knowledge, role 136
democratic society, action participation (preparation) 89
democratic strain (Chile), citizenship education 146
democratic values 108
descriptions (semantic role) 93
dialogue: promotion 73–74; value, theory/practice (interdependence) 171
digital curriculum (Norway) 134
dignity, commitment 25
(dis)ability difference 30
discomfort, pedagogy 28
discrimination: accusation 69–70; reduction 18
disinformation, spread 3–4
disorienting dilemma 55–56
diverse perspectives, recognition 103
diverse perspectives (recognition), school leader involvement (professional learning experience usage) 103
diversity 29–31, 87; awareness, raising (school need) 116; characteristics 30; collaborative professional learning 3; complexities, understanding/ appreciation 168–169; complexity/ critical co-inquiry, embracing 167; concept 67, 90, 92, 175; concept, semantic field **94**; conceptualisation

6–8; conceptual map *30*; conscious embracing 75–76; critical awareness 37; definition (creation), extracted expressions (usage) 95; descriptor, role 31; gap 66; ideas 168; identity, link 31; intersectionality 7, 34–35; issue, conceptualisation/exploration 70; meanings/connection, exploration 71–72; professional learning 10–11; promotion, aim 107; reconstructed definitions, variety/complexity 99; respect, fostering 108; respect, values (student engagement) 122; school leaders, professional learning 65; social construction 31; society basis 18; student perspective, insights (reconstruction offering) 94–95; student understanding 98–99; understanding 90–92; values 66

'Diversity and Equity in Our School': agency, promotion 73–74; anticipation tasks 81; approach foundations (shaping), intention/respect (usage) 69–70; design 70–74, 79; dialogue, promotion 73–74; equity, definitions/dimensions/challenges 82; essentialism, labels/risk 82; experiences task, sharing 82–83; implementation 70–74; intersectionality 82; issues, conceptualisation/problematisation 71–73; objectives 70, 81; one-day professional learning programme, overview **81–84**; one-day workshop, activities (sample) 81–83; participants 70; presentation/facilitator input 82; reflection, promotion 73–74; school leadership teams, professional learning programme (design) 67–74; school leadership teams, professional learning programme (development/implementation) 65; tone, setting 71

diversity, equity, and inclusion (DEI) 11; anti-DEI drive 168; anti-DEI, surveillance regime (impact) 26; exploration 12; insight, thinking/enhancing 28; research/scholarship 27

Eastern Europe (democratic society), action participation (preparation) 89

economic inequality, intensification 4

economic rights 36

education: access, ensuring 27–28; children/young people social realities, complexity 19; democracy, relationship 89; democratisation 89; equity, exploration 35; goal 103; quality 106–107

educational structures/debates, shaping 9

Education for Persons with Special Educational Needs (EPSEN) Act 66

elite dominance, majority power (upholding) 113–114

emancipatory scholarship/policies 3–4

emotional competencies, development 103

emotional repositioning 49–50

empathy: focus, impact 69; power, relationship 69

Employment Equality Acts 66

equality-focused education policy, issue 9

equal partnership 80

equal status 170–171

Equal Status Acts 66

'Equal Treatment at School Report on the Research in Schools and Quantitative Analysis of Educational and Preventive Programmes Report' (Poland) 88

Equal Treatment School Code, usage 88–89

equity 34–35, 87; awareness, raising (school need) 116; challenges, presence 76; collaborative professional identity, emergence 75; collaborative professional learning 3; complexities, understanding/appreciation 168–169; complexity/critical co-inquiry, embracing 167; concept 67, 90, 92, 175; concept, semantic field **95**; conceptualisation 6–8; conceptual map *30*; definition (reconstruction), extracted expressions (usage) 96; definitions/dimensions/challenges 82; exploration 35; interactions 36–37; intersectionality 7; issue, conceptualisation/exploration 70; literacy 37; meanings/connection, exploration 71–72; professional learning 10–11; promotion (Poland)

88–89; reconstructed definitions, variety/complexity 99; school leaders, professional learning 65; society basis 18; student perspective, insights (reconstruction offering) 95–96; success/failure, predictability 35; synthesised view 35; understanding 90–92; usage 76; work, principles 79–80
equity, diversity, and inclusion (EDI) approach 174
equity promotion 37; aim 107
equity-related classroom situation/ interaction, description 73
equivalents: category 94; semantic role 93
Erasmus+-funded BIBS project 66–67, 79, 90
Erasmus+-funded transnational BIBS project 11
escalator approach 18
essentialisation, process 32
essentialising, negative effects 71
essentialism, labels/risk 82
European BIBS project 105–106, 175
European Union (EU), anti-discrimination directives 88
Europe, political shifts 18
exclusion, patterns 32
experiences task, sharing 82–83
experiential learning 57
explicit action, disruptive potential 49–50
expression, freedom 108
extracted expressions, usage 95, 96
extracurricular activities, impact (awareness) 76

failure, individualisation 32
fairness, commitment 25
far-right ideologies, impact 49–50
fascist authoritarian extreme right, marginal political phenomenon 24
feedback 53, 76
forced displacement 4
forward-looking actions, collective planning/implementation 78
'Framework of Competences for Democratic Culture' developed by the Council of Europe' 172
freedom of choice values, student engagement 122
funding application, content 17–18

Garland, Sara 11, 12
global awareness 76–77, 80
global citizenship, emphasis 104
global health threats 4
globalisation, acceleration 29–30
globally connected outlook 80
governments, public trust (erosion) 3–4
Graham, Cáitlin 12
Great Famine (Ireland) 65–66
group, presentation 32

Halvorsen, Bård 13
Heinz, Manuela 11, 12, 13
Hernández López, Francisco Alfonso 12
holistic practices 120
homophobia, opposing 25
human dignity, core value (focus) 134
human rights: emphasis 104; promotion 25; respect 104
human values, development 116
Hungary, political shifts 18

Ibarra, Camila Jara 13
identity 31–33; core value, focus 134; diversity, link 31; formation 31; intersecting identities *33*; signifiers 33–34
implicit biases, persistence (demonstration) 69–70
inclusion: challenges, presence 76; meanings/connection, exploration 71–72; promotion, aim 107; reconstructed definitions, variety/ complexity 99; school leaders (professional learning) 65
inclusive partnership 80
individuals, professionalism (enhancement) 57–58
inequality, institutionalised workings (detraction) 69
inequity: forms 17–18; interactions 36–37; intersectionality 34–35; preclusion 34–35
integrative knowledge 50
intercultural dialogue 108
Intercultural Education Strategy 66
internal bias, awareness 76
international education policies/research 174–175
international meetings, partnership 21
international transformation agendas, attention 5
intersecting identities *33*

intersectionality *33*, 33–34, 82; collection 168; forms 34; negative effects 71
Ireland: additional educational needs (AEN) 66; Celtic Tiger name 65–66; Department of Education, action plans 54; Department of Education, Guidelines for Supporting Students 66; diversity/equity/inclusion, school leader professional learning 65; economic growth 65–66; Employment Equality Acts 66; Equal Status Acts 66; equity, existence 68; ethical approval, University of Galway research ethics committee provision 75; Great Famine 65–66; intersectionality, idea (impact) 171; longer-term objectives (achievement), assessment (issues) 74; national factors, impact 50; partner school, establishment 67; qualitative evaluation statements, personal/possessive pronoun usage 77; reflective thematic analysis (RTA) approach 74–75; school ethos statements 66; school mission statement ('Together We Will Achieve') 67; Special Educational Needs (SEN) 66; University of Galway, BIBS project allowance 129
Ireland, professional learning: day, design/implementation 70; model, school leader development 47–48; programmes 11
Irish Centre for School Leadership: continuum, proposal 53; framework development 52–53
Irish school leaders, professional learning model *55*
irreversible knowledge 50

Jensen, Ruth 13
justice work, detriment 39

knowledge: building 140; forms, valuation 172–174; role 136; types 50
Kołodziejczyk, Jakub 12
Kotlarz, Joanna 12

labeling, negative effects 71
language, importance 169–170
leadership: continuum, conceptualism 53; development, professional development components (shared understanding) 53; development, provision 52; enabling, skills/competences (development) 48; explicit action, disruptive potential 49–50; learning, reframing 167; practice, improvement 59; role 175–176; scholarship 48–49; school leadership 3, 24; studies 173; transformative leadership 6; transformative school leadership, professional learning (enabling) 47
leadership professional learning: providers, impact 167; rethinking 169
leading by example 172–174
learner, rights 71
learning: constructivist approaches, value 98; environments, establishment (contribution) 108; programmes, materials (development) 29; *see also* professional learning
legislative change, implementation 175
LGBT-free zones 95
LGBTQIA+, impact 170
liminal positionality, recognition 49–50
locally rooted action 80
'Looking at Our Schools' (LAOS): quality framework 54; use 54, 59

Mac Ruairc, Gerry 11, 12, 13
Maldonado López, María del Carmen 12
management content, predominance (concern) 53
marginalisation: forms 18; mis-characterisation 25
marginalised charities 25
Mazurkiewidz, Grzegorz 12
meaning-making process 75
meaning, reconstruction 93
men/women equality, emphasis 104
metapolitics, impact 26
misinformation, spread 3–4, 146
misogynistic language, usage 73–74
moral development, context 96
mutual trust, nurturing 174

National Action Plan for Equal Treatment 88
National Council for Special Education's (NCSE) Inclusive Education Framework 66

national curriculum: democracy, central value 12–13, 128; usage (Norway) 134
National Directorate for Teaching and Training, packages offering 139
national/regional contexts, shaping/ framing factors (recognition) 48
negative beliefs, overcoming 18
new public management (NPM), usage 129
Nihill, Mary 11
Nixon, Richard 26
non-violence, resolution 104
normality, definitions 25
Norway: action learning 138; action research models **133**; action research workshop 133; Bildung 128–129; Brandon School, description 131; Brandon School, learning initiative (structure/content) 132; collaboration, time allotment 139; common core curriculum 129; core value, focus 134; curriculum reform (LK20) 131; curriculum values/ practice connection, professional learning initiative (design/ implementation) 132–138; data, checking (workshop) 136; democracy education, assumptions/practices (workshop) 134–135; 'Democracy in Education: Connecting Curriculum Values with Practice in Schools' 129; democracy, theme (centrality) 133; democratic education, aims/ practices (workshop) 136; digital curriculum 134; discussion prompts/ recommended readings **137**; education aims/purposes 133; experiences/impact, exploration methodology 138–139; experiences, summarisation 136–138; future solutions, development 132; learning points 139; learning process, pace/ momentum 139; models, scaffolding (providing) 132–133; national curriculum, usage (workshop) 134; National Directorate for Teaching and Training, packages offering 139; new public management (NPM), usage 129; plenary presentations, appreciation 138; project, learning 139–141; rural school, professional learning programme 13; school leaders, support/engagement/ leadership 139; staff, international experiences (gaining) 139; values-based education 9; values/ practice connection, school leaders/ teachers (interaction) 128; workshops 133–136
Norway, professional learning 138; initiatives 139; models 132–133; programmes 11

'Of Mice and Men' (teaching) 73–74
O Neachtain, Art 12
operational content, predominance (concern) 53
opposition: function 94; semantic role 93
oppositional culture war, metapolitics (impact) 26
oppression, freedom 36
Organic Law 2/2006 (LOMLOE) (Spain) 103–104, 114, 123–124
otherness, monotony (opposition) 95
other, stabilisation 33
Ottesen, Eli 13

participation, core value (focus) 134
peace, long-term commitments 4
Pedagogical Coordination Committee 113–114
pedagogical situations, empathy 69
peer-to-peer discourse 37
Peña Fredes, Javiera 13
people, essentialisation 32
perestroika, democratic structure dismantling (Poland) 171
personal epistemologies 56
personal/possessive pronoun, usage 77
phrases, alignment 93
pluralism, values, student engagement 122
Poland: academics/teachers/high school students, initiative 12; anti-discrimination education, importance 88–89; civic culture, shaping 9; democratic structures, dismantling 171; education, democracy (relationship) 89; 'Equal Treatment at School Report on the Research in Schools and Quantitative Analysis of Educational and Preventive Programmes Report' 88–89; Equal Treatment

School Code, usage 88–89; equity, promotion 88–89; legislation, European legislation (alignment) 88; National Action Plan for Equal Treatment 88; political shifts 18; professional learning programme, project partner development 90; professional learning programmes 11; teachers/students (social phenomena), understanding (development) 87
policy-directed reforms, implementation 51
political instability, challenge/source 89
Political Lexicological Centre 92
political polarisation: increase 3; spread 146
political push-back, increase 19
political rights 36; popularity, increase 17–18
politics, power dynamic 38
populist movements, resurgence 3–4
Portela Pruaño, Antonio 12
possessive individualism, 'thin' market-oriented versions 128
post-programme surveys 12
power: dynamics 38; impact 69
PowerPoint presentations, usage 138
practitioner-academic interactions 6–7
pre-programme surveys 12
presentation/facilitator input 82
principals, school leader (reference) 50
problematic effects (reproduction), empathy focus (impact) 69
professional development: bodies, conceptual models/resources 10; importance, acknowledgement 53; initiative, cornerstone 90–91; models 51; provision, coherence 53; purposes 51
professionalism: concept, representation 54–55; constructions 52
professional learning 10–11, 50–53, 65; collaboration, formative experiences (development) 124; collaborative experiences, teacher motivation/ commitment/involvement 124; context 28–29; critical professional learning, commitment (sustaining) 174–176; enabling, model 47; experience (Spain) 107–110; experiences ('Democracy in Our School') 120–122; national factors, impact 50; Norway university-school project 138; power, appreciation 49–50; targeting 56; transformative professional learning 167
professional learning models 55, 132–133; development (Irish context) 54–58; factors/concepts/principles 48
professional learning programme: design 176; design/implementation (Chile) 148–153; development 20, 66–67; impact, evaluation 74–75; overview (Chile) **158–160**
professional practice: impact 76; shaping 76
programme evaluation: experiences/ impact, exploration 154–155; perspectives, change 22
project design ('Democracy in Our School') 107–108
project schools, school leaders/teachers (encouragement) 19
public policy, shaping (increase) 24
public school, CEP implementation (Chile) 147
pupils: anonymous pupil data 135; democracy/voice/activism 130; survey 140–141
Pygmalion effect 72, 76

qualification (Norway education aims/ purposes) 133
quality improvement process 107
queer (word), usage 170
questions, asking 19

racism, opposing 25
racist slurs, usage 73–74
radical democracy, experience 123
readability, ensuring 92
reciprocal learning, recognition 22
recognition system, creation 124
reconstruction: insights, offering 94–98; meaning, reconstructing 93
reflection, promotion 73
reflective practice 56–57
reflective thematic analysis (RTA) approach 74–75
reframing, stimulation 57
reimagining 51; category (Sach) 51
'Reimagining Our Futures Together' (UNESCO) report 4
relational interactions, usage 32–33
remodelling 51
respect, commitment 25

retooling 51
revitalising 51
'rights of the learner' approach, usage 170
rights, types 36
Robin, R. 92
Rodríguez-Entrena, María Jesús 11, 12, 13

Sánchez Bachmann, Macarena 13
scholarship: body, increase 55–56
Schön, Donald 56–57
school-based applications 108
school-based planning, support 13
school-identified issues, exploration/addressing 19
school leaders: conceptual models/resources 10; identity 49; perspectives, exploration 67–69; professional learning (Chile) 146; support/engagement/leadership (Norway) 139; term, reference 50; values/practice connection, interaction 128
school leadership 3; diversity/equity/democracy, impact 24; domains 49; implications 5–6; professional learning model development, Irish context 54–58; profession, distinction 50–51; team, buy-in 171; team, professional learning programme (design) 67–74; transformative approaches, focus 48
school leaders, professional learning 50–53, 65; programme, design/implementation (Chile) 148–153
schools: culture, core value (embedding) 68–69; curriculum, overloading 50; data, generation 173–174; democratic competences, reflection/analysis facilitation **116**; democratic operation 116; ethos 19; ethos statements 66; extracurricular activities, impact (awareness) 76; ideas 17; identity 33; improvement (Spain) 123–124; improvement, contribution 19; organisational conditions, establishment 124; policies, impact (awareness) 76; self-evaluations (Spain) 123–124; self-evaluations, LAOS quality framework 54; teachers, professional learning (Chile) 146; teachers, values/practice connection (interaction) 128; transformation 122; transformation sites 4
Scottish College for Educational Leadership (SCEL): collaboration 52–53; feedback/work 53
self-evaluation, process 107
self-fulfilling prophecy 72
self-learning, deepening 5
self, presentation 32
semantic roles 93
semi-structured interviews/questionnaire 112
sentence, meaning (search) 92
sexism, opposing 25
sexual orientation difference 30
sexual pluralism, embracing 25
shared humanity, sense (promotion) 18
shared intellectual journey 170–171
shared intellectual journey project 171
shared understanding: building 1023; building, school leader involvement (professional learning experience usage) 103; development 53
skills/competences, development 48
social cohesion, fostering 146–147
social competencies, development 103
social conflicts, addressing 147
social constructivism, premise 89–90
social inequalities, (re)producing 5
social injustices/exclusions, reproduction/exacerbation 69
socialisation (Norway education aims/purposes) 133
social justice: long-term commitments 4; promotion 25, 36
social media 25
social memory (preservation), language (usage) 91
social norms/realities, co-construction 37
social pluralism, embracing 25
social rights 36
social worlds, complexity (sense) 19
societal barriers, addressing 4
societal issues, in-depth deliberation 18
society, diversity (Spain) 106
socio-political orientations 38–39
Spain: Ciclo Formativo de Grado Básico 106; collaborative dialogue 122; collaborative work commissions, establishment 116; collective agreement, striving 114; curricular

diversification programmes 107; curricular pressure, feeling 104; democratic citizenship, visibility 9; democratic project-based learning approach 117; democratic schools, cultivation 122–123; democratic values/practices, understanding 120; diverse perspectives (recognition), school leader involvement (professional learning experience usage) 103; diverse voices, inclusion 114; education legislation 103–104; education, quality 106–107; elite dominance, majority power (upholding) 113–114; holistic projects 120; Organic Law 2/2006 (LOMLOE) 103–104, 114, 123–124; participatory action research 107–108; professional learning experience 107–110; professional learning programmes 11; public secondary school (Murcia), participation 106; quality improvement process 107; secondary school classrooms, critical/democratic citizenship (development) 105; self-evaluation, process 107; shared understanding (building), school leader involvement (professional learning experience usage) 103; society, diversity 105–106; training activities 117; training unit, example 118; transformation of practice 115; University of Murcia, online survey tool 120; values education 105
Spain, schools: case study, context 106–107; improvement 123–124; self-evaluation 123–124; transformation 122
Spain, teachers: collaboration, promotion 123; motivation/conviction, absence 105; questionnaire, provision 120; training 114–115
Special Educational Needs (SEN) 66, 106
speech, order 92
'sprinkle of theories' 72
status quo, questioning 38
student-centred pedagogies 76
students: attainment/achievements, portrayal 76; complex phenomena, understanding (development) 87; decision-making 108; diversity/equity/democracy perspectives, reconstruction offerings 94–98; engagement, enhancement 19; learning experiences/achievement, improvement 51; meaning (making), collaborative semantic analysis (usage) 92–94; needs 19; perspectives, exploration 67–69; treatment, equity (usage) 76; voice, incorporation 8, 35
subjectification (Norway education aims/purposes) 133
subject-specific classroom interventions, development/implementation 105–106
subtractive schooling 32
superstructure, impact 34
surveillance, impact 26
sustainability, long-term commitments 4
Sustainable Development Goals (SDGs) 4, 27, 39
sustained transnational exchange/collaboration, opportunities (providing) 19
system-wide engagement 9

teacher-centred pedagogical approaches 8
teacher educators, conceptual models/resources 10
teachers: collaboration, promotion (Spain) 123; complex phenomena, understanding (development) 87; motivation/commitment/involvement 124; motivation/conviction, absence 105; perspectives, exploration 67–69; post-action learning set questionnaire (BIBS) *121*; professional learning programme, design/implementation (Chile) 148–153; support, time/space/resource provision 124; workloads 140
teaching: constructivist approaches, value 98; methods/resources/assessment tools, identification 108
teaching practice(s) 76; democratic competence, resources list (providing) 108; teacher usage/promotion 108
terminology, explicitness 169–170
text, meaning (search) 92
theoretical frameworks, understanding (enhancement) 172–173

theoretic democratic values, translation (facilitation) 108
theory, practice (interdependence) 170–171
theory-/rationale-based chapters 10–11
thinking, space (creation) 69
third space, practitioner-academic interactions 6–7
threshold concepts 34, 70, 176; ideas, usage 169; identification 72; principles 50; working, value 48
through democracy dimension 130
tolerance, increase 18
tolerant-tolerated relation (reproduction), empathy focus (impact) 69
'Tools for Understanding Citizenship Education' (Chile) 148–153; teachers/school leaders, professional learning programme (design/implementation) 148–153; understanding/practice (enhancement), conceptual frameworks (leveraging) 149–150
traditional/hierarchy, scrutinisation 38
training: activities approach, four-level structure *110*; experience (assessment), questionnaire (example) *121*; sessions, development 110–112; unit, 'Democracy in Our School' example **118–119**
transformational leadership, development 53
transformative educational practices 28
transformative ideas, in-depth deliberation 18
transformative intentions, need 51
transformative knowledge 50
transformative leadership 6
transformative model (Kennedy) 51
transformative outcomes 48–49, 173; professional learning (foundational principles) *48*
transformative perspectives, alignment 49
transformative professional learning 13, 167
transformative purpose/orientation 51
transformative school leadership, professional learning (enabling) 47
transnational collaboration, value 21–22
transnational exchange/collaboration, opportunities (providing) 19
transnational professional learning project 17
transphobia, opposing 25
troublesome knowledge 29, 50; working, value 48
Trzópek-Paszkiewicz, Joann 12

Ukraine, refugee crisis 18
uncertainty, generation 171–172
understanding, deepening 65
United Nations 2030 Agenda for Sustainable Development 27
United Nations Convention on the Rights of the Child (UNCRC), usage 27
university-school collaboration, formative experiences (development) 124
utterance sequences, distribution 92

values education 105
values/practice connection, school leaders/teachers (interaction) 128
Vance, JD 26
victimisation, forms 18
victimsed 'other,' risk 69
Vinje, Pia Merethe 13
visibility system, reaction 124
voter turnout, declining 9

warm-up anticipation task, participants (engagement) 71
wars, outbreak/escalation 4
Whyte, Claire 12
wicked problems 49
woke, negative connotations/accusations 24–25
word: alignment 93; meaning, search 92
working material, development 110–112
work, occurrence/context 8–10
worldview difference 30

young people, life-chances 25

For Product Safety Concerns and Information please contact our EU representative GPSR@taylorandfrancis.com
Taylor & Francis Verlag GmbH, Kaufingerstraße 24, 80331 München, Germany

www.ingramcontent.com/pod-product-compliance
Ingram Content Group UK Ltd.
Pitfield, Milton Keynes, MK11 3LW, UK
UKHW021055261125
465413UK00018BB/691
* 9 7 8 1 0 3 2 6 0 1 3 4 2 *